Translating Milan Kundera

TOPICS IN TRANSLATION
Series Editors: Susan Bassnett, *University of Warwick, UK*
Edwin Gentzler, *University of Massachusetts, Amherst, USA*
Editor for Translation in the Commercial Environment:
Geoffrey Samuelsson-Brown, University of Surrey, UK

Other Books in the Series
Culture Bumps: An Empirical Approach to the Translation of Allusions
  Ritva Leppihalme
Constructing Cultures: Essays on Literary Translation
  Susan Bassnett and André Lefevere
The Pragmatics of Translation
  Leo Hickey (ed.)
Practical Guide for Translators (3rd edn)
  Geoffrey Samuelsson-Brown
Written in the Language of the Scottish Nation
  John Corbett
'Behind Inverted Commas' Translation and Anglo-German Cultural Relations in the Nineteenth Century
  Susanne Stark
The Rewriting of Njáls Saga: Translation, Ideology, and Icelandic Sagas
  Jón Karl Helgason
Time Sharing on Stage: Drama Translation in Theatre and Society
  Sirkku Aaltonen
Translation and Nation: A Cultural Politics of Englishness
  Roger Ellis and Liz Oakley-Brown (eds)
The Interpreter's Resource
  Mary Phelan
Annotated Texts for Translation: English–German
  Christina Schäffner with Uwe Wiesemann
Contemporary Translation Theories (2nd edn)
  Edwin Gentzler
Literary Translation: A Practical Guide
  Clifford E. Landers
Translation-mediated Communication in a Digital World
  Minako O'Hagan and David Ashworth
Frae Ither Tongues: Essays on Modern Translations into Scots
  Bill Findlay (ed.)
Practical Guide for Translators (4th edn)
  Geoffrey Samuelsson-Brown
Cultural Encounters in Translation from Arabic
  Said Faiq (ed.)
Translation, Linguistics, Culture: A French-English Handbook
  Nigel Armstrong
Translation and Religion: Holy Untranslatable?
  Lynne Long (ed.)
Theatrical Translation and Film Adaptation: A Practitioner's View
  Phyllis Zatlin

For more details of these or any other of our publications, please contact:
**Multilingual Matters, Frankfurt Lodge, Clevedon Hall,
Victoria Road, Clevedon, BS21 7HH, England**
http://www.multilingual-matters.com

TOPICS IN TRANSLATION 30
Series Editors: Susan Bassnett, *University of Warwick, UK*
Edwin Gentzler, *University of Massachusetts, Amherst, USA*

Translating Milan Kundera

Michelle Woods

MULTILINGUAL MATTERS LTD
Clevedon • Buffalo • Toronto

Library of Congress Cataloging in Publication Data
Woods, Michelle
Translating Milan Kundera/Michelle Woods. 1st ed.
Topics in Translation: 30
Includes bibliographical references.
1. Kundera, Milan–Translations–History and criticism. 2. Translating and interpreting. I. Title. II. Series.
PG5039.21.U6Z95 2006
891.8' 685409–dc22   2006001480

British Library Cataloguing in Publication Data
A catalogue entry for this book is available from the British Library.

ISBN 1-85359-883-6 / EAN 978-1-85359-883-8 (hbk)
ISBN 1-85359-882-8 / EAN 978-1-85359-882-1 (pbk)

Multilingual Matters Ltd
UK: Frankfurt Lodge, Clevedon Hall, Victoria Road, Clevedon BS21 7HH.
USA: UTP, 2250 Military Road, Tonawanda, NY 14150, USA.
Canada: UTP, 5201 Dufferin Street, North York, Ontario M3H 5T8, Canada.

Copyright © 2006 Michelle Woods.

All rights reserved. No part of this work may be reproduced in any form or by any means without permission in writing from the publisher.

Contents

Preface vii
Acknowledgements xii
List of Abbreviations xiii

1   Introduction 1

2   Translation 25

3   Rewriting 62

4   Writing 104

5   Reception 144

6   Conclusion 180

Bibliography 189

Index 196

Preface

Part of the research for this book took place in the depository of the National Library in Prague, a small concrete building located exactly where the city ends and the countryside begins. One day there, I began reading the 1987 French translation of Milan Kundera's novel *The Book of Laughter and Forgetting* (1979), focusing on a section about an untranslatable Czech word, *lítost*. In the novel, the fictional character of Milan Kundera, in exile in France, was reminiscing about a literary clique in an attempt to explain the word to foreign readers. The clique was made up of fictionalised characters based on real Czech literary figures still in communist Czechoslovakia, whom the narrator cannot name for fear of the consequences that may befall them. Out of respect, he 'translates' them into the names of great European authors: Goethe, Boccaccio, Lermontov, Petrarch and Voltaire. Because of this novel, Kundera's Czech citizenship was revoked; his work had been banned since 1970 in Czechoslovakia, and this novel was his first one written after his exile to France in 1975. Despite the ban, the French translation I was reading was marked by a Czechoslovak Socialist Republic stamp, and an older gentleman sitting beside me, also studying in this utilitarian reading room of the Library's Depository, was none other than the real author named Voltaire by Kundera in the novel.

The communist regime had, it turned out, collected all the French and English translations. I was comparing the 1987 French translation revised by Kundera with the 1979 French translation originally by François Kérel, the 1980 English translation by Michael Henry Heim, the 1996 English translation by Aaron Asher, and the 1981 Czech edition (Sixty-Eight Publishers) published in Toronto. All the versions differ textually from each other. Kundera rewrote elements of the text while revising the French translation in 1987, and Asher re-translated the novel from this French version; these translations became the 'definitive' versions of his novel, according to Kundera, though they differ slightly from each other on a textual basis. There is no definitive Czech version of the novel, as it has never been published in the Czech Republic. Kundera's Czech, French and English bibliographies do not coalesce: there are pre-1970 Czech works that have never been published in translation; there are Czech works that have never been published in the Czech Republic; and there are French works (Kundera began writing in French in the mid 1980s) that have not been published in the Czech Republic. Fifty-six editions (mostly differing) of six novels and eight differing editions of three books of poetry later, the scale of Kundera's obsession with translating, rewriting and reassessing his work, even after publication and before any of his work was translated, became clear. I wanted to find out why.

Another large part of my research took place in the United States in two archives: that of one of Kundera's translators, Peter Kussi; and that of one of his American editors at Knopf, Nancy Nicholas. I went into the archives with some very definite lines of enquiry. As Kundera has been critical of individual translators, I wanted to find out more about Kundera's relationships with his translators. I had questions about the publishing process, because Kundera's critique was tempered by his argument that translators were bound by social norms. Kundera did not mention the publishers as purveyors of these norms, but, in reading through the correspondence in the Kussi archive, it became clear that they had a huge influence on choosing the translator and on the way the translation was finally presented. While Kundera and Kussi frequently corresponded on the meaning of the translatorial decisions, there was no such dialogue with his publishers. My goal was to discover exactly the extent of the publisher's influence on the translated text, given that translation and literary research has often focused only on the author–translator dyad, as if this relationship existed in a vacuum. I was surprised by the influence the publishers had in choosing translators and in hiring them, and in forcing authors as well as translators to acquiesce to their decisions. The ultimate commercial intent behind the translations clearly affected the editing, and the editing radically changed the translation. Kundera's main issues with the translations seemed to be forged more in the editing than in the translation process.

I had discovered that Kundera's revisions of his translations were quite systematic, and especially pronounced in two areas: punctuation and repetition. In revising the translations, Kundera changed all the punctuation (in the novels with Czech editions) to the Czech style in which it had been written originally. Any synonyms introduced by the translator or the editor were systematically removed. *Lítost*, the untranslatable word, occurs throughout Kundera's fiction, but because it is untranslatable it was translated in a variety of ways: compassion, sorrow, la pitié, or la compassion. While Kundera knew, as he wrote about it, that this word could not have a definite equivalent in English or French, he knew that it could be referred to with consistency either by compassion or by sorrow, but not by both. Reading through all the different editions, it became clear that

Kundera was concerned with refining an authorial style that depended on a fairly unusual punctuation style and on the investigation of certain key words that occurred in texts and across them. The way in which Kundera wrote held the meaning of his text as much as did the content. The linguistic style of Kundera's work has not been investigated in English-language criticism partly because it was not wholly translated. I wanted to find out from the archives how much the style was understood and how much it was changed at an editorial rather than a translatorial stage.

The book has six chapters and investigates a variety of forms of translation. My intent with this variety was to underline that the translation process is not simply a relationship between a source text and a target text, or a translator and an author, but is a central meeting point for a mixture of relationships that are textually, culturally or personally bound. In Chapter One, titled 'Introduction', I present a general introduction to why Kundera is such an interesting case to pursue, and why translation is so central to understanding his work. A bilingual author, Kundera lost his native-language readership (apart from a small exile readership) once his work was banned in Czechoslovakia in 1970. He wrote in Czech from then on, knowing that the large majority of readers would not be Czech speakers. In the mid 1980s he began writing in French and from the mid 1990s onwards his novels have been written in French. Also in the mid 1980s, Kundera revised all the French translations of the novels written in Czech and declared these, rather than the Czech versions, to be the definitive and authentic versions of the novels. The translations in other words became the originals. Later, to produce new Czech versions, he would use *three* 'originals': the Czech manuscript, the first published Czech versions (in Toronto, Canada) and the French definitive translations.

In Chapter Two, titled 'Translation', I divide the topic of translation into two sections. In the first section, I conduct a reading of the Kussi and the Knopf archives, providing a translation history of Kundera's novels from 1969 onwards. I examine in detail the role of the translator in relation to the author and to the publishers, focusing on the triadic relationship rather than on the author–translator dyad. I also examine the extent of editorial influence on the text and the questions of power, cultural capital and commercialism as they relate to how the translation is both envisaged and enacted. The second section focuses on excerpts from the translations, not in order to rank the translations or expose their inadequacies, but to chart Kundera's revisions (either by himself, in the French translations, or through other translators, in the English translations), in order to convey the systematic changes in punctuation and repeated words and the reasons behind these changes.

In Chapter Three, titled 'Rewriting', I divide the topic into three sections. In the first section, I examine Kundera's textual rewritings of his novels, showing what he changes when he revises the translations and focusing on the importance of naming and reusing names and titles from his early Czech work, omitted from his bibliography. Secondly, I focus on the case of Kundera's rewriting of the *Laughable Loves* short-story collection (1963–70) and show how it has been amended and which stories have been omitted, and then I focus on one particular omitted story, 'Já, truchlivý bůh' / 'I, the Mournful God' (1963), which Kundera revised twice in the 1970s but never published again. In the third section, I examine how Kundera utilises the praxis of rewriting to achieve definitive versions of his novels rather than depending on one given original version, and how his bibliography differs across languages. Finally, I examine how Kundera figuratively rewrites his early omitted work, particularly his poetry, into the content and structure of his novels.

In Chapter Four, 'Writing', I focus on the issue of writing *as* translation in two ways. Firstly, in Kundera's first two novels written in exile, *The Book of Laughter and Forgetting* (1979) and *The Unbearable Lightness of Being* (1984), I discuss translation within the framework of the novels, particularly in focusing on etymology and untranslatability in novelistic essays (specifically with the Czech words *lítost* and *soucit*). Secondly, the chapter focuses on what can be translated, in examining Kundera's French-language novels, and the ways in which he has translated the linguistic style of his Czech novels across into French.

In Chapter Five, titled 'Reception', I look at the issue of how Kundera's work has been received in recent years in two cultures, the post-communist Czech Republic and Britain. The chapter focuses on how literary criticism and literary reviewing affect the dissemination of Kundera's work and questions the kinds of agenda behind views and criticism of the work. It examines how influential reviewing structures are in how a translation is received.

In Chapter Six, titled 'Conclusion', I pose the question of whether Kundera's comparison of the textual interference of communist censors with that of Western publishers can be made, through the issues of linguistic normalisation and covert censorship. Particularly, I want to pose the issue of culturally hegemonic practices in the Occident towards 'Eastern European' writing and the means by which its function in the anglophone world has been defined. Kundera's unusual writing style was deemed to lie outside accepted norms, especially in commercial terms – the interest was in the perceived political content of the work. I argue that the subversive element in Kundera's work is not the political or dissident content, but the epistemological possibilities of his writing style – a plurilingual European style, a newness, that exceeds the parameters of accepted articulation as defined by Occidental publishers, editors and newspapers. Rather than dwelling on inadequacies of translators or translations, I focus on how translations are manipulated on a variety of levels because of ideological assumptions or preconceived notions, especially, in this case, of European writing. Work on norms, cultural translation and post-colonial translation in Translation Studies informs these arguments, but I also want to stress the need in the field for further research beyond text-to-text comparisons, particularly via lesser-used languages within and beyond Europe.

There are two primary aims of this book: first, I show that translation is not a one-dimensional issue, correlating only to comparative analyses of source and target texts. While these analyses are extremely valuable in examining translatorial decisions, issues of domestication or translator style, I want to parse out the wider cultural scope of the translation issue, through using primary sources, and concentrating on third parties - the publishers, other writers, newspapers, and critics – in order to understand more about the translator–author relationship. My intent is to apply concepts of cultural translation theories (Bassnett & Lefevere, 1998; May, 1994; Niranjana, 1992; Venuti, 1998) to a particular case where such primary sources existed. The second aim of the book was to investigate Kundera's claim that, for him, 'translation is *everything*' (Kundera, 1998a: 121). Translation has been a priority of other bi-lingual exiled writers, such as Nabokov, Beckett and Brodsky – all of whom, like Kundera, have changed their own work when translating it or revising translations. I investigate whether the difference with Kundera is that not only has he written as much about translation as maybe Nabokov, but that translation has literally permeated his work, even before it was translated. Kundera's very first story – revised several times and omitted from his *oeuvre* – revolved around translation and misinterpretation, and, as Kundera lost the majority of his native-language readership, translation is paramount to any exegesis of his work. Kundera, in other words, seemed an exemplary case through which to examine translation not only as a substantive act, shot through with a variety of cultural and ideological interventions, but also as a mode of reading.

I hope that the book that follows will tempt readers to read or reread Kundera's work, with the issues of language, translation, mediation and dissemination in mind. I hope to show that translation, rather than being a minor element in his work, is one of the major keys to understanding his work, leading the reader to new insights and enjoyment.

Acknowledgments

There are many people and institutions without whom this book would not have been possible; I have been constantly amazed by their generosity and patience. I would like to thank my editors Edwin Gentzler and Susan Bassnett, whose help has been invaluable. None of the archival research would have been possible without the aid of the Irish Fulbright Commission, especially Sonya McGuinness and Carmel Coyle, and of the Fulbright programme, CRH, the Department of Slavic Languages at Columbia University, the Bakhmeteff Archive of Russian and East European History and Culture at Columbia University, especially the help of Tanya Chebotarev, and the Harry Ransom Humanities Research Center at the University of Texas at Austin. I would also like to thank Justin Doherty and the Russian Department at Trinity College Dublin as well as Petr Bílek and the Department of Czech Languages and Literature at Charles University. The Národní knihovna, the Památník národního písemnictví and the Národní filmový archiv in Prague allowed me access to their resources, and I thank them. I would also like to note the graciousness of Peter Kussi and Michael Heim, and thank them for their patience and interest in queries. A section of Chapter Five appeared in a slightly different version in *Kosmas* as 'A Very British Bohemian? The Reception of Milan Kundera and His Work in Great Britain' (vol. 16 (Spring), pp. 27–43).

The Centre for Translation and Textual Studies has provided me with a wonderful home for the last two years and I would like to thank my colleagues for their enthusiasm, interest and support, especially Rita McCann, Marion Winters, Colm Caffrey, Michael Cronin and Minako O'Hagan who all kept me on this side of sanity.

This book would not have been possible without the love and support of friends and family, especially Yvonna Woods, the Woods family, Mandy Dowdall, Kate Griffiths, Dinah Kenny, Antoin Rodgers and Kerry West. And most especially Michael Reisman, whose love and endless understanding has kept me going.

List of Abbreviations

KA: Kussi Archive: The Bakhmeteff Archive of Russian and East European History and Culture, the Peter Kussi Collection, Columbia University, New York
KENNA: Knopf Editors: Nancy Nicholas Archive, Harry Ransom Humanities Research Center at the University of Texas at Austin
PNP: Památník národního písemnictví, Prague

Chapter 1
Introduction

The Franco-Czech novelist Milan Kundera is adamant about how important translation is to his work. 'Translation', he writes, 'is *everything*' (Kundera, 1988a: 121). Kundera now writes in French, but for the majority of his writing career he wrote in Czech, though soon after he published his first prose work, his writing was banned in the only country in the world where the language is spoken. As a result, for 20 years Kundera wrote in a language that few people could read, yet in that time he became a best-selling international success thanks to the wide-ranging translation of his novels. Although Kundera gained a world-wide readership as a result of translation, his reactions to the process have never been positive: 'Translation is my nightmare', he told one interviewer. 'I've lived horrors because of it' (Elgrably, 1987: 17–18); a year later he wrote that for him translation was a 'trauma' (Kundera, 1988a: 121). His negative public statements on translation and translators have invoked a flurry of criticism, with Kundera painted as an irascible pedant causing trouble for the sake of an impossible ideal: to have exact copies of his Czech originals rendered in the foreign languages.

At the same time, the original Czech text of his novels, which Kundera described as a 'matrix', were left in the drawer, because most of them – *Life is Elsewhere* (1973), *Farewell Waltz* (1976), *The Book of Laughter and Forgetting* (1979), *The Unbearable Lightness of Being* (1984), *Immortality* (1991) – were first published in French, as *La vie est ailleurs*, *La valse aux adieux*, *Le livre du rire et de l'oubli*, *L'insoutenable légèreté de l'être* and *L'immortalité*. Until the ban on Kundera's work was lifted in Czechoslovakia, following the fall of the communist regime in 1989, his only work published in Czech was by a small publishing house named Sixty-Eight Publishers, based in Canada and owned by fellow Czech writer and émigré Josef Škvorecký. However, the editions ran to print runs of no more than 9000, and all the novels were published after they had been translated into French. Since 1989, Kundera has published only some of his work in the Czech Republic (a fact which has caused great consternation and criticism) – *Žert/The Joke* and *Směšné lásky/Laughable Loves* in 1991, *Jakub a jeho pán/Jacques and His Master* in 1992, *Nesmrtelnost/Immortality* in 1993 and *Valčík na rozloučenou/Farewell Waltz* in 1997. His defence of the slow publication of work that had never been read by the Czech public was that he was rewriting the Czech 'originals'. There are, in Kundera's words, three originating versions for each potential Czech version: the manuscript (the 'matrix'), the Škvorecký version and the revised French translations, from all of which Kundera would construct a Czech version (Kundera, 1993b: 345–346).

Between 1985 and 1987, Kundera, who had been living in France for a decade, revised the French translations of all his Czech novels and declared them to be the authentic version of his body of work – *more* authentic than the originals themselves. In response to the fact that many translators were already translating from the French rather than the Czech versions because of the dearth of Czech-language translators worldwide, Kundera undertook this authenticising of the French translations with the express purpose of creating new 'originals' from which translations into other languages could be made. Also, French was becoming Kundera's second writing language: he began writing critical essays in French in the early 1980s and published *L'art du roman/The Art of the Novel* in 1986 – his first book written wholly in French. His first novel written entirely in French, *La lenteur/Slowness*, was published a decade later, in 1995. He has since published two more novels, *L'identité/Identity* in 1997 and *L'ignorance/Ignorance* in 2003 (though the novel was first published in Spanish in 2000) and another book of essays, *Les testaments trahis/Testaments Betrayed*, in 1993 in French.

As with other émigré writers who adopted a second language in which to write, such as Vladimir Nabokov (to whom, in terms of a preoccupation with translation, Kundera compares himself) and Samuel Beckett, Kundera has not only undertaken the translations in the second language but has blurred the boundaries of what can be constituted as an 'original' and a 'translation' because of his interventions (Kundera, 1991c: 325). The process of revising the French translations not only addressed problems with the transference from one language (Czech) to another (French), but also allowed an opportunity for Kundera to rewrite the novels. In some cases, where the material was too culturally specific, Kundera deliberately altered the translation to make it more accessible to a French readership. In other cases, he dealt with elements of the novel – and not the translation – with which he felt dissatisfied by omitting, altering and adding material.

The French translations did not wholly replaced the Czech versions as the new 'originals', although they did become the new original versions for the English translations. In the 1990s, Kundera supervised and collaborated on the retranslation of all the English translations of the Czech novels from the French translations. However, in the cases in which Kundera published a new Czech edition of a novel – for example, *Valčík na rozloučenou* / *Farewell Waltz* in 1997 – the new edition, while revised and altered, does not entirely correspond to the 'definitive' and 'authentic' French revised translation. The history of the evolution of *Farewell Waltz* (1976) is symptomatic of Kundera's working and translation process. First circulated in a *samizdat* edition in 1970 under the title *Epilog*, the novel, with some changes to the content, was first published in France in 1976 as *La valse aux adieux*. It was then published in Czech in 1979 by Sixty-Eight Publishers in Canada, with further changes to the content, some included (and some not) in the revised (by Kundera) French translations of 1984 and 1986. In 1997, Kundera published a new Czech edition in the Czech Republic, which contains some changes made in the revised French translations but also some changes unique to the new 1997 Czech edition.

As Kundera deliberately differentiated the Czech and French versions in content – as he has also done with *The Joke* (1967), *Laughable Loves* (1970), *Life is Elsewhere* (1973), and *The Book of Laughter and Forgetting* (1979) – the issue of fidelity has become increasingly more complex. If there is no one untouched original version of the novels, if even the manuscript is a 'matrix' (Kundera, 1977: 3), then with what justification can Kundera demand fidelity? The answer would seem self-explanatory, i.e. that Kundera demands fidelity to the definitive French version, because with novels such as *Life is Elsewhere* (1973), *The Book of Laughter and Forgetting* (1979) and *The Unbearable Lightness of Being* (1984), which have not been published yet in the Czech Republic, the French version is the most recently revised version, the closest to the author's current vision of the novel. The English translations of *Farewell Waltz* serve as a possible example: the novel was first translated from Czech by Peter Kussi in 1976 as *The Farewell Party* and corresponded to the 1970 Czech edition, with the changes that would appear in the 1979 Czech edition. It was retranslated in 1998 from French by Aaron Asher as *Farewell Waltz*, which was closer – or more 'faithful' – to the 1986 French edition than to the 1997 Czech edition (Asher speaks no Czech). The new English edition is considered more definitive because it includes some of the content changes that Kundera made to the novel while revising the French translation, but it also slightly differs, in content, from both the French and Czech editions.

Kundera has been criticised for his policy of fidelity on two counts: firstly, because he rewrites the translations and deliberately alters them so they do not necessarily correspond to the Czech 'originals'; and, secondly, because 'fidelity' – in the traditional translation sense – is now widely regarded to be an impossibility. The translation theorist Lawrence Venuti characterised Kundera as 'naïve' because he apparently refuses to accept that a translation automatically incurs changes because of the cultural differences between languages – each language containing culturally untranslatable differences that need to be transformed in order to make the translation understandable (Venuti, 1998: 5–6). Kundera has, indeed, claimed that a translation is only beautiful if it is faithful and, strangely for a writer living and writing in two languages, apparently asserted that such fidelity is possible (Kundera, 1986a: 85–87), which seems curiously odd and even hypocritical given that Kundera deliberately alters the translations once he has control of them, an act which paradoxically implies that Kundera is both unaware of cultural difference between languages, demanding exact fidelity from his translators, while simultaneously cynically exploiting cultural differences in his own translation process.

Some critics believe that Kundera had a very specific agenda in at once complaining that translators were being unfaithful while he himself altered the novels in translation (Stanger, 1997), i.e. that Kundera tailored his translations for a specific audience. Allison Stanger argued that Kundera deliberately removed certain material from the English and French translations of *The Joke* (1967) in order to ingratiate himself with those readerships by simplifying Czech history to comply with Western assumptions, for instance by removing a passage that suggested Czech collaboration with the Red Army (an image that ran contrary to Western perceptions of Soviet domination and Czech victimhood), or by removing passages that, though acceptable to a Czech readership, would potentially be seen as sexist in the West. These allegations would be mitigated, Stanger argued, only if Kundera genuinely felt that his changes made for an aesthetically superior vision of the novel. But because Kundera made no such changes in the Czech original, Stanger intimated that this was not the case. In an article indicting Kundera's 'betrayal' of his translators and readers, Caleb Crain pointed to Stanger's assertions as proof that Kundera's alterations to the translations were cynical acts of contingency (Crain, 1999: 45).

These views echo a certain strand of Czech literary criticism which suggests that Kundera not only altered his translations for a Western audience, but also altered his own writing. In his widely circulated 1988 *samizdat* essay *Kunderovské paradoxy/Kunderian Paradoxes*, Milan Jungmann made similar arguments, stating that *The Unbearable Lightness of Being* (1984) was written with the intention of becoming a Western bestseller novel, because of the erotic content and because of the simplification of Czech history in the novel. Jungmann also accused Kundera of rewriting his image, presenting himself to the West as an unknown writer and a critic of the regime. However, because of his poetry and plays, Kundera had been an important literary figure in Czechoslovakia in the 1960s. He later removed this work, some of which was strongly communist, from his bibliography by not translating it (Bauer, 1998a: 12–13). The suspicion that Kundera betrayed his Czech readers and his own talent has been reinforced by his decision to write in French, regarded by some Czech critics (including Jungmann) as a conscious decision to move from the periphery of European culture to its centre, and, in doing so, seeking fame and recognition.

As if shaking a kaleidoscope and not waiting for it to settle, these criticisms have told only part of the story. To gain some insight into Kundera's search for 'fidelity', his rewriting instinct, his awareness of audience and his blurring of the original/translation boundary in his work, some assumptions need to be challenged. The first is this original/translation distinction, a binary echoed in the search for authenticity/inauthenticity in Kundera and his work. Stanger criticises Kundera for his privileging of the translation of *The Joke* (1967) over the Czech original, yet goes on to do the same thing by detailing the changes in the translations but not identifying any changes in the Czech version between 1967 and 1991. In fact, Kundera rewrote *The Joke* three times in Czech – in 1968, 1969 and 1991. Not one critic – Czech or otherwise – has made any systematic comparison among the different Czech editions Indeed, Kundera has rewritten the bulk of his work in Czech. His rewriting reflex began with his very earliest work, which he published in different and substantially rewritten editions, suggesting that, while translation has provided an opportunity to rewrite, it is not the sole reason for it. Based on Kundera's own comments that his Czech manuscript serves as a 'matrix', any new Czech edition would have to be rewritten from three originating versions. Thus, there are no sole source Czech originals. Kundera's own formulation could in fact be reversed: *everything* is translation.

Kundera has also translated himself. His personal withdrawal from media contact, in order to avoid reductive assumptions about himself that might cloud his work, has resulted in an intensification of the search for the authentic Milan Kundera. He has become, as was once written about J.D. Salinger, 'a story demanding resolution, intervention and exposure' (Remnick, 1997: 42). Because he rewrote his bibliography, the contemporary 'authentic' representation of him might be characterised as that of a Czech turncoat and an opportunist in the West. This chameleon move was further enhanced by his embrace of France, regarded by some as an opportunistic move into the centre of Western European literary discourse and a further denial of his Czech heritage. By dwelling on Kundera's reinventions, some Czech and Anglo-American journalists and critics, such as

Milan Jungmann, Michal Bauer, Caleb Crain and Allison Stanger, have neglected serious evaluation of his work. The question is whether Kundera's rewriting of himself or, in connection, of his bibliography, makes him or his work any less authentic. Kundera has played with reinvention in his fiction, inserting himself into his novels as a character and demystifying the notion of the authentic author. In addition, using translation as a theme in his fiction, Kundera suggests that rewriting one's past is an existential reaction to the creation of the present self. Kundera is continually preoccupied with the problems of the themes and forms of his early work, much of which has been removed from his official bibliography, in his later authorised fiction. Kundera has not exercised a contingent 'forgetting' of his past work (and his communist or Czech past); rather, as Jan Lukeš has argued, he is one of the few Czech writers to deal with the consequences of the past by making it art (Lukeš, 1997: 82). The reconsideration of his authentic original past as art is both inauthentic (fiction) and authentic (existential enquiry). Kundera's past is his life's work.

The second issue, in the light of the above-suggested complexities, is fidelity, which is a vexing one for critics in view of Kundera's claim that a translation must be faithful while he simultaneously is rewriting the translations *and* his Czech originals. The general view has been that Kundera demands fidelity for the simple reason that he is difficult and that he intends to antagonise his translators almost for the sport of it, feeding the constructed image of Kundera. Another possibility has been suggested by his long-time American translator, Peter Kussi, who wrote that Kundera was searching for a fidelity to his *ideal* of the novel, which is also an unattainable fidelity, especially for the translator, for whom it is impossible to know the author's intent (Kussi, 1991: 70). Perhaps there is yet another type of fidelity, one which Kundera proposed in the 1990s (though he had made it clear to his translators from the first translations) but which critics have so far ignored, which is a fidelity to the 'author's style'. Such a fidelity is markedly different from demanding a fidelity to meaning or content, both of which have little relevance within the context of Kundera's revision praxis. A fidelity to the author's style refers to transferring the way in which the author uses language into the target language. For Kundera, this is the most difficult aspect of the translation because it is the most threatening aspect of the work of the art – Kundera argues that each work of art *qua* art is a transgression of the given cultural norms of style. When the work is translated into another language, its style is often assimilated automatically into the target culture's stylistic norms in order to render the work less foreign and more accessible, but, in doing so, the translation removes or dilutes what makes it art in the first place (Kundera, 1996b: 99–120).

In all the talk of translation, Anglo-American literary criticism has not focused on the language *in* Kundera's novels (as opposed to the language *of* the novels). Unlike other Czech writers, such as Bohumil Hrabal, Kundera is still overlooked as a real Czech language stylist. As Kussi pointed out, Kundera is regarded as having a 'classic' style that owes more to the rational than the poetic literary mind (Kussi, 1991: 69). Yet Kundera has a very specific linguistic project that connects all his prose work and indeed connects his prose work to his earlier experience with poetry. The use of an intricately constructed language owes much to Kundera's musical education (his father, a pupil of Leoš Janáček, was a professor of music), especially his use of melody, motif and polyphony. In his use of ordinary language and dialogue, which is infused with beauty because of the manner of its usage, Kundera, a great admirer of Janáček, attempts an aesthetic quite similar to that of the composer. Words are used constantly in refrain not only in each novel, but also intertextually with his other novels and his other yet untranslated work. Some of these words are what Kundera has defined as 'theme-words', functioning again on a musical model – that of Schoenberg's 'tone-row' – words that reoccur throughout a novel (or novels) to set off an existential enquiry into the word in its constantly new and different context (Kundera, 1988a: 84–85). Words are also repeated in smaller frameworks within passages that often include several different repeated words and phrases, which lend a tonality to the character's or narrator's voice. Some of this melodic repetition is of course untranslatable – Czech vowel sounds and the uniform endings of Czech verb conjugations are impossible to reproduce in English – but as a whole the stylistic repetition is a translatable element of the text. Kundera does not believe the words' meanings to be absolutely translatable, but the repetition of the same word is. The manner in which the word is used – as a motif, as a refrain – is a large part of the textual meaning. Also translatable is the way in which the melody breathes, and that can be helped by the punctuation. Received opinion is that punctuation should be culturally translated; for instance English sentences tend to be much shorter than Czech sentences, and the translation should take this into account. However, Kundera argues strongly against this acceptance, pointing to English-language novelists who do not adhere to accepted punctuation norms – Joyce, Faulkner and Hemingway, who all use English punctuation in vastly different ways. Kundera's own use of Czech punctuation (the signature of his long, long sentences interspersed with brief halting ones, his use of semi colons and his use of parentheses) pushes the envelope of normal Czech punctuation, a transgression that is as valid an act in any language as it is in Czech. The problem, though, is that it does not make the translation in the target language particularly accessible, and from the first translation of his work into English it has been one of the strongest areas of assimilation – and appropriation – of his novels. This is an issue not simply between author and translator, but also between the translator and the publisher. Kundera's novels, once translated, often underwent a form of second translation in which the editor or copy-editor reworked the translator's manuscript to make it sound less literal and more 'English'. The first casualty was punctuation, altered without the slightest understanding of its aesthetic role in the text. That the linguistic style of Kundera's body of work – central to its meaning – has never been examined attests to this assimilation.

The Threshold of Untranslatability: Kundera and Translation Studies

'Kundera's thinking about translating is remarkably naïve for a writer so finely attuned to stylistic effects', writes Lawrence Venuti. 'He assumes that the meaning of the foreign text can avoid change in translation, that the foreign writer's intention can travel unadulterated across a linguistic and cultural divide' (Venuti, 1998: 5). Venuti's criticism of Kundera is an interesting starting point from which to consider how Kundera's case may be informed by or may inform current debates about how to theorise translation in order to reconsider its praxis. Venuti levels his charges against Kundera in two categories that have come under reconsideration in the past decade: the question of fidelity and the role of the translator. These categories can be subdivided into certain issues that are pertinent to understanding both Kundera's work and contemporary translation theory: the dangers of fluency, cultural hegemony maintained and constructed through translations, the effects of cultural dualism within the text and the reconsideration of what a translation is.

The questioning of fidelity or equivalence is one of the central repositionings of contemporary translation theory. Once seen as a necessity for a translation, its relevance has been questioned on two levels. Firstly, as Venuti and André Lefevere have argued, such terms are historically determined. Lefevere argued that the adherence to the construct of fidelity in the West is related to religion, that the 'ideal of the unchanged translation of the word of God, because it is the word of God, still lives on in the West in the concept of the faithful translation'. He argues that, in contrast to Chinese society, the tradition of translation in the West is tied into its oral beginnings, where the ideal (fidelity) is subsumed by pragmatic goals of communication (Bassnett & Lefevere, 1998: 24). Fidelity became a marker in the West rather, Lefevere suggested, of how well the translated text fitted into the domestic culture's prevailing poetological and ideological norms, becoming faithful to the target readership's expectations rather than to any original text.

Secondly, the 'cultural turn' (Bassnett & Lefevere, 1998: 123) in translation studies has questioned, as Venuti does above, the possibility of one language being able to be absolutely faithful to another language because of the cultural differences inscribed in all languages. These differences function on a very basic quotidian level – as pointed out by both Walter Benjamin and Roman Jakobson, both of whose work has been central to contemporary theory: 'The words *Brot* and *pain* "intend" the same object', Benjamin writes, 'but the modes of this intention are not the same. It is owing to these modes that the word *Brot* means something different to a German than the word *pain* to a Frenchman, that these words are not interchangeable, that, in fact, they strive to exclude each other' (Benjamin, 1967: 74). 'The English word "cheese"', Jakobson writes, 'cannot be completely identified with its standard Russian heteronym "сыр" because cottage cheese is a cheese but not a сыр' (Jakobson, 1990: 429).

Each language is 'culture bound' (Álvarez & Vidal, 1996: 2) and contains, as Benjamin argued, some elements of untranslatability. These preclude an absolute fidelity because there will always be some elements of the text that either cannot be translated, or are left out or domesticated. Despite Venuti's claim that Kundera is 'naïve' and unaware of the impossibility of fidelity, because Kundera lived and wrote in a second language after going into exile he cannot but have been aware of the cultural differences between languages. Kundera articulates this in a poignant passage citing the fundamental difference between the word 'home' in French and Czech (which does not appear in the English translation):

> CHEZ-SOI. *Domov* (en tchèque), *das Heim* (en allemand), *home* (en anglais) veut dire: le lieu où j'ai mes racines, auquel j'appartiens. Les limites topographiques n'en sont déterminées que par décret du cœur: il peut s'agir d'une seule pièce, d'un paysage, d'un pays, de l'univers. *Das Heim* de la philosophie allemande classique: l'antique monde grec. L'hymne tchèque commence par le vers: «Où est-il mon domov?» On traduit en français: «Où est-il ma patrie?» Mais la patrie est autre chose: la version politique, étatique du *domov*. Patrie, mot fier. Das Heim, mot sentimental. Entre patrie et foyer (ma maison concrète à moi), le français (la sensibilité française) connaît une lacune. On ne peut la combler que si l'on donne au chez-soi le poids d'un grand mot. (Kundera, 1986b: 149)

CHEZ-SOI. *Domov* (in Czech), *das Heim* (in German), *home* (in English) means: the place where my roots are, to which I belong. Topographical limits can only be determined by the heart's decree: it can be a question of just one room, of a landscape, of a country, of the universe. *Das Heim* for classical German philosophy: the ancient Greek world. The Czech national anthem opens with the words: 'Kde domov můj' (Where is my home?). This would be translated in French as '*Où est-il ma patrie?* '. But *la patrie* is something else: the political, state, version of *domov*. *Patrie*, a proud word. *Das Heim*, a sentimental word. For French (French sensitivity) there is a lacuna between *patrie* and *foyer* (one's actual home). The gap can only be bridged if *chez-soi* is given the weight of a *grand mot*. [my translation]

Yet, equally, Kundera does demand fidelity, and the question has to be whether fidelity can still be a word used with the knowledge that the same text by the same author in different languages can never be the same. In his essay 'The Measure of Translation Effects' (Lewis, 1985: 31–62), Philip E. Lewis suggests that the term 'fidelity' could still be used, but coins the phrase 'abusive fidelity'. Lewis, writing on the translation of his own essay on the translation of Jacques Derrida's *La mythologie blanche* (1972), suggests that

> the abusive work of the translation will be oriented by specific nubs in the original, by points or passages that are in some sense forced, that stand out as clusters of textual energy – whether they are constituted by words, turns of phrases, or more elaborate formulations ... the translator's aim is to rearticulate analogically the abuse that occurs in the original text, thus to take on the force, the resistance, the densification, that this abuse occasions in its own habitat ... (it is as if the translation sought to occupy the original's already unsettled home, and thereby, far from 'domesticating' it, to turn it into a place still more foreign to itself). (Graham, 1985: 43)

Lewis argues that the English translator could have engaged with Derrida's text more radically but chose instead, understandably, to produce a comprehensible text that articulated Derrida's arguments rather than his prose style. The problem lies in that Derrida's prose style *is* his argument, for instance in the return of motifs, phrases and punctuation. This is elided in the translation but could, if translated, provide an active, performative text in English. The difficulty is not in finding the right words that mean the same as those in Derrida's text – this would be nonsensical, as his point is to underline the polysemy of the words and the endless deferral of meaning (appositely enhanced by the translation process) – but to use similar linguistic strategies with English words. In other words, the style of the text contains its meaning.

Reading Kundera's essay 'The Sentence' (in which he compares three French translations of one of Franz Kafka's sentences), Venuti critiques Kundera's assumption – that Kundera might know what Kafka would have wanted in his French translation: 'With Kafka, he criticizes the French use of "marcher" ("walk") to translate "gehen" ("go, walk") because the resulting effect "is surely not what Kafka wanted here". But a translation can't give what a foreign writer would want if he were alive and writing in the translating language and culture. What Kafka would write in French can be no more than another French interpretation, not a rendering more faithful or adequate to the German text. The fact that the author is the interpreter doesn't make the interpretation unmediated by target-language values' (Venuti, 1998: 5–6). Venuti is right in the sense that Kundera cannot presume an author's intention. However, Kundera suggests that a grotesque sense arises from the use of 'marcher', which stands out in the sentence, not from the translation of 'gehen' as 'marcher'. This choice is, of course, as Venuti suggests, a matter of taste, but the thrust of Kundera's essay from which Venuti extracts this comment is that the translator is not faithful to Kafka's *style* in the sentence: his use of repetition, his punctuation and the layout of his prose (without paragraphs). In the essay, Kundera does not suggest that one would be able to find exact meanings in French for the German words, but that one could find a style faithful to the author's, because this is potentially translatable, even though it may seem to transgress the style of the domestic language. What distinguishes it as a work of art, Kundera argues, is that it transgresses the style in its own language – an abuse occasioned in its own habitat that needs to be translated.

Such transgression is, in effect, also one of Venuti's central arguments and one of his proposed strategies against fluency in translations, once regarded to be the marker of a translation's success. Fluency, Venuti argues, engenders 'an illusion of transparency' (Venuti, 1995: 1) that makes the translator and the threats of the foreign text invisible: 'The aim of translation is to bring back a cultural other as the same, the recognizable, even the familiar; and this aim always risks a wholesale domestication of the foreign text, often in highly self-conscious projects, where translation serves an appropriation of foreign cultures for domestic agendas, cultural, economic, political' (Venuti, 1995: 18). A fluent translation imposes the style of the domestic culture for domestic ends. In answer to this, Venuti has advocated translations that emphasise the 'foreignness' of the translated text, which allows for points of resistance at, as Lewis argued, 'the nubs of the original', making the domestic reader aware of the text as a translation, of the translator as a mediator, and of the displacement of the domestic language which cannot elide the foreign language at particular junctures of the text. Kundera actually makes the same argument against fluency or 'flow': 'Partisans of "flowing" translation often object to my translators: "That's not the way to say it in German (in English, in Spanish, etc.)!" I reply: "It's not the way to say it in Czech either! My dear Italian publisher, Roberto Calasso, declares: The mark of a good translation is not its fluency but rather all those unusual and original formulations ["not the way to say it"] that the translator has been bold enough to preserve and defend. Including unaccustomed punctuation. I once left a publisher for the sole reason that he tried to change my semicolons to periods"' (Kundera, 1988a: 129–30).

The rewriting or acculturation of the text is not just a matter of style, but a matter of interpretation informed by domestic agendas, and a recognition of this has been perhaps one of the most important contributions by translation theorists to the study of translation – the emphasis on how a text is manipulated and by whom. Susan Bassnett underlines this central importance 'that a study of the processes of translation combined with the praxis of translation could offer a way of understanding how complex manipulative textual processes take place: how a text is selected for translation, for example, what role the translator plays in that selection, what role an editor, publisher or patron plays, what criteria determine the strategies that will be employed by the translator, how a text might be received in the target system. For a translation always takes place in a continuum, never in a void, and there are all kinds of textual and extratextual constraints upon the translator' (Bassnett & Lefevere, 1998: 123). Such rewritings for domestic agendas are, Lefevere argued, endemic in modern culture – rewritings of an author, a work or a body of work by translators, publishers and patrons, media, the academy: 'rewriters adapt, manipulate the originals they work with to some extent, usually to make them fit in with the dominant ideological and poetological currents of their time. Again, this may be most obvious in totalitarian societies, but different "interpretative communities" that exist in more open societies will influence the production of rewritings in similar ways' (Lefevere, 1992: 8). Lefevere gives a series of examples across time and cultures, for instance, in how the English-language translations of Aristophanes' *Lysistrata* omitted or toned down the sexual element – the central element – of the play because of the domestic proscription of such references or in how the figure of Anne Frank has been re-presented in German-language translations.

Lefevere emphasised the implicit conservatism in such rewritings, a weeding out of the subversive i.e. any element that may seem to threaten the domestic aesthetic or ideological norms. For Venuti, this awareness suggests another strategy for translators – to focus on minoritising translations, that is either in translating texts from 'minor' literatures or in selecting minor texts from within well-translated literatures. In such a way, he argues, translators can challenge the rather top-down approach to translation, in which only approved texts are translated, i.e. texts that are bestsellers in their original language (and thus attractive to publishers) or texts that will consolidate a given image of a culture. This, he argues, would challenge the accepted cultural and aesthetic norms within the target culture, and introduce or reveal foreignness in it.

The question of cultural hegemony, as constructed and upheld by translation, is increasingly being examined via a combination of post-colonial and translation studies. Prasenjit Gupta, for example, provides a telling anecdote – when reading an English translation of Bengali stories, *Stories of Bengalee Life*, he noticed that the backing to the spine of the book was made of an old Bengali script: 'There could scarcely be a more apt metaphor for the domesticating act of translation. The Bengali had provided the backbone for the English artefact, and in doing this it had been all but effaced' (Gupta, 1998: 170). Such re-presentations of colonial languages and cultures became the justification for dominance over them, at once consolidating the image of the colonised and the image of the coloniser. This was not limited to individual texts but extended to bodies of text. Writing about the cold-war period, Rachel May shows how images of Russia were created, altered and recreated through the English-language translations of Russian and Soviet literature and used for ideological effect:

> As in earlier periods of international tension, the politics of fear and mistrust again colored the selection of works for translation and the quality of translations. Works from the earlier Soviet period were revived, or brought out for the first time, primarily if they had 'informational' value in the fight against communism. New works by unofficial or dissident writers were rushed into print, while others languished. (May, 1994: 45)

May, quoting John Malmstad, goes on to point out that Western choices were often aesthetically conservative: by ignoring aesthetically 'difficult' and potentially non-commercial writers or writers who did not fit into the dissident mode, the West effectively mimicked some of the censorship underway in the Soviet regime. The former USSR was both in and outside Europe, but May's examples remind us that the post-colonial definition of the world has, as Michael Cronin has argued (with respect to Ireland), 'shortcomings' in its positioning of Europe against the colonies, because Europe itself is a heterogeneous entity which does not have a common cultural or linguistic experience and which contains its own hegemonic intercultural relationships (Cronin, 1996: 3). Piotr Kuhiwczak strongly emphasises this point in reference to Central Europe and to Kundera in particular, arguing that the Western expectations of Central European writers contributed to translations that were appropriations because they chose to reduce the work to a political level (Kuhiwczak, 1990: 124). This fed into, as May pointed out, the ideological needs of the West. Charting a part of the British translation history of Kundera's first novel, *The Joke* (1967), Kuhiwczak argues that the translators and publisher (Macdonald) dismissed parts of Kundera's text as it was seen to be aesthetically inferior because it was Czech and different from the accepted norms at that time within British culture. That Kundera was published in 1969 for the first time in English is not arbitrary; the interest in the Prague Spring and sympathy after the 1968 Soviet invasion of Czechoslovakia created a market for Czech voices (as long as they were seen to uphold a digestible view). Even today, the only Czech literature in wide circulation in English can be reduced to a handful of names, almost all of which are tied in some way to the Prague Spring and the memory of the Soviet invasion of Czechoslovakia in 1968.

Post-colonial studies scholars have argued that resistance to potential ideological acculturation can be found within the text itself. Tejaswini Niranjana, for example, in focusing on the theoretical relationship between post-colonialism, deconstruction and translation, examines how the coloniser's discourse was effected and maintained by translation, but also how translation can be used as a subversive force in exposing the *aporia* within such inscriptions (Niranjana, 1992). Samia Mehrez suggests that the cultural mix within post-colonial societies can often result in an already subversive text:

> By drawing on more than one culture, more than one language, more than one world experience, within the confines of the same text, postcolonial anglophone and francophone literature very often defies our notions of an 'original' work and its translation. Hence, in many ways these postcolonial plurilingual texts in their own right resist and ultimately exclude the monolingual and demand of their readers to be like themselves: 'in-between', at once capable of reading and translating, where translation becomes an integral part of the reading experience. In effect, this literary production is in and of itself plurilingual and in many instances places us, as Khatibi has suggested, at the 'threshold of the untranslatable'. (Mehrez, 1992: 122)

Kundera, something of a *scriba duplex*, has also identified this potentially plurilingual element of his texts – the Czech language cleansed in the mirror of Diderot's tongue, or the French language with a Czech accent – as a subversive and resistant element to domestication. In effect, Kundera tangibly enacts Derrida's suggestion that writing is in and of itself an act of translation, an act of positing meaning while being indubitably aware of the trace of other meanings on the words used. By leaving words in the original Czech in the translation, tracing the difference in cultural etymologies of the same word and repeating words as motifs in the text which return with different meanings for different characters, Kundera demands an awareness from the reader of the novels as translations. As with Derrida, the style is a vital element of the content – the long sentences (more familiar in Czech), the repeated words and phrases, the layout – which may seem awkward, but which is a transgression that points to the cultural differences in the text and to a transgression within the domestic language. Kundera is not only not unaware of cultural difference in language (as Venuti argues), but he deliberately exploits it, and here he is in good company with other bilingual exile writers, such as Vladimir Nabokov, Samuel Beckett and Joseph Brodsky.

All three of these writers have deliberately used the opportunity of translation to rework and experiment with their texts and to produce and disseminate different versions of ostensibly the same text in different languages. The case of the self-translator or auto-translator is interesting because the traditional binaries of fidelity/betrayal and original/translation are dismantled. The authority of the author allows the translation an autonomy from the initial 'original' text. Of Nabokov, Jane Grayson writes, 'where the author and the translator are one and the same person, the requirements of "faithfulness to the original" no longer apply. In translating his own work, Nabokov is under no obligation to reproduce his original exactly. He is at perfect liberty to emend, to elaborate. And this Nabokov does in many of his translations' (Grayson, 1977: 22). In analysing Beckett's publication of *Quatres poèmes* (1961) in French and English on facing pages but with different content so that the English version was 'not just a rewriting but a complete rethinking of the original concept', Susan Bassnett writes, 'If they were published separately, we could perfectly well read just one of them and be satisfied. But the moment we are told that the English is a translation of the French, we are thrown up against the problem of the "authenticity" of the "original". One solution to the dilemma is to deny the existence of any original here, and consequently to deny the existence of a translation, assuming instead that we have two versions of the same text that simply happen to have been written by the same author in different languages' (Bassnett & Lefevere, 1998: 31). The autonomy of the translation, however partial or great, gives it an authenticity that is not reliant on a comparison with the original version – it may be a newer version of the text, simply a different one, or an attempt by the author to get closer to a platonic and perhaps unattainable ideal of the text (as Kussi argues is the case with Kundera). For Jon Theim, this is itself a form of fidelity 'to some trans-text or *Ursprache* or *Ur*-idiolect' (Theim, 1995: 212).

However, the author's version may suppress the translator's and may not appear to be aesthetically better – there have been criticisms of Brodsky's 'odd' English and his lack of diplomacy with his translators (Weissbort, 1998) and of Nabokov by one of his translators, Michael Scammel, who argued that his efforts were very mediated by Nabokov's because of the primacy of the author in the relationship (Scammel, 2001: 52–60). Kundera's efforts have likewise been criticised, especially because he has openly used the efforts of his translators for his own translations. In some ways, he is more of a ghost-translator, and his translations are a response to or a dialogue with earlier translations rather than simply independent translations of the 'original' texts. However, Kundera is not, as Venuti suggests, acting through naïveté of the translation process or of the translator's role. Kundera was and is a translator – he translated poetry into Czech in the 1940s and 1950s and as such is well aware of the uses of translation for ideological ends (Bauer, 1998b: 6–7); he underlined the dominant role of the translator in Czech culture in a seminal speech in the 1960s as a mediator towards and creator of a new national culture; he has retranslated his own work and contends that he was translating it while writing it. These experiences may not have made him more sympathetic to his own translators, but it is likely that they have given depth to his consideration of the matter.

Venuti suggests that Kundera's choices of which translations are better is purely arbitrary: 'Copyright law permits Kundera to get away with his questionable uses of translation by giving him an exclusive right in works derived from his. The law underwrites his view that the author should be the sole arbiter of all interpretations of his writing. And that turns out to mean that he can be arbitrary as well'. He argues, taking Allison Stanger at her word, that Kundera 'is not above the domestications that he attacked in the previous English versions', suggesting that Kundera's revisions are simply domestications that will endear him to his foreign audience (Venuti, 1998: 6). Ultimately, however, it is Kundera's right to rewrite his own novels in any way he wishes (Garfinkle, 1999), and it is debatable whether his rewrites are simply cynical ploys to make his novels more commercial or more acceptable in a foreign market. Kundera's claim that there are problems with the earlier translations, and his revisions of them, must also be studied in order to make or contest such dismissals. That Kundera has been disingenuous about his own changes to the translations and to the Czech 'originals' is partly true; there are only playful indications towards this in English (his statement that the French translations were more faithful to the originals than the Czech originals themselves). Kundera has been relatively honest to his Czech readership in asserting that there are no real originals for his work, certainly since *Life is Elsewhere* (1973), because these works existed in different versions in Czech and in different languages. Rather than condemning this blurring of boundaries between the original and the translation, it may be more fruitful to compare the versions and analyse the frictions among them. This may provide a way not only to analyse Kundera's translation praxis – more similar than oppositional to Venuti's call to a foreignising praxis – but also to rehabilitate the work of his translators. It may also provide an entry into reading his work. As Marilyn Gaddis Rose writes, 'If we do not juxtapose a work and the translations it elicits, we risk missing many a gift inside the borders. Each phrase, each sentence, each paragraph has a boundary that is more a threshold than a barrier' (Gaddis Rose, 1997: 7).

Everything is Translation

In reading Kundera's work, it becomes apparent that there are a series of 'translations' happening all at once. The word 'translation' itself is notoriously multifaceted, not easily reduced, and in this book I analyse four types of 'translation' in order to establish an awareness of its centrality to Kundera's work: translation, rewriting, writing and reception. Though these 'translations' are analysed separately for sake of clarity, they are intrinsically linked and are of an equal importance in coming to any understanding of Kundera's claim that 'translation is *everything*'.

In Chapter Two, 'Translation', I analyse the most straightforward and traditional concept of translation, Jakobson's interlingual translation (Jakobson, 1990: 429) – the process of transferring language from one language to another and the cultural barriers faced – and I provide a case study of the translation of Kundera's work from Czech into English, concentrating firstly on the translation history and then on Kundera's revisions of the initial translations of his work. The translation history is vital not only to an understanding of Kundera's current position on translation but also to an understanding of the various mediative agendas involved in the process for any writer. Often, and especially with Kundera, the dynamics of power in the translation process have been read as a hegemonic interaction solely between the author and the translator, with the author in the position of power. This conveniently effaces the role of the publisher – the site of real power – in the translation process. It is the publisher who inevitably controls what is published and when it is published, and who employs the translator and controls the dissemination of the translation. An awareness of this triangular – rather than dual – relationship is crucial in understanding the translation history of Kundera's novels in English because it reveals a set of cultural and power agendas which have not been considered in judgments of Kundera's reaction to the translation process. In the light of the history, Kundera's revisions demonstrate a consistency that relates back to the publishers' demands on the aesthetic rewriting of the novels to domesticate them for an English-language (primarily American) readership. By examining the revisions that Kundera makes to the English translations of some of his novels – *The Joke* (1969, 1982, revised 1992), *Life is Elsewhere* (1974, revised 1987, revised 2000) and *The Book of Laughter and Forgetting* (1980, revised 1996) – Kundera's attempts to move beyond this assimilation, and to allow as much of the original style of his novels to be translated as can be, become apparent.

In the third chapter, 'Rewriting', I focus on three forms of rewriting concurrently undertaken by Kundera: the literal rewriting of his work, the rewriting of his *oeuvre* and finally the figurative rewriting of his early work in his later work. I examine the writing that Kundera removed from his bibliography, but also show how he reworked this writing before omitting it and how he consistently returns to it in his later work as a figurative rewriting of themes and style. One of the most important examples concerns the first prose fiction piece Kundera ever wrote, his first story 'I, the Mournful God' (1963) – a story in which Kundera repeatedly said he found his true writing voice. The story was removed from the *Laughable Loves* collection (1970) before it was translated into French, but Kundera returned to it in the 1970s when he began writing the 'stories' that were to become part of his novel *The Book of Laughter and Forgetting* (1979). A story centred upon a false Cyrano-like translation, it – and Kundera's rewritings of it – presages and experiments with the signature narratorial voice in his later fiction *The Book of Laughter and Forgetting* (1979) and *The Unbearable Lightness of Being* (1984). An examination of the rewriting of his other translated fiction, *The Joke* (1967) and *Farewell Waltz* (1976), reveals how Kundera rewrote the Czech version before, while and after he rewrote the novels in translation. These rewritings challenge the traditional duality of original and translation, with Kundera introducing a new category of 'definitive' edition. Because of Kundera's acceptance and use of cultural differences to experiment with his work, this definitive edition is not an original but a specific authorised version in each language that may differ from definitive editions of the same work in other languages. Thus, in Spain and Germany, the definitive edition of *Laughable Loves* (1970) is a novel, but, in the Czech Republic (altered several times in its form in Czech), the United States and Britain, it is a collection of short stories. Kundera has also produced a definitive body of work – a second form of rewriting – that has substantially altered his bibliography. Translation allowed for this rewriting because Kundera was able to prevent published translations of his early work, but, since 1989, he has also effected a rewriting in the Czech Republic by authorising certain work and preventing the republication of other work. His argument for this reappraisal of his bibliography is an aesthetic one; he claims that the early work is of inferior quality and does not answer to his present-day aesthetic, that of the novel not only as a genre but as an 'attitude' to life. His justification has been greeted with scepticism, with some critics arguing that Kundera is airbrushing his early work from his bibliography as an organised 'forgetting', just as Kundera describes Clementis being airbrushed (from a photograph with Gottwald once he fell foul of the communist regime) in *The Book of Laughter and Forgetting* (1979). Yet Kundera's third form of rewriting suggests that although he deliberately suppresses the physical editions of his early work, it reappears again and again as both theme and form in his fiction, Kundera effecting a figurative translation of the early work. Certain themes recur from his poetry – the Great March from his first 1953 collection *Člověk zahrada šírá / Man, the Broad Garden* is reconsidered in the Great March section of *The Unbearable Lightness of Being* (1984) and as the theme of the Great Return in his latest novel, *Ignorance* (2000). The valorisation of Julius Fučík, a Czech Communist martyr, in Kundera's second 1955 collection of poetry, *Poslední máj / The Last May*, is reconsidered in his first novel *The Joke* (1967), and the 'Variation' poems in his third collection, *Monology / Monologues* (1959), become a theme all through Kundera's fiction. Furthermore, Kundera claims that the novel has become poetry, because of the importance of language in it. This reconception of the novel as an 'anti-lyrical' poetry creates a dialogue between his fiction and his poetry, in form (linguistic usage and layout) as well as themes reconsidered through the lens of the novel.

In the fourth chapter, 'Writing', I focus on writing as a form of translation. Post-structuralist theorists, notably Jacques Derrida, argue that all acts of writing are translations because a writer is choosing and imposing a certain interpretation of a language as they write. In this way, all original texts are already translations (Derrida, in Graham, 1985: 165–207; Gentzler, 1993: 145–80). Kundera certainly made similar claims, and from the point at which his books were banned in Czechoslovakia he was conscious of his novels as translations as he was writing:

> I too was forced from then on to write for translators only. And, paradoxical as it may seem, I feel it has done my mother tongue a lot of good ... I am very concerned that I should be translated faithfully. Writing my last two novels, I particularly had my French translator in mind. I made myself – at first unknowingly – write sentences that were more sober, more comprehensible. A cleansing of the language. I have a great affection for the eighteenth century. So much the better then if my Czech sentences have to peer carefully into the clear mirror of Diderot's tongue. (Kundera, 1977: 4)

The self-awareness of the ensuing translation did not result in a different language or an absolutely different writing style. Rather, with Kundera's exile fiction – beginning with *The Book of Laughter and Forgetting* (1979) – a careful emphasis on style lending it more predominance actually clarifies it for both translator and reader. In effect, Kundera began writing as a *reaction* to his experiences of translation. This is most clearly discernable in three areas of his first two exile novels: the *Litost* section of *The Book of Laughter and Forgetting*, the essay on the etymology of 'soucit' and the 'Words Misunderstood' section in *The Unbearable Lightness of Being* (1984). *Lítost* and *soucit* are two Czech words: the first 'untranslatable' according to Kundera because it contains so many meanings and tones, and the section of the novel that bears it as a title concerns an enquiry into how the sense of the word can or cannot be translated. Kundera looks at the etymology of the word *soucit* in different languages, showing how the different etymology affects not only the perception of the word but also its emotion (comparing the root of the English version, 'compassion', with that of the French, 'pitié'). The two words saturate *all* Kundera's fiction; fellow Czech writer Jiří Kratochvil argues that Kundera's fiction describes a journey from *lítost* to *soucit*, and that these are two of his central and repeated theme words throughout his fiction (Kratochvil, 1995: 182–84). The difficulty in translating them, however, has tended to efface the effect of their repetition in his translated work, leading Kundera to include the Czech versions of the words and the impossibilities of translating them as a theme, a response and a resistance in the novels.

The 'Words Misunderstood' section again consciously emphasises the untranslatability of language, this time within one common language but from two different personal cultural approaches – first, the Czech exile Sabina; and second, her lover, the Western European Franz. The misunderstandings between them echo a theme that reverberates throughout

Kundera's fiction (and in his plays), which is that of misunderstanding itself. This is often emphasised, as Květoslav Chvatík has pointed out, in the trope of lost 'texts' that disappear in Kundera's fiction: Mirek's lost letters and Tamina's lost diaries in *The Book of Laughter and Forgetting* (1979); the diverted postcard in *The Joke* (1967); the mistaken pills in *The Joke* and in *Farewell Waltz* (1976); the Cyrano letters in *Identity* (1997); or Josef's diary in *Ignorance* (2000) (Chvatík, 1989: 29–31). The theme is metastasised when translation becomes an issue in writing, as the misunderstanding becomes cultural as well as personal. The emphasis on the foreignness of language, its loss, is engendered by writing in a Czech language un-moored from its cultural references, but the subtlety and humour with which Kundera approaches it as a theme shows the gain of translation – that of insight into misunderstanding rather than communication as the human norm of language.

If Kundera has 'translated' his Czech language in writing, it is a theme of his fiction and this is one element that he has translated into much of his French-language fiction, including *Slowness* (1995), *Identity* (1997), and *Ignorance* (2000). The essayistic enquiry into the etymology of the word 'nostalgia', for example, is the central point of *Ignorance*, as the anonymous letters are central to *Identity*. With each of the French-language novels, Kundera deliberately appropriates a part of the French or Western European literary discourse and interprets it thematically, in his words, as a 'variation': with *Slowness*, he reinterprets Vivant Denon's *Point de Lendemain* and Choderlos de Laclos's *Les Liaisons Dangereuses*; with *Identity*, he re-interprets Edmond Rostand's *Cyrano de Bergerac*; and with *Ignorance*, Homer's *Odyssey*. It could be said that he is writing into a European homeland but with a 'foreign' style. While it may be tendentious to suggest that Kundera has given his French writing a Czech accent, he has certainly translated his linguistic style into the novels, in the use of theme-words, repetition and syntactical style suggesting, to quote Seamus Heaney, '... some unpartitioned linguistic country, a region where one's language would not be simply a badge of ethnicity or a matter of cultural preference or an official imposition, but an entry into further language' (Heaney, 1999: xxv). Writing about the Martinique author Patrick Chamoiseau, who also approaches the French language from an inflected viewpoint (with the meeting of Creole and French), Kundera similarly argues that 'Chamoiseau does not make a compromise between French and Creole, as if to mix them. His language is French, if altered; not so much creolized (no Martiniquan speaks like that) but Chamoiseau-ized' (Kundera, 1993a: 198). This 'further language', as 'Kundera-ised language', is the translatable and translated authorial linguistic style.

In the fifth chapter, 'Reception', I suggest certain border points of entry for readers into Kundera's writing, working from the arguably untranslatable elements of his fiction. To do so, I find it necessary firstly to analyse the question of misinterpretation. The trope of lost letters in Kundera's novels extends beyond them, with Kundera constantly anxious not only that the physical letters he sends to translators and publishers are received (the misunderstandings over the first English translation of his work arose from two lost letters – sent by the publisher for permission to edit – which never were never received) but also that the figurative letters he sends – his fiction and his paratextual writing – are *not* received, are mislaid and misinterpreted. Paradoxically, for a writer so concerned about misunderstanding within his texts, Kundera has generated a great deal of misunderstanding himself that has affected the reception of his work both abroad and in the Czech Republic. That Kundera identifies with the 'misunderstood' in terms of his 'old homeland' is clear from his essay on Janáček, 'The Unloved Child of the Family' in *Testaments Betrayed* (1993), in which he argues that the treatment of Janáček in his home country, by his 'family', who 'tolerated' him, smothered his music and his legacy, in contrast to the likes of Joyce and Strindberg, who escaped such fates through exile (Kundera, 1996b: 179–98). Kundera is unrepentant in his view that exile was an escape for his art from potential parochialism, and that, in exile, the French language has improved his art. Kundera, in other words, gained from the loss of exile.

With cunning and rewriting, if not silence, Kundera has alienated himself from some Czechs who think that he 'ran away', that his novels are a justification for this flight and that his adoption of French is the final betrayal (Garton-Ash, 1987: 217). The fragile relationship with Czech readers has been further weakened by the slow publication of his novels (his Czech publishers have no current plans to publish any further novels in the future) because he is 'rewriting' them, contributing to a sense that Kundera does not regard his Czech readership with due importance. The lack of a public and published Kundera in the Czech Republic has led to a great deal of speculation, which has in turn reverberated into literary criticism and media criticism of his work. On the other hand, some of the finest literary criticism of his work has been published by Czech critics post-1989, and these are inevitably critics who themselves were exiles. It is interesting that little notice has been taken of this literary work abroad, with British and American media focusing on the negative reaction to Kundera post-1989, a reaction that has affected both Anglo-American media and academic readings of Kundera and his work.

The inseparability of the Kundera persona from the work has been engendered to some extent by Kundera himself. His withdrawal from public life has been more than adequately balanced by the strong voice in his paratextual writings – essays, articles and author's notes appended to new editions that he uses to control interpretations of his work. For instance, in each of the post-1989 Czech editions of his work, Kundera appended not only long author's notes but also essays by others on the work which Kundera has chosen and, in doing so, approved. This practice is nothing new with Kundera: in the mid 1960s, he appended a note onto his play *Majitelé klíčů / The Keepers of the Keys* (1962), in response to what he regarded as the critics' failure to understand the play (Kundera, 1962: 82–91). Their misunderstanding (reading it as a political play) galvanised the success of the play, and this is one of the most interesting paradoxes of Kundera's consistent sense of being misunderstood – he believes that his success is based on reductive readings and misunderstandings. This has specifically involved reductive political readings of his work, especially *The Joke* (1967) and *Life is Elsewhere* (1973), where in both cases the initial positive critical reception focused on the political import of the novels to Western readings of Eastern Europe. The way in which the novels were translated, Kundera suggested, aided such an interpretation, especially in the case of *The Joke*, when the initial British publishers removed swathes of material that seemed irrelevant to such an interpretation.

The barriers of language have affected the interpretation of Kundera's work most notably in the disregard in the English-speaking world of his linguistic project. This disregard has a direct correlation to problems with the translations (though not necessarily with the translators), which were commissioned, controlled and published by publishing houses that demanded accessible English-language texts. This mediative agenda, ripe with given cultural assumptions, then carried into the media and critical reception of Kundera's work, where only passing reference was made to the fact of translation at all, as if the processes of both translation and critical reception were transparent. A familiar foreignness of Kundera, on the other hand, has always been underlined in the perceptions of the intellectuality, eroticism (and sexism) and political nature of the work, reinforcing the stereotype of an 'Eastern European' author. Kundera's move into the French language, along with the political changes in the ex-Czechoslovakia, has complicated this stereotype, and has been partially responsible for the negative reactions towards his work. Any move to interpret Kundera needs to read the agendas involved in doing so.

It is possible to regard Kundera's interventions as heavy-handedly posing a correct way to read the novels, whether by revising the translations or by adding paratextual work, but it could be reasonably argued that he is not imposing a correct interpretation, rather a way of reading. Congruent to Kundera's whole novelistic enterprise is the revelation of the plurality of language and of interpretations of this language. Because of the interpretations of the text by the translators or/and the editors, some choices in the translating and editing of the novels have attenuated or even closed down thesepluralities. In reading what Kundera has attempted to revise when returning to these translations, possible entry points appear into what these interpretations were and how they affected the reading of the language and, concurrently, the reading of the novels.

The actual act of interlingual translation is the nexus of a series of 'translations' that need to be explored to enlighten the manipulations and transformations going on before even one can begin begin to interpret Kundera's work. These translations are not a controversial side issue but a path into the heart of the work that has been obscured because of interlingual translation. A reading of any author's work involves assumptions that are borne on a series of manipulations, and Kundera's case is vitally important because it is a direct response to these layers of manipulation of language and ideas. Looking at the translation of his work does not centre solely on the question of what understanding is, but on where the understanding comes from and from where to begin understanding.

Chapter 2
Translation

'An exaggerated obsession with translation?' Kundera writes, 'I cannot say. When Carlos Fuentes writes a novel, he knows that eighty per cent of his readers will read it in the original, in Spanish; he can calmly wave off his translations. But after the Russian invasion, Czech readers made up one in a hundred, in the nineteen eighties finally not even one in a thousand, of my public. It was perverse and sad, but I had to reconcile myself with it; my books lived their lives as translations; as translations, they were read, criticised, judged, accepted or rejected. I am unable not to care about them.' (1993b: 345–56, my translation). Kundera argues further that, with the exception of Vladimir Nabokov, few authors have been more involved in the translation process of their novels, but it is Kundera's involvement that has caused controversy. In the last decade, he has been criticised for this involvement: for his antagonism to his translators, for demanding an impossible and absolute fidelity to the originals, for articulating a 'naïve' and impracticable translation theory, for producing his own inadequate translations, and for revising his translations (and not his Czech originals) to pander to a 'Western' readership (Crain, 1999; Stanger, 1997).

I suggest that these criticisms have ignored certain factors: the role played by the publishers in the translations, Kundera's actual translation theory and praxis, the working relationship with his translators and, finally, Kundera's reasons for assuming ultimate authority over his own texts. Translation is not a transparent process, and Kundera has always been suspicious of any potential manipulation of his work, attributed largely to his experience with censors in the former Czechoslovakia and to his own experience as a translator. The mediating party in a translation is often regarded to be the translator, but publishers also play a central role in choosing what is translated and how it is translated. Kundera has had a troubled history with his English language publishers, which has had an effect on both the translators and the translating process, with many of the problems stemming from editorial rather than translatorial decisions. The roots of these problems lay in the publishers' needs, which were at times in direct opposition to those of Kundera. The publishers invariably sought an accessible and fluent translation, one which would recoup a cultural and preferably commercial dividend, with a consequent emphasis on assimilation to the current norms of literary style. A translator's command of English was considered more important than their command of Czech, and Kundera, though nominally granted his choice of translator, was largely overruled. Kundera's aim was to work with a translator who was a native Czech, and who was sensitive to the linguistic style of the novels. He consistently argued that any novel worth its name transgresses the norms of literary style, however subtly, and it is this transgression that makes it art.

The disparity between the translation and proper English is not automatically a question of the translator's incompetence or of problems with the author's style, but it is the site where the 'foreign' style, both in the sense of the foreign language and in the sense of the author's different style, which defines the individuality of that author, challenges the accepted one. Kundera's frustration was that the central and most translatable element of his language style was one that was not in the interests of either the translator or the editor to re-produce. He was not seeking an absolute transference of meaning between his different language texts but rather a consistency of language usage. This is an important distinction because, as he wrote and revised his translation, Kundera began to consciously realise his novelistic poetics in the repetition of key terms, the repetition of words for their tonality and the structure, including the punctuation. Kundera's major impetus for revising the translations focused on these areas of concern, but his compositional style and poetics were frequently ignored, in large part because they ran counter to the publishers' needs for fluent and accessible translations.

Kundera consistently explained this compositional style to his translators, in order to avoid its effacement, in long and numerous letters. Because of Kundera's involvement and interest, the working relationship with his translators was initially a positive one, but was often hampered by physical distance. When his first books were translated into English, Kundera was still in the former Czechoslovakia and a *persona non grata* there – this meant that correspondence and reading and editing of manuscripts were often haphazard owing to possible censorship, and called for a smuggling of manuscripts or a roundabout articulation of needs in correspondence. When Kundera moved to France in 1975, the physical distance was often frustrating to him because it did not allow the relationship to be close enough for in-depth explanation and understanding. In the 1980s, Kundera began to meet his translators, and in the 1990s, he consolidated this close collaboration with his new translator, editor and publisher, Aaron Asher. It took a change in status, however, for Kundera to establish the kind of relationship he wanted with his translators. As an unknown quantity Kundera only had nominal control over translatorial decisions, whether in choosing his translators or in challenging editorial decisions. His arguably obsessive control, over his novels, and the revision of the translations, was in part a reaction to the early lack of control, and changed with his growing international success. The establishment of authority over his own novels enabled him to take certain liberties with the foreign-language versions, resulting in different versions of the same novel existing across languages, whose fidelity was found more in the conveyance of style rather than in the exact reproduction of content. Kundera's reasoning cannot be dismissed as quixotic because to do so, is to fall prey to the same assumptions about what a translation should be as Kundera's initial publishers held – that it should only be fluent and 'understandable' from a domestic cultural viewpoint, thereby concealing the manipulations inherent in any mediation of literary texts, a manipulation that lies at the heart of Kundera's novelistic enterprise.

Straight Lines: Publishers and Translators

> What translation has in common with censorship is that both operate on the basis of the 'what's possible' principle, and it must be noted that linguistic barriers can be as high as those erected by the state.
>
> Joseph Brodsky (1987: 47–48)

Through the 1950s and 1960s, the censors in Czechoslovakia removed material from artistic work deemed to have an ideological threat to the communist regime, attempting to make the work conform to the imposed political and ideological norms. Kundera's stubborn attitude in defence of his work against such editing was not one borne of fame and status, but, according to Dušan Hamšík, was a strategy learnt at the censor's table:

> Kundera, as I have said, was a difficult customer. For a long time he had refused even to acknowledge the existence of the Central Publications Board, and with fastidious perseverance he had avoided any meetings or dealings with its staff. As a result, his manuscripts for the most part failed to get published. Even in cases where the censor only asked for minor changes and the damage could be kept to a minimum with a little skilful editing, Kundera would refuse ... he would rather take his copy back and once more forgo publication. We often remonstrated with him ... But Kundera's rather eccentric consistency bore surprising fruit ... [the censors] would often turn a blind eye ... In this

way Kundera procured for himself, albeit at a high price, slightly more dignified treatment than was normal. (Hamšík, 1971: 86–87)

Hamšík goes on to describe how Kundera, having agreed to minute and inconsequential changes, is later 'racked with misgivings' (Hamšík, 1971: 93) and is relieved when the censors telephone to retract their approval of the text and refuse to allow it to be published because it contained these small changes. The text in question, a reproduction of Kundera's 1967 speech to the IV. Congress of Czech Writers in *Literární noviny*, passionately argued, among other things, against censorship and also for a recognition of the centrality of the translator as a mediator and constructor of Czech culture. The translators, Kundera argued, introduced work from abroad as a basis from which to establish modern Czech cultural traditions, with the possibility that Czech culture once established would begin to nourish the cultures that had inspired it.

Kundera was no stranger to the effects of translation into Czech culture; in the 1940s and 1950s he translated and published a number of poems into Czech by poets whose work was inflected with some communist values. His translations showed a certain amount of manipulation of the poems to conform to regime standards. In doing so, Kundera contributed to the construction of a socialist canon, influencing his own poetic work as well as that of other Czech poets at the time. Such actions were indicative of the period, but it may have implanted in him an awareness of the social as well as the literary complexity of translation.

Nothing, however, seemed to prepare Kundera for the experience of being translated in the 'West', the initial experience of which he later described as a 'trauma' (Kundera, 1986a: 85) and a 'nightmare' (Elgrably, 1987: 17–18). He discovered that foreign publishers had an agenda similar in form to that of the former Czechoslovakian censors, prioritising the alteration of the 'foreign' work to conform to domestic cultural norms over the aesthetics of the work. His first novel *The Joke* had lain in the censor's office in Czechoslovakia for several months, but was finally published in 1967 without a single change – remarkable given the sense of disillusion with the regime within the novel. In 1968 it was published in France and in 1969 in England. The novel was altered considerably in both translations, without any consultation with Kundera. Ironically, whereas the French translator, Marcel Aymonin, freely added his own material to the novel, the English publishers removed a substantial amount of material. Just after the English translation's publication in 1969, Kundera wrote an open letter to the *Times Literary Supplement*, comparing the actions of the British publishers Macdonald with the 'Moscow censors':

Individual chapters have been shortened, rewritten, simplified, some of them omitted. Their order of sequence has been changed. The whole text has been cut up into pieces and put together in a daring 'montage' so as to form a completely different book ... [at the censors] I had to witness with rage how whole paragraphs were disappearing. For a certain time I am not willing to accept the slightest intervention in my texts, even if this should mean that they will not be published owing to my attitude... I do not doubt that the English publisher has broken up my book in good faith that this would improve the sales. (Kundera, 1969a: 1259)

Both the editor, James MacGibbon (Macdonald, 1969a: 1312; Macdonald, 1969b: 1282), and one of the translators, Oliver Stallybrass (Stallybrass, 1969a: 1339; Stallybrass, 1969b: 1282–83), wrote letters in reply explaining the reasons for the changes, but in attempting to exculpate themselves they served only to make matters worse. Stallybrass did not translate the novel but rewrote a word-for-word translation by David Hamblyn, removing segments of the novel because he judged them to be irrelevant to a British readership, just as, he pointed out, a relay of the county cricket averages would not be important to a Moravian readership. Both MacGibbon and Stallybrass argued that the book had artistic faults that needed to be rectified, but, as Piotr Kuhiwczak argues (Kuhiwczak, 1990), these were read to be faults because they were seen as foreign and thus inferior to the British norms. This resulted in a complete rearrangement of the novel into a semi-linear chronology and the removal of 300 sentences.

What MacGibbon and Stallybrass achieved was a rewriting or reinterpretation of the novel that consequently affected its British and American versions. The United States version, published soon after the British version, used the Stallybrass–Hamblyn translation, but made even more omissions and included more colloquial and Americanised slang. The front cover of the 1969 American edition explained the source of the original reinterpretation – with the addition of a subtitle: *The Joke: A Novel about Life in Czechoslovakia Today*. Kundera believed that the novel, published in such close proximity to the Soviet invasion of Czechoslovakia in 1968, was deliberately translated and read in terms of that political event. *The Joke* (1967) was seen, in other words, as a protest against the insufficiencies and illusions of communism, all of which was particularly suited to a Western view of the real story of life in the former Eastern Bloc. This, in turn, affected the aesthetics of the text, in which many of the experimental devices included by Kundera, such as the non-linear narrative and Jaroslav's discourse on polyphony, were seen as clouding the real message and the relevance of the book to an English-language readership.

Kundera's public chastisement of the British publishers in the *Times Literary Supplement* led to a second edition appearing in 1970, with all the omissions and the original chronology reinstated. It also left Kundera without an English-language publisher, just as his books were banned in the former Czechoslovakia. Although *The Joke* had been a best-seller in Czechoslovakia and Kundera was a well-known figure there, he was almost unknown elsewhere. In some ways, what would attract publishers to an obscure literary writer were the same reductive reasons that Kundera had protested against, that is, his political and 'dissident' post-invasion situation. To be translated, there needed to be some market for his work, and the process of translation was inevitably linked to the publisher's needs for that work. This led to an uneasy truce, frequently broken, between Kundera, his publishers, his editors and his translators.

***

Kundera's attributing of a commercial motive to Macdonald's editing of the novel was astute and subsequently relevant to all his English-language publications. Macdonald of course claimed that their priority lay in the fiction and not in the money, but a large publisher, having acquired the rights to a novel, and having paid a translator, wishes to receive some return on its investment. This return is not necessarily always financial – widespread critical success lends a prestige to a publishing house which can be as valuable as direct financial return. However, their choice of author has to be justified, especially in the case of unknown foreign authors. The risk in taking such an author on is not likely to be offset by producing a challenging translation.

The publishers' needs were central to Kundera's translations in two distinct ways: firstly, in how their concern for the market affected the translations; and, secondly, in how their power over the translators and Kundera himself affected the decision-making process of the translations. The first involved taking a literary writer, relatively unknown in the English-speaking world and establishing him not simply for the altruistic furthering of literature but to garner either prestige or financial reward, or both. This resulted in asking translators for quick and accessible translations that would satisfy the critical elite, resulting in a dual policy by the publishers, who on the surface allowed Kundera a certain discretion in choosing translators and in requesting changes to the translation, but who ultimately often overruled him. This included choosing and dismissing translators who did not conform to the publisher's needs, whether that be with regard to deadlines or linguistic style.

Alfred A. Knopf, Kundera's main English-language publisher between 1971 and 1982, realised that they needed to establish Kundera in the English-speaking world in order to sell his books. This meant firstly establishing a critical awareness of Kundera's value, and secondly capitalising on that critical success. The first book for which they bought the rights was Kundera's short-story collection, *Laughable Loves* (1970). Hearing that he had also completed a novel, *Life is Elsewhere* (1973), Knopf's strategy was to publish both at the same time with two intentions, according to Kundera's editor at Knopf, Nancy Nicholas, in a letter dated 27 September 1973 (KENNA 903.2: 1979): firstly, that each book would arouse interest in the other for a potential reader; and, secondly, that the novel would sell the stories (stories traditionally being worse sellers than novels). The short stories had their own critical and commercial use in that they could be sold individually to magazines and could be sent individually to people of cultural influence, as seen by letters to Nicholas recommending names from Philip Roth and Peter Kussi, dated 8 and 24 June and 22 July 1974 (KENNA 901.3: 1974).

The strategy of publishing the short-story collection and the novel concurrently had immediate implications for the translations themselves. In his 1971 contract with Knopf, Kundera's one stipulation, as evidenced in a letter from Gallimard (Kundera's French publishers) to Knopf on 16 March 1971 (KENNA 901.3: 1971), was that he wanted to choose the translator, which he did. This was a problematic process, because Kundera had to choose from behind closed Czechoslovak borders and was reliant on recommendations from émigré Czech writers, such as Antonín Liehm and Josef Škvorecký, rather than on personal knowledge. He was also something of a victim of his own anxiety as he provided four names, in two letters dated 20 April 1971 (KENNA 903.1: 1971), two of whom had already been contacted before Kundera supplied his decision to choose Peter Kussi. Knopf accepted his choice, but Kussi, in a letter to Nicholas dated 29 May 1971 (KENNA 903.1: 1971), stated that he could not translate both the stories and the novel in the time frame allowed. Kundera failed in his attempt, via two letters dated 9 May and 29 July 1971 (KENNA 903.1: 1971), to persuade Knopf to publish them separately in order to allow Kussi to translate both. Because they were judged to be less important, Knopf chose one of the initially contacted translators, Suzanne Rappaport, on 15 September (KENNA 903.1: 1971), to translate the stories, so that the novel and stories could be published simultaneously. By this time, however, Kundera had read her translation of one of the stories, 'Nobody

Will Laugh', and, on this basis, he wrote to Nicholas on 29 September (KENNA 903.1: 1971), strongly objecting to her. Kundera felt Rappaport's Czech was not good enough for the task, as opposed to Kussi, who was a native Czech speaker. Nicholas, however, supported the choice of Rappaport and chose her to translate the stories, because she felt that Rappaport's sample was 'really very good'. She wrote to Kundera on 25 October (KENNA 903.1: 1971), that:

> You were not convinced about her because her Czech isn't perfect, but her English is very good and fluent and literary and because she is translating into English that is really more important.

Not perhaps good enough, as Nicholas complained to Rappaport, in a letter dated 2 August 1972 (KENNA 903.1: 1972), that the translation was 'too literal':

> You have done well on the specific words, that isn't what I mean, but there must be a stylistic way around the awkward (in English) underlinings and parentheses. Also my guess is that you pretty much translated phrase by phrase which makes for accurate but translated-sounding prose. And finally in both of the stories but particularly in Edward and God could you look over them again with an eye toward eliminating some of the very repetitious 'he said', 'she said'. I don't think the answer is the bad biographer gimmick of 'he expostulated', 'she crooned', but maybe you can rearrange the sentences a bit to avoid 'that. You may not be able to get around that awkwardness, but if you could try rethinking it a bit in English it would probably help.

Rappaport was finally praised for her translation and reported to Nicholas on 13 February 1973 (KENNA 903.1: 1973), that the Kunderas liked it. However, when the subject of choosing a translator arose again for *The Book of Laughter and Forgetting*, in a letter dated 15 May 1979, Kundera (who acquiesced to Nicholas's choice of Rappaport in a letter dated 9 November 1971 [KENNA 903.1: 1971], because of pressure from Gallimard), was adamant that she could not be used (KENNA 903.2: 1979).

Knopf's commercial strategy ultimately failed because Kussi's translation of *Life is Elsewhere* was a year overdue, thus beginning a somewhat strained relationship between Kussi and Nicholas, as Nicholas threatened, in a letter dated 16 May 1973, to take the translation elsewhere (KENNA 903.1: 1973). In contrast, meanwhile, Rappaport's translation had gained an admirer in the influential American novelist Philip Roth, who began to champion the stories, and had two published in *Esquire* and wrote an introductory essay for the initial editions of the stories. Roth also provided

Knopf with a list of influential names to whom the stories should be sent in order to create an awareness of Kundera. In 1974, another story, 'Edward and God', was published in the highly regarded *American Poetry Review*. Knopf was laying the basis for both a cultural acceptance and a commercial market for Kundera's work. Roth regretted his actions upon reading the translation of *Life is Elsewhere* (1973), a novel he intensely disliked. Nicholas suggested that this was because of the translation by Kussi, but Roth, in a letter to Nicholas dated 13 December 1973 (KENNA 903.1: 1973), did not attribute his dislike to the translation. His reaction, however, possibly did influence Nicholas in her animosity towards Kussi. In the end, Kussi was nominated for a National Book Award for his 1974 translation of *Life is Elsewhere*.

On the next novel, *The Farewell Party* (1976), Kundera was satisfied with Kussi's work and collaborated closely with him via letters, in which he elaborated his views on translation, on his previous work (Kussi was writing his PhD dissertation on Kundera) and in which he gave detailed page-by-page comments on aspects of the translation. Knopf, however, was less satisfied because neither *Life is Elsewhere* nor *The Farewell Party* sold on the scale they had in France, where both were quite critically and commercially successful. While Nicholas admitted that Kundera was now a prestigious author, she expressed her frustration to Gallimard about the situation, indicating that Knopf was still waiting for a 'breakthrough' novel from Kundera, in a letter to them dated 24 July 1979 (KENNA 903.2: 1979). Finances had also become an issue with the translator, and Nicholas's relationship with Kussi was deteriorating, as Nicholas questioned Kussi, in a letter dated 30 June 1975 (KA: [13] A-Kn5 1975), on his invoice for translation and typing services for *The Farewell Party*.

In 1980, the breakthrough novel, and farewell break with Kussi, came with Kundera's *The Book of Laughter and Forgetting*. When he first started working on the book, Kundera thought he was writing a book of short stories, or, in his own words, 'a sort of *Laughable Loves II*' (Kundera, 1996b: 167). According to Kundera, in a letter to Nicholas dated 25 May 1979 (KENNA 903.2: 1979), Kussi began translating three of the stories independently: 'The Cap of Clementis', 'Mother' and 'Don't Be Yourself' (the latter a new version of 'I, the Mournful God'). According to a letter to Kundera dated 28 June 1979, Kussi thought of trying to place the first two stories in *The New Yorker* magazine in the summer of 1978, with which Kundera concurred (KA: [14] 1979). The magazine had a policy of paying half the fee to the translator and half to the author, with which Kundera also concurred, telling Nicholas, in the letter dated 25 May 1979, that he had agreed to these conditions to keep Kussi happy and that this was important, given the lack of Czech-language translators (KENNA 903.2: 1979). Meanwhile, Kundera had met directly with the British publishers John Murray, who had published *Life is Elsewhere* and *The Farewell Party* in the United Kingdom, and shown them 'The Cap of Clementis'.

Nicholas disliked Kundera's meeting separately with a British publisher, and, as the stories had now been transformed into a novel, bought the English-language rights to the novel in 1979, effectively subverting Kussi and Kundera's attempt to sell the stories directly elsewhere. Nicholas expressed her anger by presenting Kussi with a less than satisfactory contract to translate the rest of the novel, sent on 10 May 1979 (KENNA 903.2: 1979). John Murray meanwhile refused to buy the British rights on the grounds that they disliked Kussi's translation and, in a letter sent to Nicholas on 23rd May 1979 (KENNA 903.2: 1979), requested a 'united front' with Knopf to oust him. John Murray's agenda was far from being based solely on objective literary judgment; they also expressed their desire to buy a translation that reflected the needs of their British market. When presented with a second translation, this one by Michael Henry Heim, who had come to Gallimard's and Kundera's notice and been suggested to Knopf as an alternative translator, John Murray objected in even stronger terms in another letter to Nicholas dated 12 July 1979 (KENNA 903.2: 1979), arguing that his translation was:

> ... an accurate version of the original that fails to recreate it in terms of a successful piece of writing in <u>English</u>. The structure of the sentences, the very order of the words, is still dictated by the original, and while this may work in French, in English it results in a stilted writing that immediately suggests that it is a translation.

Murray, similarly to Knopf, wanted a fluent and accessible English-language translation that implicitly – and here explicitly – was not syntactically accurate to the original version. However, how to define fluent English was debatable, depending on British or American English and depending finally on a subjective view. Upon reading Heim's translation in 1980, a copy-editor at Knopf remarked in an undated memo (KENNA 903.2: 1980) that 'your celestial is very fluent', a remark that favoured Heim, especially with Kussi's impending dismissal, due to his translation's needing too much editorial work. The fluency of the translation is a mark of the editor's work, and it is a part of the work that Nicholas at Knopf took to heart.

Yet there were two distinct but unspoken problems with the editing: first, by which means could an editor compare their editing to a Czech version; and secondly, to what extent was a knowledge of the artistic vision of the text necessary and considered? The first problem was overcome by both Nicholas and John Murray in what appeared to be a straightforward way: by comparing the English translation with the French translation, as evidenced in letters sent by John Murray to Knopf on 23rd May 1979 and by Kundera to Nicholas on 5 July 1979 (KENNA 903.2: 1979). In Kundera's letter, however, he warned Nicholas about the hazards of using the French version as an intermediary text, telling Nicholas that her issues with Kussi's translations were based on her comparison with a faulty French translation (Kundera revised the French translation in 1985). John Murray, in their letter, also showed that they judged Kussi's and Heim's translations through a reading of the same French translation and wanted to go further and translate directly from French, because they argued, it would be easier to find a talented French–English translator.

Kundera's worry was that the prioritisation of fluency and the use of what he regarded as a flawed translation would potentially efface his writing style. In the case of *Life is Elsewhere*, Nicholas questioned Kussi's translation, in a letter to Kussi dated 11 July 1973 (KA: [13] A-Kn5 1973) on the basis of the punctuation:

> The one thing I think you should watch is the punctuation. The Czech (I gather) runs to long sentences with semicolons. In English it is more graceful to have periods setting them off. It is also clearer.

In a letter to Nicholas dated 17 July 1973 (KENNA 903.1: 1973), Kussi agreed that the punctuation was unusual even given the difference of syntactical norms in the Czech language, but Kundera was quick and adamant in explaining his reasons for his use of unusual punctuation to Kussi from the beginning of their correspondence (KA: [2] KB1 1973). Kundera, in later translations, kept persuading Kussi to use some latitude to preserve his style of punctuation because of its aesthetic function (KA: [11] KF7 1990). Kundera had argued against the attitude that punctuation needed to be culturally translated, asking whether Hemingway or Faulkner displayed a normal English style of punctuation when both had such distinctly different ways of using punctuation (KA: [2] KB1 1973; KA: [4] KC3 1976). If there was no correct style, then surely his punctuation had as much artistic validity as theirs. Kundera also intimates that a translation of an unusual form of punctuation could challenge and benefit the English language. Kundera knew, from receiving the translator's manuscript covered in further pencil marks, that many of the punctuation changes were implemented by Nicholas rather than Kussi. He depicts, with some humour, an anthropomorphised pencil blithely crossing out any semicolons in the manuscript and replacing them with periods (KA: [2] KB2

1973; KA: [6] KD10 1979). The pencil has a great deal of affinity with the censor's pencil because the changes are made in ignorance of the novel's meaning expressed in its syntactical structure.

Whereas Kundera had written at length to Kussi about his poetics in Czech from 1973 onwards (KA: [2] KB1 1973), his letters to his editor only briefly touched on the aesthetic questions raised by the translation process, partly because Kundera had to communicate with her in English – a language he felt he was not competent in (KENNA: 901.3 1974). Kundera and Nicholas began corresponding in French from May 1979 (KENNA: 903.2 1979), at which point Kundera seems to express himself with more clarity. He approached the question of punctuation with Nicholas in a letter dated 3rd February 1974 (KENNA: 901.3 1974), suggesting it was a problem with the translations rather than the editing, though the fact that he raises this as a primary issue suggests he was attempting to gain her attention without directly blaming her. However, in a direct postscript to an otherwise flirtatious and cajoling letter dated 7 March 1976 (KENNA: 903.3 1976), he finally asked her to cease her editing of his punctuation. How successful Kundera was is debatable, as Nicholas never showed an awareness of prioritising the aesthetic needs of the text over the needs of the final English translation.

Nicholas had the final choice over whether Heim or Kussi would be commissioned to translate *The Book of Laughter and Forgetting* (1979) because Kundera, in letters dated 25 May and 5 July 1979 (KENNA: 903.2 1979), delegated it to her, arguing that he was unable to judge how their English read. In doing so, he knew Kussi would not be chosen because of Nicholas's strained relationship with the translator. He admitted this to Kussi in an apologetic letter soon after (KA: [6] KD10 1979), claiming he should have pressurised her to choose Kussi. Kundera also claimed that he investigated the possibility of breaking his contract with Knopf so that he could work with Kussi, but was advised by Gallimard that he could not. In the letter of 5 July 1979 to Nicholas (KENNA: 903.2 1979), Kundera stated his preference for Kussi because he was a native Czech speaker and he was writing a PhD dissertation on Kundera's work. He warned her, in the same letter, that Heim, a non-native Czech speaker, did not have the same awareness of Czech idiom and expressed his wish that if Heim were chosen, then he, as the author, should have the final say over the translation. Kundera, entirely aware of Nicholas's preference, bargained with her – acceding to her choice of translator in exchange for more editorial control.

Whether or not he received this control is debatable, but the relationship with Heim was certainly more beneficial to Nicholas because much of the correspondence between Kundera and Heim was passed through her, and in French, giving her a greater sense of involvement (KENNA: 903.2 1980). Kundera had lost several years of explanation of his aesthetics to Kussi and had to begin the process again with Heim, sending him lengthy notes on the translation (KENNA: 903.2 1980). Heim, in a letter to Nicholas dated 20 March 1980, told her that he felt he could incorporate Kundera's suggestions into the text with 'little violence' to the version agreed upon by himself and Nicholas, though Kundera continued to make further suggestions (KENNA: 903.2 1980). The novel proved to be the breakthrough book that Knopf had been waiting for, Nicholas writing to Kundera, on 13 May 1981, that it 'has finally established you in the place you belong in the forefront of American literary consciousness' (KENNA: 903.2 1981).

Nicholas's policy of pursuing fluency appeared to have paid off, critically and commercially. Knopf later sold the rights of *The Book of Laughter and Forgetting*, according to a letter from Nicholas, dated 7 November 1980 (KENNA: 903.2 1980), to the 'Other Europe' series, edited by Philip Roth, for double the amount they had sold Kundera's previous work for, though Kundera, in letters to Nicholas in 1980 (one dated 29 November and the other undated) (KENNA: 903.2 1980), wrote that he felt Knopf was not pursuing an aggressive enough marketing strategy to sell the book. However, it proved something of a pyrrhic victory for Knopf. The book's success attracted other publishing houses to Kundera's work and he began to receive offers for his next novel. Though Gallimard assured Knopf that they had first option on any new novel, Nicholas was beginning to hear rumours that Aaron Asher at Harper and Row had made an offer to Kundera. She received assurances from both Gallimard and Roth, in letters dated 26 and 27 November 1980, that they had not heard these rumours (KENNA: 903.2 1980). Discovering what that offer was (not from Kundera), she offered to match it, in a letter to him on 11 June 1981, because Random House, Knopf's parent company 'has lots [of money] and now that *The Book of Laughter and Forgetting* has established you it is available as it hasn't been before'. She offered to come to Paris to 'woo' him (KENNA: 903.2 1981).

Asher's main enticement was not financial but was a promise to publish a retranslation of *The Joke* (Kundera, 1993c: viii), a promise that Nicholas wanted to match. In an earlier letter to Kundera on 13 May 1981, she wrote that 'we [would] have it translated by the translator you would choose (as you know my vote goes to Michael Heim) and bring it out with your next novel' and offered to consider his suggestion of publishing a non-fiction book based on his lectures (KENNA: 903.2 1981). Nicholas, with this statement, fell into the trap that Kundera no doubt recognised from previous work – Nicholas promising to allow him to choose a translator while clearly showing her preference from her editorial position, and also tying the re-publication to the publication of another novel, a policy that was disastrous when she attempted it in the early 1970s with *Laughable Loves* and *Life is Elsewhere*.

It seems Kundera realised that he needed to act quickly in order to exploit his new found bargaining power, a direct result of the success of the novel. Once he had moved to Harper and Row, Kundera did choose Heim again, and Heim appeared to be the obvious choice to retranslate *The Joke* (1967). In 1972, Heim had translated and published a small section of *The Joke* that had been omitted from the 1969 United States version (*The Joke* had only been published in its entirety in Britain in 1970) in a small, scholarly folklore journal (Heim, 1972). A decade later, Heim's entire translation was published and, in a comparison of the journal version of this section with the published version, the evidence of Kundera's influence on this translation can be seen in its greater precision (in Kundera's terms) and removal of some idiom (Woods, 2002: 102–03). Kundera, in a sign of new editoral freedom, appended an author's note to the edition, giving a history of the translation of the novel, a history which still clearly rankled, praising Heim for producing 'the first valid and authentic version of a book that tells of rape and has itself so often been violated' (Kundera, 1984c: xvi). Heim translated Kundera's next novel, *The Unbearable Lightness of Being* (1984), which remains the only English translation Kundera has chosen *not* to revise, which may have to do with its success, as with this novel Kundera was catapulted into major international best-selling status (Woods, 2002: 277).

In a further precipitous development, both Kundera and Asher began work with Grove Press to publish Kundera's next novel, *Immortality* (1991). The move also allowed Kundera to choose his translator, and this time he went back to Kussi. In the 1980s, Kundera and Kussi continued working together, primarily on a revised version of Kussi's translation of *Life is Elsewhere*. Kundera had expressed his dissatisfaction with the translation to Nicholas in a letter dated 25 May 1979 (KENNA: 903.2 1979), but perhaps attributed this to two factors, rather than to Kussi's abilities: the heavy editing; and the geographical distance when he had attempted to collaborate on the translation. This time, Kussi met Kundera in Paris, and they worked on the translation together, aware that they would not receive the same kind of editorial interference. The revised version of the novel was published in 1987. Again, Kundera appended an author's note both explaining his notion of lyricism in the novel and also praising (and perhaps mollifying) Kussi: 'Kussi is by far the best translator from the Czech. The fact that he returned to this novel after many years in order to revise it and make it even more faithful to the original shows that he is possessed by a longing for perfection; in other words, that he is a true artist among translators. I thank him from my heart for his beautiful piece of work and clasp his hand as a friend' (Kundera, 1987c: vii). In a letter dated 19 August 1983, Kundera had also asked Kussi to work on some of the essays he was beginning to write in French, because, as he told Kussi, he felt his French was the French of a Czech person and that Kussi, knowledgeable in both languages, would be the logical choice to do the translation (KA: [8] KF1 1983). However, after asking Kussi to translate one of the essays, Kundera also gave the same translation to the Paris-based American novelist Edmund White. Kussi told Kundera, in a letter dated 11 April 1984, that he discovered White's involvement only when he saw the essay in print, translated by White (KA: [14] 1984). Kundera sent an apology (undated letter), explaining that White was at hand in Paris and the work had proceeded more easily and quickly because of his proximity (KA: [8] KF3).

Kundera's choice of Kussi for *Immortality* (1991) and published praise of Kussi as the best American translator from Czech suggested a distancing from Heim. Soon after the publication of *Immortality*, Kundera published another revised translation of *The Joke* (1993) in which, in another author's note, he criticised Heim's 1982 translation, though the criticism seemed aimed at editorial decisions:

> In the beginning there was nothing seriously wrong, and Part Two, 'Helena', was quite good, but from the start of Part Three, I had the increasingly strong impression that what I read was not my text: often the words were remote from what I had written; the syntax differed too; there was inaccuracy in all the reflective passages; irony had been transformed into satire; unusual turns of phrase had been obliterated; the distinctive voices of the character-narrators had been altered to the extent of altering their personalities ... I was all the more unhappy because I did not believe that it was a matter of incompetence on the translator's part, or of carelessness or ill will: no; in good conscience he produced the kind of translation that one might call translation-adaptation (adaptation to the taste of the time and of the country for which it is intended, to the taste, in the final analysis, of the translator). Is this the current, normal practice? It's possible. But unacceptable. Unacceptable to me. (Kundera, 1993c: ix–x)

The 1993 version was not attributed with a translator, the translator ostensibly being Kundera and Asher, who worked from, as Kundera admits, 'faithful renderings', 'good formulations', and 'fine solutions' from the previous Heim and Hamblyn–Stallybrass versions. This version, published in hardback by HarperCollins, was published in paperback in 1993 by HarperPerennial, formerly Aaron Asher Books.

Since 1993, revised translations of *The Book of Laughter and Forgetting* (1999), *Laughable Loves* (1999), *Farewell Waltz* (formerly *The Farewell Party*) (1998) and *Life is Elsewhere* (2000) have been published by HarperPerennial, translations attributed to Aaron Asher. HarperPerennial has also published Kundera's new novels, *Slowness* (1995), *Identity* (1998) and *Ignorance* (2000), all three written in French and translated by Linda Asher, Aaron Asher's wife, who also translated his books of essays written in French, *The Art of the Novel* (1986) and *Testaments Betrayed* (1993). All of the revised translations have been translated by Asher from the French translations (which had been revised by Kundera and declared to be more faithful to the originals than the originals themselves). Though Peter Kussi and Michael Heim had been approached to revise *The Farewell Party* and *The Unbearable Lightness of Being*, both declined.

Asher, Kundera's editor since the early 1980s, is now also both his publisher and his translator. There is a great deal of logic in this, given the publishing and translation history and Kundera's need to control the mediation of the novels. Asher had provided Kundera with an editorial freedom he had not received previously and, in becoming the translator, eliminated another mediative obstacle – Kundera is now dealing with one person who is willing to work closely with him and to respect his wishes. Added to this, Asher, as the commercial publisher (with the backing of a huge publishing conglomerate), has the ability to publish what Kundera wants, including the revised translations. Much of Kundera's freedom has to do with the commercial success achieved by *The Unbearable Lightness of Being* (1984) and *Immortality* (1991) and the ensuing status, which contrasts with his lack of power when a relative unknown in the English-speaking world.

The possible drawbacks of such a relationship are also evident. One could argue that the author has too much control, and, with the lack of an outside eye, Asher and Kundera are collaborating in a kind of vacuum. Also, Asher was the editor of editions – Heim's translation of *The Joke* (1983) for instance – that were not, in Kundera's terms, any better than those at Knopf. Critics have also questioned the validity of translating from French rather than from the Czech originals – a double translation designed to cause confusion. This seems in direct opposition to Kundera's earlier view that this was a fault of translations in some languages – writing about how he discovered that his novels were being translated from French rather than Czech in *The Art of the Novel*:

> I meet my translator, a man who knows not a word of Czech. 'Then how did you translate it?' 'With my heart'. And he pulls a photo of me from his wallet. He was so congenial that I almost believed it was actually possible to translate by some telepathy of the heart. Of course, it turned out to be much simpler: he had worked from the French rewrite, as had the translator in Argentina. (Kundera, 1988a: 121)

His discovery that his novels were being translated by non-Czech speakers from French engendered a change of policy. Kundera revised all the French translations of his novels between 1985 and 1987 so that they could be used as originating versions rather than the Czech. Asher's translations are from these 'definitive' and 'authentic' French versions. The authenticity of the French versions is one conferred by Kundera, and this is not to say that they are more faithful to the Czech versions in content. The result is that Asher's English translations differ from both the Czech and the French versions, some of these differences being inevitable given culturally untranslatable elements, some of these resulting from Asher's choices and some resulting from some loss of tone through the second translation. Another potential issue is Asher's editorial control over interpretations of Kundera's work: he has commissioned two books on Kundera – Maria Němcová-Banerjee's *Terminal Paradoxes* (1990) and François Ricard's *Agnes's Final Afternoon* (2003), the latter of which he also translated from French. While the first does not display any editorial influence, the second includes fundamental errors that may suggest deliberate editorialising, such as the assertion that all of Kundera's books have been published in the Czech Republic (when they have not), the assertion that Kundera is correct to rewrite his bibliography without an analysis of what he omitted and why, and the now axiomatic assertion that Kundera's language is 'simple' and 'classic' and only 'entirely dedicated to the meaning it must transmit' rather than to any transgressive style (Ricard, 2003: 165). The sanctioning of interpretative work, therefore, must be approached with a modicum of wariness. What is important to Kundera, however, is his ultimate authority over the English translations because of his relationship and *modus operandi* with his publisher-editor-translator, Asher. Whatever the qualities or drawbacks of the new translations, Kundera has achieved an empowerment over his own texts denied to him previously in the English-language context.

Devious Routes: Author and Translators

> Anyone familiar with Kundera's habits, his constant rewriting of manuscripts, his requests for changes phoned in from Brno and his subsequent lamentations when he saw the result, can imagine how delighted he was at this proposal for a rapid revision 'in peace'. I still have the pages that emerged from this melancholy labour. The reader will see, alongside the censor's straight lines, drawings of hideously misshapen cripples and weird primitive faces – not illustrations, but subconscious by-products of what was going on in Kundera's mind. Some of the sentences have been crossed out and replaced by fresh ones, then these in turn crossed out until, word by word, the author returned by devious routes to his original version. (Hamšík, 1971: 91)

Kundera has been ruthless in pursuing textual integrity for his novels, a choice that has alienated his translators. The critical reaction has been to castigate Kundera for betraying his translators for a quixotic and whimsical game of irrelevant textual changes. No effort has been made to understand the impetus behind Kundera's changes to the translations, which have reinforced the perceived view that they are irrelevant. Yet reading Kundera's changes not only clarifies a stringent and mainly consistent translation revision policy, it also provides entry into an understanding of his poetics. His personal treatment of his translators can be criticised, but the textual reasons for his criticisms need to be understood before one can comprehend why and where these problems actually arose.

The central myth that needs to be dispelled is that Kundera has no translation policy other than one based on disagreement with his translators' interpretations and choices. The perceived wisdom on Kundera's ideas about translation is that they are 'remarkably naïve', that Kundera's dissatisfaction with his translators lies in the fact that he actually believes that his work 'can avoid change in translation, that the foreign writer's intention can travel unadulterated across a linguistic and cultural divide' (Venuti, 1998: 5). Kundera did make the bald statement that 'a translation is only beautiful if it is faithful', but it must be noticed that he omits to add *to what* the translation should be faithful (Kundera, 1986a: 86). Kundera does not believe that a translation can be absolutely faithful to the original text on two levels: firstly, as a writer writing in one language and being read almost exclusively in translation, as a writer living in one language and writing in another. The untranslatability of language because of cultural differences inherent in it is a paradox that Kundera focuses on again and again, through his own exile experience and in his writing. Secondly, as we shall see in the next chapter, Kundera has rewritten almost all his

Czech 'originals' so that the translations have no original text to be faithful to. The concept of original has been subverted further, as the French translations have become originating texts even for the more recent Czech editions.

Kundera does present an answer to this question of fidelity in *Testaments Betrayed* (1993), writing that a translation should be faithful to the author's style. He maintains that an author's style is translatable but is often not translated well because of the need imposed by the power structures of the target culture to assimilate the incoming text in order to retain a status quo in the domestic language. The problem, Kundera argues, is that this is fundamentally at odds with the very core of what true art attempts – to transgress the norms of artistic style.

On several occasions, Kundera repeats to Kussi and Nicholas that because of his limited English the only way in which he can judge a translation is through its accuracy. This accuracy mainly relates to two things: to specific terms and specific words used in the novels and, secondly, to the punctuation in the novels. Both of these elements were not merely overlooked in the early translations but were aggressively revised in the editing, if not the translation. Kundera has never been regarded as a consummate language stylist in Czech or in translation. Indeed, the simple and lucid style of his prose has often been seen as a reason to disregard the fact of translation. Kundera does, however, have a concrete linguistic project and style evident both in his novels and also in his critical work. He discusses the question of the author's style and the threat posed by translators, who are required to impose a 'good style' in the their domestic language on the text, in *Testaments Betrayed*:

> ... every author of some value transgresses against 'good style' and in that transgression lies the originality (and hence the raison d'être) of his art. The translator's primary effort should be to understand that transgression. That is not difficult when it is obvious, as for example with Rabelais, or Joyce, or Céline. But there are authors whose transgression against 'good style' is subtle, barely visible, hidden, discreet; as such, it is not easy to grasp. In such a case, it is all the more important to do so. (Kundera, 1996b: 110–11)

In the essay, Kundera examines different French translations of one of the latter types of author, Franz Kafka, arguing that certain elements of his style – repetition of words, punctuation, paragraph layout – have been overlooked in translation and, as a consequence, in criticism because these elements are not regarded as fundamental to prose style (in contrast, it could be added, to poetry). 'When one artist talks about another one,'

Kundera writes elsewhere, 'he is always talking (indirectly, in a roundabout way) of himself, and that is what's valuable in his judgment' (Kundera, 1996c: 12). Indeed, the whole book of essays relates to Kundera's work without much of mention of it. However, his analysis of Kafka's translations is instructive in any analysis of his own. The linguistic and syntactical elements underlined in the essay are ones that Kundera repeatedly returns to in his instructions to Kussi – respecting the repetitions that are there for an aesthetic reason, respecting his use of punctuation which like the bars in a stave controls the rhythm of his prose, and even the layout (respecting the use of italics and underlining). The use of repetition is two fold: firstly, to repeat throughout a work the principal words which guide its existential enquiry; and, secondly, to repeat words in close succession for melodic and epistemological purposes.

Kundera claims to have fully realised his own aesthetic only when revising the translations of his novels, commenting in *The Art of the Novel* (1986) on the recurrence of the word and theme of 'lightness' throughout his work: 'Only when I reread my books in translation did I see, with consternation, all those recurrences! Then I consoled myself; perhaps all novelists ever do is write a kind of theme (the first novel) and variations' (Kundera, 1988a: 137). However, Kundera had described and analysed the use of repetition as a device already in the late 1950s (when he was first beginning to write prose fiction) in his critical work on Czech writer Vladislav Vančura (also entitled *The Art of the Novel / Umění románu*). In that book, Kundera argued that Vančura uses the repetition and 'return' of different words that defer the plot but construct the tonality of the narrative (Kundera, 1960: 128–31).

With reference to the quote above, Kundera's sense of transgression (echoing the theme of betrayal in all of the essays) is clearly stated not only in the word but in its repetition, woven around the repetition of other elements of the paragraph, the notion of 'good style', which is repeated throughout the essay, and the repetition of 'chez' in the French version, which is not entirely translatable into English but also refers to the concept of the artist's artistic homeland in the final essay 'You're Not in Your Own House Here, My Dear Fellow'. This is Kundera's poetry in prose and it is a carefully composed poetics (Kundera, Jiří Kratochvil writes, is 'a poet of construction, syntax, composition, architectonics, structure' (Kratochvil, 1995: 184)). It is directly confronted by the demands placed on the translator to provide a more English-sounding text which may eschew – or even not see – the constant repetition or words and which cannot colloquially sustain the long sentences more familiar in the Czech language. Kundera consistently laments the heavy-handedness of the translators and editors in dealing with these elements, and in his and Asher's revisions of the translations he consistently returns to remove what he calls the translators' 'synonymising reflex' (i.e. the automatic implementation of synonyms to produce a 'good style') and the imposed punctuation.

The 'return' of a word, whether within a passage, within a novel or within all the novels, was often effaced by synonyms, and Kundera maintains a clear policy in his revisions of removing the synonyms to reveal the architectonics of his novelistic enquiries. 'Return' – and the concepts that surround the word – is itself one of these key words. For example, in *The Unbearable Lightness of Being* (1984), Kundera investigates man's inability to return to their acts (playing on a demystification of Nietzsche's concept of eternal return); in his latest novel, *Ignorance* (2000), he demystifies the illusion of the 'Great Return'. Here he argues that return is not necessarily the grand gesture it has been assumed to be since Ulysses' return. The theme – and the word – appears also in his first novel, *The Joke* (1967), in which the protagonist returns to his home city and attempts to return to his past in order to change it. One of the other main characters, Jaroslav, also returns to the past but to the past of Czech culture, lost in the illusion his subjective view of the past gives him. Yet at one moment in his narrative he realises the impossibility of return, of changing one's actions, and Kundera constructs a beautifully composed passage in which the realisation is enhanced not only by the repetition of the word 'nenávratnosť' (non-return, never-to-return) but by the repetitions that surround it, which do return. The word 'nenávratnost' is repeated four times and is used once in its adjectival form, 'nenávratné'. Several other words are repeated: skutecny/real, švindlovat/cheat, základní/basic, věnec/garland, věneček/little garland, člověk/man (person), and some phrases are also repeated: 'Viděl jsem před očima ten věnec'/I saw before my eyes that garland, and 'Nesmí'/ It is not allowed. There is also a sense of repetition in collusion of the repeated words and alliteration of : 'podává potok říčce, říčka řece, řeka Dunaji a Dunaj moři'/the brook passing it on to the stream, the stream to the river, the river to the Danube, and the Danube to the sea.'

In an analysis of the three English translations of the passage (see **Translation Example 1**), Kundera's problems with translation and his solution to them become evident. Stallybrass and Hamblyn translate the central concept of the passage only three times and in two different ways, as 'irrevocability' and 'beyond recall'. Heim translates it five times and includes the common root though using two different terms, as 'never to return' and 'no return'. Kundera's translation brings uniformity to the reference, this time including six references to 'never-to-return', one more than the Czech 'original'. The additional reference is further from the Czech version than the Stallybrass and Hamblyn formulation, which is closer as a direct translation. This is a clear example of Kundera not only desynonymising the passage but tailoring the English version by emphasising the repetition specifically for it in two ways: through his use of the awkward and 'foreign' translation 'never-to-return' and through adding in the additional reference to the word-phrase that does not exist in the Czech version. The awkwardness and repetition of the word-phrase serve to draw the reader's attention to it.

Kundera's translation, following Heim's, does not repeat the skutečný/real of the Czech version (as the Stallybrass–Hamblyn does), nor does he translate 'Nesmí' as the usual 'It is not allowed' (again as the Stallybrass–Hamblyn does) but chooses Heim's formulation of 'No', which is repeated, underscoring the primacy of the repetition over a faithful translation of the Czech-language version. However, Kundera also adds in repetitions not translated in the previous two translations – the four references to 'garland' (little garland), the repetition of: 'I saw before my eyes the garland', the repetition in 'aby byl člověk člověkem'/for a man to be a man (removing Heim's colloquial formulation 'Any man worth his salt') , emphasising the repetition of 'než' in 'víc než … než' (translated faithfully by Stallybrass and Hamblyn as 'more than … than') as 'more than … more than'. Kundera changes Heim's translation of 'lidový' from 'traditional' to 'of the people' which, although not repeated in the passage, is repeated throughout the section. Kundera corrects a small misreading of 'rozplétat', translated by Stallybrass and Hamblyn and Heim as 'weaved' but which really indicates its opposite, to untie.

Kundera's actual alterations show a number of qualities emphasised within his translation policy: firstly, the intricacy of the construction of the writing belies its simplicity, an intricacy ill-served by translators and editors because it does not provide fluency in the text. Secondly, his revisions promote this repetition, giving a primacy to the repetition over fidelity to the Czech text – he deliberately changes the English version to emphasise this style (reflecting his claim that the translations are closer to the original than the Czech). The style of the passage is not merely an exercise in style but is elemental to the construction of Jaroslav's voice, which, as Czech critics have pointed out, is narrated in a particularly lyrical and dream-like manner, reflecting his illusions of the idealised folk world. This lyricism, reflected in his language, was misunderstood by Stallybrass as rambling irrelevance and therefore subject to omission.

Translation Example 1

Bože, co je to, že mne vzpomínka na rozmarýnový věneček dojímá víc než naše skutečné první milování, než skutečná Vlastiččina panenská krev? Nevím, jak to, ale je to tak. Ženy zpívaly písně, v nichž ten věneček odplouval po vodě a vlny mu rozplétaly červené pentle. Chtělo se mi plakat. Byl jsem opilý. Viděl jsem před očima ten věnec, jak pluje, jak ho podává potok říčce, říčka řece, řeka Dunaji a Dunaj moři. Viděl jsem před očima ten věnec a jeho nenávratnost. V té nenávratnosti to bylo. Všechny základní životní situace jsou nenávratné. Aby byl člověk člověkem, musí tou nenávratností projít s plným vědomím. Vypít ji do dna. Nesmí švindlovat. Nesmí se tvářit, že ji nevidí. Moderní člověk švindluje. Snaží se obejít všechny mezníky a projít zadarmo od života k smrti. Lidový člověk je poctivější. Dozpívá se až na dno každé základní situace. Když Vlastička zkrvavila ručník, který jsem pod ni položil, netušil jsem, že se setkávám s nenávratností. Ale v této chvíli jsem jí nemohl nikam uniknout. (Kundera, 1967: 145)

God, why is it that the memory of that garland of rosemary affects me more than our first real love, than Vlasta's real virgin blood? I do not know why but it does. The women used to sing songs in which the garland floated off across the water and the waves weaved it into ribbons of red. I felt like weeping. I was drunk. I saw before my eyes the floating flowers, I saw the brook handing them onto the stream, the stream to the river, the river to the Danube and the Danube to the sea. It was in this irrevocability that the essence of the whole thing lay. All basic situations in life happen only once and are then beyond recall. To be a real man, a man must go through to the end with full knowledge of what he is doing. He must drink to the dregs. He must not cheat. He must not pretend he does not see what he is doing. The modern man cheats. He tried to get round all the turning points and walk on aimlessly through life till death. The man of the people is more honest. He sings himself to the bottom of every basic situation. When Vlasta stained with blood the towel I had placed beneath her I had no idea that something had been done which was beyond recall. Now there was no escaping it. (Kundera, 1970b: 148)

Good Lord, why is it the memory of that garland of rosemary affects me more than our first embrace or Vlasta's real virgin blood? I don't know why, but it does. The women sang songs about the garland floating off across the water and the waves weaving it into red ribbons. It made me want to weep. I was drunk. I could just see the flowers floating and the brook passing them onto the stream, the stream to the tributary, the tributary to the Danube, and the Danube to the sea. I saw the garland go, never to return. No return. That was what brought it home to me. The basic situations in life brook no return. Any man worth his salt must come to grips with the fact of no return. Drink it to the dregs. No cheating allowed. No making believe it's not there. Modern man cheats. He tries to avoid all milestones on the road from birth to death. Traditional man is more honest. He sings his way into the heart of every basic human situation. When Vlasta's blood stained the towel I'd placed beneath her, I had no idea I was dealing with the fact of no return. Now there was no way out. (Kundera, 1984c: 128–29)

Lord, why is it that the memory of that garland of rosemary affects me more than our first embrace, more than Vlasta's real virgin blood? I don't know why, but it does. The women sang songs, and in the songs, the garland floated off across the water and the current untied its red ribbons. It made me want to weep. I was drunk. I saw before my eyes the floating garland and the brook passing it on to the stream, the stream to the river, the river to the Danube, and the Danube to the sea. I saw before my eyes the garland going, never to return. Yes, never to return. All the basic situations in life occur only once, never to return. For a man to be a man, he must be fully aware of this never-to-return. Drink it to the dregs. No cheating allowed. No making believe it's not there. Modern man cheats. He tries to get around all the milestones on the road from birth to death. The man of the people is more honest. Singing on the way, he goes to the core of every basic situation. When Vlasta's blood stained the towel I'd placed beneath her, I had no idea I was dealing with never-to-return. But at this moment of the ceremony and the songs, the never-to-return was there. (Kundera, 1993c: 148)

***

The problems with punctuation and with repetition are often linked, recurring in lyrical passages which populate Kundera's novels and often underline the character's unawareness or awareness of illusion. In the sixth section of *Life is Elsewhere* (1973), a new character is introduced, complementing the main character, Jaromil, who is defined by his actual and metaphysical youth. The novel, as Kundera writes in his introduction, is a critique of youth, or the 'lyric age', an age of absolutism and illusion. The new character is known only by his age reference 'the forty-year-old' (also the title of the section), and the reader discovers in the section that he had also been Jaromil's girlfriend's lover. She turns to him after being released from prison (incarcerated because of Jaromil's information), and the whole section contrasts with the rest of the novel in its sense of calmness (Kussi interestingly connected Kundera's unusual use of punctuation in the rest of the novel with the staccato phrase-making of an inarticulate youth). In one passage the redhead realises that the ordinary action of making supper with her lover is the most beautiful moment of her life. The narrator questions this in two staccato interrogatives, followed by a torrent of reason, in which the word 'safety' is repeated several times supported by the secondary repetition of a series of words and sounds:

> Nejkrásnější? Proč?
> Byl to kus života plný bezpečí. Tento muž k ní byl hodný a nikdy po ní nic nepožadoval; není před ním ničím vinna ani povinna; byla u něho vždycky v bezpečí, jako je člověk v bezpečí, když se octne na chvíli z dosahu vlastního osudu; byla tu v bezpečí, jako je v bezpečí postava dramatu, když spadne opona po prvním aktu a je pauza; i ostatní postavy odloží masky a pod nimi jsou lidé, kteří si bezstarostně povídají. (Kundera, 1979c: 324)

> Yes, the most beautiful. It was a piece of life that was completely safe. This man was kind to her and never demanded anything. There was nothing she had to feel guilty or obligated about. She was always safe with him. It was the kind of safety people feel when they are momentarily out of the reach of their own fate. She was as safe as a figure in a play, when the curtain falls after the first act and there is an intermission. The other characters, too, put down their masks and become ordinary people carrying on casual conversation. (Kundera, 1974: 264)

The tonality and melody of the intricately constructed passage is, in elements such as alliteration, almost impossible to translate. Yet the sense in which the initial translation is not faithful where it could be is clear. The two interrogatives are altered to an assertion that effaces the intervention of the narrator and removes the contrast between the suddenness of the sound of that intervention with the lyrical flight of the rest of the passage. Except the lyrical flight is not present, because the passage has been cut up into eight sentences rather than the two of the Czech version. It is a prime example of the kind of editorial influence that Kundera had suspected, and it affects the meaning of the novel by rendering the girl's reflection as a detached, cold and utterly rational one. The repetition of 'safe' is more or less intact (bar one reference to 'safe' and the inclusion of 'safety'), as is that of 'when' and 'She was', but some is lost, the repetition of 'as/like' and the translatable echo in 'vinna' and 'nevinna' – guilty and not guilty – is not employed.

Kundera's intervention can be seen immediately in the revised translation of 1986, in which the content of the translation remains the same, but the punctuation is changed to reflect the Czech punctuation and the original rhythm of the passage. The second revision in 2000 by Aaron Asher is not necessarily closer to the Czech version (he omits part of the last clause 'pod nimi jsou lidé' and does not translate 'plný' or 'nikdy' ('completely' and 'never' in the Kussi translation), but he does include the extra repetition of 'safe', 'her', 'as' and 'character' which had been removed previously in the English translations. While not choosing to include the repetition of sound in 'vinna'/ 'nevinna', Asher and Kundera include repetitions that do not appear in the Czech version but which bolster the sense of melody in the English language, '**as one** is **safe when one** finds **oneself** for the moment beyond the reach of **one's** own destiny':

> The most beautiful? Why?
> It was a piece of life that was completely safe. This man was kind to her and never demanded anything; there was nothing she had to feel guilty or obligated about; she was always safe with him; it was the kind of safety people feel when they are momentarily out of the reach of their own fate; she was as safe as a figure in a play, when the curtain falls after the first act and there is an intermission; the other characters, too, put down their masks and become ordinary people carrying on casual conversation. (Kundera, 1987c: 279–80, translation by Peter Kussi)

> The most beautiful? Why?
> It was a part of life in which she was **safe**. This man was good to **her** and required nothing from **her**; in his eyes she was neither guilty of nor responsible for anything; **she was** always **safe** with him, **as one** is **safe when one** finds **oneself** for the moment beyond the reach of **one's** own destiny; **she was safe as** a **character** in a play is **safe when** the curtain falls after the first act and the interlude begins; the other **characters**, too, remove their masks and chat casually. (Kundera, 2000: 238, translation by Aaron Asher; my emphasis)

The intrinsic effects of the punctuation and repetition in such passages on the meaning of the novel cannot be understated, nor can the effect of interference with it. Examining Kundera's two interventions in this passage, it is obvious that he is not searching for an exact rendition of each of the words in the Czech version, but is deliberately attempting to convey the sound and the melodic effect of the Czech version even if this requires moving the English version away from the Czech in terms of content. In another example, this time from *The Book of Laughter and Forgetting* (1979), the same process is evident.

In the 'Litost' section of the novel, the poet Petrarch narrates a story of a schoolgirl's obsession with him – a story the sceptic (and father of the novel) Boccaccio refuses to take seriously. Petrarch poetically describes the schoolgirl as she declares her love for him, thus dramatising events. Her declaration, in Czech, is conveyed through its sound rather than simply through what she is saying. The baroque extravagance–which Petrarch takes for poetry–strengthens the irony in the text:

> Petrarka pokračoval: 'Přál bych vám, přátelé, slyšet, co mi **říkala**. To bylo nezapomenutelné. **Říkala** a bylo to **jako** modlitba, **jako** litanie, *já jsem prostá, já jsem úplně obyčejná dívka, **nic na mně není**, ale já jsem přišla, protože mne sem posílá láska, já jsem přišla*–tiskla mne v té chvíli za ruku–***abys poznal***, *co je pravá láska,* ***abys** to jednou za život **poznal**!'* (Kundera, 1981b: 144; my emphasis)

The repetition of the long and short '-a' layered in with the alliteration of 'přišla', 'protože', 'posílá', 'poznal' and 'pravá' and then also the alliteration of 'nic na mne není' imitates what Petrarch calls a hymn or a litany. Heim's translation conveys a much more earnest account of the girl's declaration, because the punctuation is altered, so that the girl's irrational flow of speech – according to Petrarch – is presented in a series of short sentences, producing a far more matter-of-fact tone in the declaration. The tonality of the Czech version is again impossible to translate, but some of the repetition is possible to convey. In the 1996 Asher translation, it is again clear that the alterations attempt to instate some of the repetition as well as the long final sentence (Asher does not include the easily included repetition of 'poznal'/ 'recognise', translating it as both 'know' and 'experience' – Heim translates it as 'feel' and 'taste' – Asher is following the French version from which he translated the novel, which uses 'saches' and 'connaisses'):

> 'Let me tell you what she said to me, friends', continued Petrarch. 'It was unforgettable, like a prayer, like a litany. "I'm a simple girl, a perfectly ordinary girl. I have nothing to give you, but I have come at love's behest. I want you to feel"–by now she was squeezing my hand– "real love, I want you to taste it once in your life."' (Kundera, 1988b: 135, translation by Michael Henry Heim)

> Petrarch went on: 'Listen, all of you, my friends, to what **she said to me**, it was unforgettable. **She said to me**, and it was **like a** prayer, **like a** litany, "**I'm** a simple girl, **I'm** quite an ordinary girl, I have nothing

to offer you, but **I came** here because I was sent by love, **I came**"–and now she squeezed my hand very hard – "**so that you'll** know what real love is, **so that you'll** experience it once in your life."' (Kundera, 1999b: 185, translation by Aaron Asher; my emphasis)

This is not to say that Kundera's policy is entirely successful when he returns to his translations. For example, in *The Farewell Party* (1976) / *Farewell Waltz* (1998), one of his characters, Růžena, is literally saved by Bertlef, to whom Kundera has playfully given heavenly powers. The chapter in which they first talk privately is resonant with repetitions of ordinary language which is promoted to poetry. One of these refers to Bertlef's heavenly provenance, as he appears always at the right time. The Czech version plays again with alliteration in the repetition of 'proč?' 'přišel' and 'právě včas'. Kussi's translation omits the repetition of 'přišel'/ 'arrived/came', translating it as 'arrived' and 'come' and through omitting the last sentence. From an editorial point of view, the omission makes sense, because it is superfluous except for its sound and emphasis. Asher includes the sentence in his translation, but although this allows the extra 'Why?'; he translates 'přišel' as three different words, 'arrived', 'came' and 'looking for'. Asher to some extent is following the French version again, 'Pourquoi avez-vous cherché à me voir?', but the French version had otherwise translated 'přišel' as 'venu':

> ... **jsem přišel právě včas** [...] Ano, **přišel jste opravdu právě včas** [...] Ale **proč? Proč jste přišel** za mnou? (Kundera, 1997b: 168; my emphasis)

> ... I arrived just at the right time [...] It's true, you really did come at the right time [...] But why? (Kundera, 1976b: 151, translation by Peter Kussi)

> ... I arrived at the right time [...] Yes, it's true, you came at the right time [...] But why? Why were you looking for me? (Kundera, 1998a: 199–200, translation by Aaron Asher)

> ... je suis venu à temps [...] Oui, c'est vrai, vous êtes venu à temps [...] Mais pourquoi? Pourquoi avez-vous cherché à me voir? (Kundera, 1986c : 239, translation by Milan Kundera)

Similarly, Kundera, in contrast to his rigorous revision policy, decides not to retranslate Heim's translation for a new edition of *The Unbearable Lightness of Being* (1984). Two brief examples illuminate the incongruity because Heim's translation is no closer to Kundera's style than any of the other unrevised translations. The second chapter of the 'Words Misunderstood' section opens with three very short sentences that emphasise Sabina's isolation within her love affair with Franz, Kundera again employing assonance with the short and long 'a/á':

> Sabina zůstala sama. Vrátila před zrcadlo. Byla stála jen v prádle. (Kundera, 1985b: 81)

> Sabina was now by herself. She went back to the mirror, still in her underwear. (Kundera, 1985c: 86, translation by Michael Henry Heim)

In Heim's translation, the second and third sentences become one, in contrast to the ending of the previous chapter, which contained long sentences describing Franz's misguided happiness and which in Heim's translation is cut up into a series of shorter sentences. The contrast between the closing of one chapter and the opening of the next contrasts the two characters. Even the most minute changes in the punctuation can have a strong effect on meaning: in the second example, Sabina comments on Franz's arms, realising as she does so the inherent metaphysical weakness of his character. In this, she echoes the questioning of the duality of weakness and strength through the novel, and her comment conveys a melancholy irony in Czech:

> 'To je neuvěřitelné', řekla, 'jaké ty máš svaly'. (Kundera, 1985b: 103)

The English translation adds exclamation marks to this: 'The muscles you have! They're unbelievable!' (Kundera, 1985c: 111), which transforms Sabina into a simpering admirer of Franz's physique (exactly as he mistakenly understands it), removing the irony which introduces her insight into the paradox of his muscles and his existential weaknesses.

The changing of two full points for exclamation marks can affect the novel, as can the revision of one word. This is particularly true of key words that resonate throughout a novel or novels (such as the notion of 'return' above). In *Life is Elsewhere* (1973), one of the key words in the tone 'row' of the novel is 'moderní/modern'. Kussi had chosen to translate it as 'progressive' rather than 'modern', arguing that modern invoked a certain historical context used in an artistic sense in the United States (i.e. inter-war art) which would detract from its meaning in the novel. Kundera replies that 'progressive' also has certain negative political connotations but provides his defence for the use of 'modern' rather than 'progressive' mainly because its repetition echoes the famous citation from Arthur Rimbaud's *Une saison en enfer* (1873), 'Il faut être absolument moderne'. He argues that this is the leitmotif of the novel and signposts an enquiry into the impetus for the need to be absolutely modern. The novel, Kundera explains, contains the word as a refrain, which attempts to demask the illusion of this absolutist and grosteque drive. He suggests using the citation as an epigraph to the whole novel in order to awaken the reader to the reference – and specifically the American reader, because he suggests they will not comprehend the reference already in the title (another quote from Rimbaud), as French readers would. He makes this suggestion also to Nicholas, on 3 February and 11 March 1974, but, receiving no reply, writes that if 'progressive' is used then there is no point in including the epigraph (KENNA: 901.3 1974). The epigraph was included in the first English-language edition in 1974, but was omitted in the revised definitive edition in 1986 (the novel was published in a third revised English language edition, also declared 'definitive').

Asher – under Kundera's direction – pursues a different policy from that of the earlier translators (partly because he has no editor to answer to and partly because Kundera has the commercial and cultural currency to demand it now), and that is of 'foreignisation'. This is a popular critical concept which holds that a translator should underline, even exaggerate, the foreignness of the translation rather than effacing it, especially at points in the text that seem to be untranslatable. This is a policy he has been criticised for, and on a superficial reading of the translations there is a real sense of jarring at points, yet it can be argued that this is the consequence he intends. One of the more obvious examples of this occurs in his retranslation of the *Laughable Loves* (1970) story 'The Golden Apple of Eternal Desire'. The story revolves around two men and their chasing of women, a game which has its rules set down. Two of the rules are of 'reportáž' and 'kontaktáž': the first, writing down the names of women they meet, and the second, contacting the women. Rappaport translated these as 'registration' and 'contact', and the initial French translator, François Kérel, translated them as 'le repérage' and 'une prise de contact'. Kundera decides to change the French 'une prise de contact' to 'l'abordage', which both removes the common root and introduces an oddity, which is directly translated into English by Asher as 'boarding' (he also follows the French translation when revising 'registration' to 'sighting').

In the 1974 translation, therefore, the narrator explains 'kontaktáž': '*Contact* is a higher level of activity and means that we will get in touch with a particular woman, make her acquaintance, and gain access to her' (Kundera, 1975: 100). This is altered to: '*Boarding* is a higher level of activity and means that we will get in touch with a particular woman, make her acquaintance, and gain access to her' (Kundera, 1999a: 55). Again, in the 1974 translation, Martin asks 'Have you contacted that medical student yet?' and the narrator adds, 'Martin was satisfied and he urged me to contact her' (Kundera, 1975: 105). These sentences are changed in 1999 to: 'Have you boarded that medical student yet?' and 'Martin was satisfied and he urged me to board her' (Kundera, 1999a: 61).

The distinct oddness of the formulation in English, however, attempts to translate the foreignness of the terms in Czech, in which the 'abstract and latinate terms' (Němcová-Banerjee, 1990: 59) signpost a clinical – and as a result laughable – categorisation imposed by the hapless Martin. 'Boarding' seems ridiculous, and it is meant to be, adding the humour lost in the otherwise perfectly legitimate and, at first glance, seemingly closer translation of 'contact'. For the translation of *Life is Elsewhere* (1973), Kundera urged Kussi to avoid latinate terms because they appear too harsh and that the Czech language has the advantage in that it often uses Czech and latinate terms for the same thing, but the meaning in using either choice changes (KA: [4] KC5 undated).

Kundera's urge to literally go against the flow is apparent in the other main focus of revisions – the removal of overly colloquial language in the translations which does not reflect the tone of the novel. Heim describes Kundera's Czech language as 'classical'; one element of this style of language allows for the abstract concerns of the novels and divests it of over identification with a particular cultural context (though not entirely divesting the language of its cultural connotations). The problem for the translators is that they were pressured to make the translation sound more authentic in the English translation, but this led to divisions as to which authentic English should be used. For instance, Rappaport uses formulations such as 'Say, kid …' for which she is criticised in British reviews of *Laughable Loves*, because they locate the book too strongly in an American context. John Murray's call for a British translation echoes this division. It must equally be noted that British and American English is no longer so divided by a common language and that some of Rappaport's idiomatic choices are probably more familiar to a non-American English-speaking readership today than when first published – such as her choice of words such as 'butt', 'strip joint' and 'big shot'. However, the initial choices resonated with American influences, especially the hard-boiled male voice, which does not reflect the tendentious tone of the male character in 'The Hitchhiking Game' (Kundera, 1975: 100, 111, 123, 112, 125; Lewis, 1977: 11).

While some American slang may have become more familiar to British readers, other idiomatic language can lose its meaning over time, rendering an outdated feel to the translation which does not reflect the style of the work. An inadvertently humorous example of this occurs again in Rappaport's translation of 'The Hitchhiking Game'. In Czech, the third chapter opens: 'Mladlík byl vždycky rád, když byla jeho dívka veselá ...' (Kundera, 1991b: 66) which literally translates as: 'The young man was always happy when his girlfriend was cheerful'. In 1974, Rappaport translated this as: 'The young man was always glad when his girlfriend was gay' (Kundera, 1975: 7). While this may titillate anti-Kundera enthusiasts as an example of his phallocentric eroticism, it clearly underlines the change of usage and meaning in the English language across time. Kundera and Asher revised the translation in 1999 to: 'The young man was always glad when his girlfriend was in a good mood' (Kundera, 1999a: 84). It can be seen here that Kundera is not aiming for complete accuracy to the Czech version – though Asher is following the French translation that Kundera had made: 'Le jeune homme était toujours content de la voir de bonne humeur' (1986d: 94).

Despite the removal of idiomatic material, Kundera has a very limited perspective from which to judge the translations. He spent time in Switzerland and England learning English, and his wife taught English in Czechoslovakia and appears, from Kundera's letters, to have been instrumental in advising him on the translations. However, he made it clear from the start to both Nicholas and Kussi that his command of the English language was not good enough to make an appraisal of the translation as a whole; that this was their job. He approached this in a humorous way, parodying himself for wanting to control a translation that he could not even understand.

Yet what he made clear from the outset was that there was a level on which he could understand the English translations, and that was one of accuracy. By accuracy, Kundera did not necessarily mean fidelity in the traditional sense of the word, i.e. that the words, phrases and sentences were the best (in his view) English-language rendering of the original Czech ones. In his letters to Kussi, Kundera tended to concentrate on what he perceived to be the more translatable elements, largely the repetition of words and punctuation. The accuracy of rendering the repetition is consistently challenged by Kundera and consistently explained. Kundera also called for accuracy in clear cases of mistakes or changes, for instance, missing pieces of text – whether due to the translator or to Kundera and or the italicisation of areas of the text (for instance the whole 'Xavier' section of *Life is Elsewhere*) against Kundera's wishes.

Kundera was both clear and consistent in his interventions from his first contact with his translators, and yet problems arose, leading Kundera to blame the translators and editors without accepting responsibility for any of the translations himself. However, despite the clarity of his vision for his translated texts, there were two major barriers against his comments actually being implemented. The first of these was the editors, certainly at Knopf. While nominally inviting and encouraging Kundera both to choose and to work with the translators, Nicholas consistently gave primacy to her vision of a fluent English-language text. Part of this, to be fair, was a result of the second obstacle: the means of communication. It is important to realise that, during the period of the first translations, Kundera, his translators and editor were all communicating via letter. Owing to Kundera's anxiety about the efficacy of letter-sending (whether because of possible censor interception while he was still in Czechoslovakia or not) and to the different languages being used – Kundera writing at length and in detail to his translators in Czech and in stilted brief English to Nicholas (later more fluently in French), there was always some confusion as to who was receiving what information. The bottom line, however, was that while the translators were getting instructions and comments sometimes in duplicate from Kundera, they were also being employed by Nicholas, who was very definite about the kind of translation she wanted.

This meant that while Kundera was communicating with the translators and working with them, he could not co-operate to the extent he wanted to given the physical distance. Recently Kundera has been regarded as an author who merely opposes his translators, but he always tried to work with his translators and to work with them in great detail. This was hampered by the lack of close proximity and by the central figure of the editor, leading Kundera to acquiesce over translations more times than he cared to. This unfortunately led to Kundera praising translations immediately upon their completion, only to disparage them later on, with the translators ultimately in the firing line. Kundera's consistency bore fruit only when he was not being undermined by the needs of the publishers and when he had the cultural and commercial currency to allow him authority over his own novels. His 'close collaboration' with Asher makes sense within this history, when Kundera can work closely with the translator (editor and publisher) knowing that his decisions will not be reversed. Kundera has taken responsibility for these translations; whether he changes his mind has yet to be seen.

Kundera's authoritarian stance belies a certain amount of openness with his translators, revealed in his correspondence with Kussi throughout the 1970s and 1980s. While Kundera at times was extremely tough on Kussi, underlining what he regarded as faults with the translation, he also allowed him a surprising amount of autonomy over the translation. The toughness was often related to his ideas of accuracy, Kundera being frustrated that notions he had already explained were not being implemented. Yet Kundera also invariably apologised to Kussi if he felt his tone had been too strong in its criticism. On the other hand, he also sought Kussi's advice not only regarding the translation but also regarding the novels, at one point asking his advice about a passage towards the end of *The Farewell Party* (1976), which Kundera worried was too long. When Kundera questioned parts of the translation or certain phrases, he encouraged Kussi to make the final decision on them. In some cases, these were considerable decisions. For example, when Kussi was still scheduled to translate *Laughable Loves* (1970), Kundera told him to choose whether to follow the French translation (which contained seven stories) or the 1970 Czech version (which contained eight), though Kundera stated his preference for the former. Kussi was ready to defend and explain his decisions, and a real dialogue grew up between the two, a dialogue that developed into friendship. Despite the fallout over *The Book of Laughter and Forgetting* (1979), the two worked face to face on the revised translation of *Life is Elsewhere* (1973, first English translation 1974) and on *Immortality* (1991), in the contract for which it was stated that some of the translation process must take place on a personal basis rather than via letter.

The experience of translating *Immortality* (1991) led to two things: firstly the end of Kussi and Kundera's professional relationship and secondly, perhaps ironically, Kussi's short but seminal essay on translating Kundera. While the translation and the novel were successful, Kussi objected to changes made to the translation after he had requested that no further changes be made (the translation was also altered for a British readership), and when in 1994 Kundera sent an impersonal letter asking Kussi whether he would revise *The Farewell Party*, the friendship came to an end. Kundera apologised for the tone of the letter and wrote that he understood Kussi's reluctance to return to a previous work; unfortunately, he added with melancholy, he felt he himself could not escape from doing so.

In his essay *Několik poznámek o překládání Milana Kundery / A Few Notes on Translating Milan Kundera* (1991), Kussi discusses working with Kundera, Kundera's poetics and the effect of translation on these poetics. He is absolutely clear about the process being painstaking and difficult and about translators' feelings of anger towards Kundera because of his 'ingratitude' towards their aid in launching him to 'worldwide fame': 'Translating Milan Kundera', he adds, 'is obviously not easy.' Kussi attributes Kundera's dissatisfaction with his foreign-language texts to his dissatisfaction with his novels, pointing out Kundera's rewriting instinct as practised in the Czech-language versions as well as the foreign-language ones: 'The perfect Kundera novel is the Idea, which is never fully realised and finished …' (Kussi, 1991: 70, my translation). The perfectionism that makes Kundera so impossible, in Kussi's view, is paradoxically what also makes him an ideal author for a translator. 'Precision is Kundera's passion', he writes, arguing that this precision enables the translator to understand what the author wants, and Kundera does not stint on time or effort in enabling the translator to understand why he makes certain choices. Kussi points to his own experience translating *Immortality* (1991), when they revised the text together at great length and detail, even though Kundera had just finished doing the same with the German translation. One of the main difficulties, Kussi writes, in translating the novels is the translation of the 'musical form of Kundera's novels – articulating the polarity of precision and freedom by the polarity of theme and variation' (Kussi, 1991: 69, my translation). He argues that this can be subtly defined by the choice of two seemingly unimportant words, repeated through the text, and he cites Kundera's polarisation of 'cesta/path' and 'silnice/road' in *Immortality*, one representing slowness and a certain approach to life and the latter, speed and an opposite approach to life (a formulation which is central to his next, 1995, novel, *Slowness*). The problem is also in the fact that *cesta* has no 'elegant' translation in English, meaning either 'path' or 'way', whereas its meaning is more concrete in Czech. Similarly, Kussi focuses on Kundera's repetition of the word, 'boj', which, depending on the context in English, can mean 'struggle, battle, fight', but which needs to be translated as one of these consistently (Kussi, 1991: 68–70).

Kundera's perfectionism is summed up in Kussi's comment that he 'suffers over details' and by his editor at the Czech publishing house that has published some of his novels post-1989, who commented that Kundera was hard on himself when it came to perfecting his texts (Uhdeová, 1993: 4). Kundera parodies himself in a letter to Kussi, begging for Kussi to indulge the author in his crazy belief that a misplaced semi colon would destroy the whole novel, even if he is convinced the readers would never notice. He was consumed by the worry that the smallest misreading by the translator would result in misreadings by the readers – Kundera writes in length to both Kussi and Nicholas on how he felt *Life is Elsewhere* (1973) was misunderstood by the French critics, intimating that the way the novel was translated into English might try to avoid such misunderstandings, to the extent that Kundera requested that a sentence be omitted because it had been misunderstood in reviews. In many ways, the success of the novels in translation raises Kundera's suspicions, leading to his feeling with *The Joke* (1967) and *Life is Elsewhere* (1973) that the novels had been received well critically precisely because they had been reductively read as political dissent. With the translations (and revised translations) of both, Kundera takes this into account, changing small details that he fears may give cause for misunderstanding.

Such misunderstanding begins, Kundera feels, at the translation stage, and he has some justification in arguing this. Nicholas's editing showed little sensitivity towards Kundera's language, regarding it as irrelevant as long as it read well in English. This echoes Stallybrass's actions in removing so much text because it seemed too culturally specific, and awkward rather than innovative, Stallybrass being little impressed as to the aesthetic reasons behind the use of such language (in the establishing of Jaroslav's lyrical voice). It is no surprise then that American and British critics and reviewers have seldom commented on Kundera's language, characterising it by its simplicity and lucidity. In contrast, the majority of critical work in the Czech language has focused on the language of his novels, with Květoslav Chvatík succinctly summing up his view in writing that 'For Kundera, the art of the novel is the art of the word' (Chvatík, 1994: 80, my translation). For Czech critics – Helena Kosková in *Milan Kundera* (1998), Jiří Kratochvil in *Příběhy příběhů/Stories of the Stories* (1995) and Sylvie Richterová in *Slova a ticho/Words and Silence* (1986), as well as Chavtík in *Svět románů Milana Kundery/The World of Milan Kundera's Novels* (1994) – Kundera has initiated a linguistic project that connects all of his work intertextually and which is central to an understanding of the construction of his novels. Kundera's attention to detail has proved necessary because these details – the altered punctuation, the synonyms, the omitted material – have affected the critical reception of his novels abroad.

It is easy to dismiss Kundera as a pedant, demanding changes simply in order to assert his authority, but his instinct to control all aspects of the text generates valid and important questions about how texts are mediated before we get to read them and how it affects our reading. So while Jitka Uhdeová, Kundera's Czech editor, judiciously opts not to answer a journalist's question of whether it is easy working with Kundera, she points out that what is positive about working with him is his profound respect for the text, this perfectionism extending to the graphics and cover design. This is nothing new – in 1957 Kundera gave an ultimatum to the editor of *Basnický almanac (Poetry Almanac)*, Ladislav Fikar, that he should either get rid of the cover or leave out Kundera's poetry (PNP: Fond Ladislav Fikar, č. inv.257–261, c.přír.39/78). He complains further that the type is too small, which would result in readers not reading every single word with attention, thus invalidating the point of the whole book (Kundera makes this point about typeface with relation to Kafka in *Testaments Betrayed* (1993)). For Kundera, everything to do with the physical book is, to use a phrase from Gérard Genette, a 'threshold of interpretation' (Genette, 1997), whether it be the cover, the typeface or an epigraph. He has a point: all the new revised translations brought out by Kundera's

British publishers, Faber, carry Kundera's own illustrations, surreal and humorous cartoons. This contrasts with earlier Penguin editions which carried erotic art, which certainly aided the perception of Kundera as being interesting primarily for his eroticism.

Kundera's lack of grace and ingratitude to his translators is one issue, but it does not abrogate the validity of his claims and should not be used to obfuscate the problems that did exist in the translations or to obfuscate the manipulations of the novels for the publishers' interests. Such fastidiousness reveals a series of manipulations taking place that may have cultural agendas behind them however innocent on a conscious level. What was assumed to be irrelevant – whether it be the punctuation, the repetition of words or even the cover design – presented a false transparency, lulling the reader into the belief that they were reading the author as intended. In 1967 Czechoslovakia, Kundera pointed out to his censors the irony of the fact that they wanted to censor a speech decrying censorship. Through the 1970s and 1980s he urged his editors not to strike out the authorial imprint of his language because what they were doing was attacking the integrity of work, which is constructed to persistently reveal how language is manipulated and used as a tool of illusion to incite and justify, to create love and to murder.

Chapter 3
Rewriting

From the Sketch to the Work

> *From the sketch to the work one travel's on one's knees*
> Vladimir Holan (Kundera, 1988a: 153)

There is no 'original version' in Kundera's work in any traditional sense. For *The Book of Laughter and Forgetting* (1979), Philip Roth suggested the title, *A History of Undoing*, which succinctly describes Kundera's working practice, as he returned to almost all of his published work in order to rewrite it. 'The perfect Kundera novel', Peter Kussi writes, 'is the Idea, which is never fully realized and finished; if you take his expression from *Immortality*, his novels are like the *eternal court*. Even when a novel is published, Kundera changes and revises it not only in the translations, but also in the Czech original. The French translation of *Immortality* states that it is an authentic text, which is from every view equivalent to the Czech original. The English version might have the same imprimatur. Each translation, however, has its own character, its own linguistic and cultural constructions, so that the 'genuine' novel exists only as a cumulative approximation of all the possible translations or as an ideal in the author's mind' (Kussi, 1991: 70).

Rewriting is not an afterthought for Kundera, it is a *modus operandi*. Several forms of rewriting are concurrent in his work, and in this chapter I explore the following forms: the physical rewriting of his work; the rewriting of the translation paradigm both because of the constantly rewritten original and because of the rewriting of the translation as an original text; the rewriting of his bibliography; and finally the rewriting of his early work within his later work. It is important to analyse the interaction between these different forms of rewriting, not only because, seen together, they show a certain pathology of rewriting, but also because, focusing on one form would recount only a part of the story.

Kundera argues that rewriting is as creative an act as writing, and that an author has every right to reconsider and re-evaluate his or her work. If some of the writing or some of the work does not come up to the standard of the rest of the work, then it is the author's duty to omit or rewrite it:

... aesthetic wishes show not only by what an author has written but also by what he has deleted. Deleting a paragraph calls for even more talent, cultivation, and creative power than writing it does ... What obtains for deletions within the microcosm of a particular work also obtains for deletions within the macrocosm of a complete body of work. There too, as he assesses his work, and guided by his aesthetic requirements, the author often excludes what doesn't satisfy him. (Kundera, 1996b: 268–69)

The author's act of rewriting, for Kundera, is in direct opposition to rewriting enacted upon a writer's work or words by others, because he argues of the dangers of reductive interpretation and manipulation for the ends of the rewriters. He defines this type of rewriting in his dictionary, 'Sixty-Three Words', under the heading 'Rewriting': 'Interviews. Adaptations, transcriptions for the theater, for film, for television. Rewriting as the spirit of the times' (Kundera, 1988a: 147). 'Rewriting', he writes elsewhere, 'eliminates the author' (Kundera, 1986a: 87). This is a central struggle for Kundera – between the freedom that he demands for himself to rewrite his work or his language and his utter objection to others doing so. Kundera sees no obstacle in allowing for different versions of the same work to exist across languages as long as he himself is involved in the changes, because of his fear that changes implemented by others are made for the wrong reasons and for manipulation to a certain end. A good example is the 1969 English translation of *The Joke* (1967), which approached the text with a very definite interpretation and led to the omission of swathes of text because of an inherent misunderstanding of the novel's aesthetics.

A good example of Kundera's own rewriting can be found in his definition of 'Rewriting' in 'Sixty-Three Words'. The dictionary, which appears in *The Art of the Novel* (1986), was put together for an article in *Le Débat* in response to Kundera's frustration with his translators and readers – he wanted to define certain theme-words that appeared in or related to his fiction. These are not definitions in the OED sense, but serve as starting points from which to consider elements of his work with a playfulness in utter seriousness of Gustave Flaubert's *Dictionnaire des idées reçues* (1911). The dictionary in *Le Debát* was entitled 'Quatre-Vingts Quatre Mots' (Eighty-Four Words), but was republished in the first, French, version of *The Art of the Novel* as 'Soixante-Treize Mots' (Seventy-Three Words). The next year it was published in the English-language version of *The Art of the Novel* as 'Sixty-Three Words'. While Kundera has not published *The Art of the Novel* in the Czech Republic, in 1999 he published the dictionary in a journal, *Host*, under the title 'Slova' ('Words'). This dictionary has 27 definitions, and one of the ones omitted is 'Rewriting'. The French entry for 'Rewriting' uses the English word, and is twice as long as the English-language entry.

Kundera has also substantially rewritten his bibliography. This happened somewhat organically, beginning with the ban on his work in the then Czechoslovakia in 1970. Following this ban, Kundera's novels began to be published in the West, and by the time there was interest in publishing his early work – his poetry, plays and criticism – he refused to allow it to be translated. The barrier of language allowed him to jettison work and to concentrate his *oeuvre* round his novels. This became problematic in 1989 when the ban was lifted on his work in Czechoslovakia, where the early work was still extant though obviously not in print. Immediate efforts to produce his plays were rebuffed, and in his author's note to his first work published in his old homeland since 1970 – the 1991 Czech version of *The Joke* – Kundera clearly set out a manifesto on how his bibliography should be regarded. His authorised bibliography was to become the bulk of his fiction and one of his three plays. However, since 1991, Kundera has only published five (of a possible 14) of his books in the Czech Republic: *The Joke* (1991), *Laughable Loves* (1991), *Immortality* (1993), *Jacques and His Master* (1993) and *Farewell Waltz* (1997). He justified the delay in publishing the rest of his novels in the Czech Republic by arguing that he needed to rewrite the Czech versions before they could be published.

Along with his poetry and some stories, Kundera declared that his one book of literary criticism, published in 1960, was also to be omitted. This book, on the Czech writer Vladislav Vančura, was called *Umění románu – The Art of the Novel*. His reuse of the title for his 1986 book of essays, *L'art du roman/The Art of the Novel*, is a deliberate reference to this 1960 monograph: 'I retained the title for a personal, almost sentimental reason ... This book, at once likeable ... and immature, will never again be reissued and I wanted to keep the title as a memory of years past' (Oppenheim, 1989: 11). While Kundera has removed his authorisation of certain work in his *oeuvre*, this has not entirely led to its disappearance. This early work becomes the source of and motivation for his later fiction and features in the fiction in a variety of ways. Kundera reuses material (titles and phrases) directly from earlier work and he reuses and returns to themes from there, albeit from a different vantage point and with a view to exposing the absolutism of his poetry. His choice of the novel form is a direct result of his experience with poetry. The early prose work that has been omitted shows an experimentation with a narratorial voice that will be familiar to readers of *The Book of Laughter and Forgetting* (1979) and *The Unbearable Lightness of Being* (1984). Kundera experiments with form and language by working in a novel form that is poetic but in an anti-lyrical sense (in direct opposition to the lyricism of his early verse). This aesthetic and anti-ideological rewriting gives no pretence of judgment of or apology for Kundera's personal past, but suggests that he is returning again and again to the Idea and its Form that consistently elude him, as Kussi suggests, in his pursuit of them.

Kundera's first two collections of poetry, *Člověk zahrada širá / Man the Broad Garden* (1953) and *Poslední máj / The Last May* (1955), resonate with communist imagery (Kundera was thrown out of the Communist Party in 1950 but his membership was reinstated in 1956). His book *The Art of the Novel / Umění románu* (1960) also pays lip service to communist aesthetic theories prevalent at the time. However, his third collection of poetry and the three *Laughable Loves* stories, which he also de-authorised, are not political, nor is his 1968 play, *Ptákovina* (a difficult title to translate; 'pták' is the Czech for 'bird', but also slang for 'penis', the '–ovina' ending indicates playful nonsense. The play was initially entitled *Dvě uši, dvě svatby – Two Ears, Two Weddings*), or particularly his 1962 stage success, *Majitelé klíčů / The Keepers of the Keys*. Nonetheless, these critics believe that Kundera deliberately eschewed this work to present a different and less compromised image of himself and his work in the West.

This notion ties in to the criticism of his rewriting the translations. Between 1985 and 1987, Kundera retranslated all the French translations of his novels, and, when doing so, introduced rewrites. He omitted passages, added material and introduced some deliberate acculturation into the novels, removing references that he felt were too specifically rooted in a particular Czech historical or political context. He then declared the French translations to be more authentic than the Czech originals, in part because they presented a newer version and vision of the novels. Stanger and Crain view this as an attempt to pander to a Western audience by making the novels more palatable to them through the omission of certain material. They read his privileging of the Western audience by, at best, giving them a new and improved version of the work as a snub and a betrayal of his original Czech readership. Kundera is seen as deeply hypocritical because of his accusations that his translators are rewriting his novels.

These criticisms can lead the reader down a blind alley. Kundera's Czech critics, such as Michael Bauer, consider his socialist work often in isolation from his later work, ignoring the innate links between the two. Although Kundera may censure his early work in a physical sense, it is everywhere in his later fiction. He may be one of the few Czech writers who have deliberately faced their past in a profoundly metaphysical sense. No believer in autobiography, Kundera does not dwell on the subject of his personal or his generation's guilt but on the question of its consequences. Many readers are unaware that, while Kundera has rewritten his novels when revising the French and English translations, he has also rewritten many of them in Czech. This is not to say that, in respect of content, a novel will be the same in two languages, but that Kundera's pathology of rewriting is expressed partly separately and partly in synchronisation in each language. There are four differing editions of *The Joke* in Czech alone (1967, 1968, 1969, 1991), three versions in French (1968, 1980, 1985) and five different versions in English (1969 (UK), 1969 (US), 1970, 1983, 1993). The definitive editions in all three languages are, with regard to content, different.

Kundera is entirely aware of his different audiences across cultures and across time and uses the opportunity new translations provide to change his work. His rewriting allows him to experiment simultaneously with different versions of the same text and points to, as both Kussi and Hamšík suggest, an intense disquiet in his writer's soul with any of his writing. It also points to a willingness to watch his work evolve as he attempts – in an attempt doomed to failure – to perfect it.

***

'It is an inviolable right of the novelist', the narrator says in *The Book of Laughter of Forgetting* (1979), 'to rework his novel. If the opening does not please him, he can rewrite or delete it' (Kundera, 1999b: 15). Kundera rewrote and republished Czech versions of *Laughable Loves* (1991) *The Joke* (1991) and *Farewell Waltz* (1997). He published the first two in rewritten editions in Czech before they were translated, and made further changes in the translated versions and then again in Czech following some, but not all, of the changes made in the translations. *Life is Elsewhere* (1973), *The Unbearable Lightness of Being* (1984) and *The Book of Laughter and Forgetting* (1979) have not been published yet in the Czech Republic because Kundera has not rewritten them and intimates that he may not. His rewriting after initial publication began with his poetry – he published his second collection of poetry, *Poslední máj/The Last May*, in three substantially different editions in 1955, 1961 and 1963, and he published his third, and last, collection of poetry, *Monology/Monologues*, in four substantially different editions in 1957, 1964, 1965 and 1969.

The rewrites fall into several categories: the first, Kundera's consistent changing of names of novels and characters, suggests a certain pathological element to his rewriting that he himself satirises in letters to his translator Peter Kussi, presenting an author who quixotically thinks that each word is of equal importance and that the choice of the wrong one is capable of ruining the entire novel. The second category, sometimes linked to this, is his alteration of details in the work that he considered to be too rooted in a specific historical or political context. Stanger criticises him for this, suggesting that these changes were contingent on his Western audience and were entirely opportunistic, geared towards selling more books. These changes are indeed contingent on the time and place of publication, whether in ex-Czechoslovakia, the Czech Republic today or France or the United States, because Kundera is entirely aware of a non-homogeneous and temporally differentiated audience. However, they do also show a reasonably consistent policy of paring down specific detail. The third, and the most aesthetically profound, category is that of rewrites that show Kundera experimenting with and changing the narrative voice, whether through a metafictional narrator in direct contact with the reader or through reflective passages presented by an omniscient but more concealed narrator. The narrator in Kundera's work is one of the radical elements of the art of his novel-writing, one that he links back to the narrative experimentation in the works of Sterne, Diderot and Rabelais. This is a voice that is knowingly artificial and which attains an intense irony through this exposure of the artificiality of the structure, the fiction of it. The use of the voice is apparent from his first prose work but comes to fruition only through rewriting and experimentation.

Kundera makes his anxiety about names and naming public, ruminating at several points about the titles of his novels in his essays and prefaces and even within the novels themselves. He tells an interviewer that *The Art of the Novel* (1986), purposely named after his 1960 *The Art of the Novel*, was supposedly to be named *Man Thinks, God Laughs*, a title that Aaron Asher dissuaded him from using (Oppenheim, 1989: 11). Similarly, in the preface/postscript to *Life is Elsewhere*, Kundera told the reader that the novel was to be called *The Lyric Age* but his publishers felt that it was not a marketable name (Kundera, 1987c: v). His publishers also baulked at *The Book of Laughter and Forgetting* (1979), which Kundera dwelt on in his author's note to the 1991 Czech edition of *Laughable Loves*, a title he insisted on keeping because he wanted to retain an ambiguity as to whether the *Book* was a novel or not. In *The Art of the Novel* (1986) he wrote that *The Unbearable Lightness of Being* (1984) was to be called *The Planet of Inexperience*, and in *Immortality* (1991), the character Milan Kundera tells his friend Avenarius that the novel he is writing (the same *Immortality*) should have been called *The Unbearable Lightness of Being* rather than the novel that did have that name. There is a lot of playfulness in Kundera's assertions but also a serious point about the importance of names (think of the resonance of *The Unbearable Lightness of Being*, having been much punned and appropriated by other writers and journalists) and the people who have the power to choose them other than the novelist.

Kundera's ambivalence in naming his novels is indicative also of a consistent ambiguity about names in his novels. For example, the doctor (and one of the main characters) in Kundera's *samizdat* novel *Epilog* (c.1970) is called Dr Škréta. In the French and English translations he is also called Dr Skreta (without the diacritics), and the novel's title was changed to *Valčík na rozločenou* (1979); it had been translated as *La valse aux adieux* (1973) and *The Farewell Party* (1976). Kundera explained the change to his Czech readers in an author's note to the 1997 Czech edition, writing that the title was initially *Epilog* because he thought at the time that it would be his last novel and an epilogue to his novelistic career. However, he was dissuaded by his French publisher, Gallimard, from the title because there was another novel in print in France with the same name. The new title was the same as Chopin's *Opus 69*, written to celebrate his engagement to Maria Wodzinska (whom he never married) and to herald the end of his soloist career. It has obvious connotations within the novel's theme of farewell and within the musical construct of the novel's structure. The novel was first published in the Czech language in 1979 by Škvorecký's Sixty-Eight Publishers in Toronto under the title *Valčík na rozločenou*, but the doctor's name was changed to Dr Sláma. This name was never used in translation, and in the next Czech language edition – the 1997 one – he is once again Dr Škréta. Dr Škréta's wife, a very incidental character in the novel, is called Květa in the Czech *Epilog* version of the novel (and in the first English translation), Mimi in the 1979 Czech version and Suzy in the 1997 Czech version. Kundera and Knopf maintained a long discussion about the English title of the novel, with Knopf not keen on *The Farewell Waltz* and with various suggestions from Kundera (*The Farewell Polka* being one) and Kussi (*Nocturne*) but it was initially given the title *The Farewell Party* by Philip Roth. This worked on the level of the 'party' as a social and a political entity, and it was jokingly suggested by Roth that it should be *The Party Farewell*. The revised English translation of 1998 was entitled *Farewell Waltz*.

Such changes are also apparent in *The Book of Laughter and Forgetting* (1979), in which Tamina's husband, who is dead, undergoes a series of name changes in different editions. He is called Mírek in the first edition – the first French-language edition (1979) – and first English-language edition (1980), Petr in the first Czech-language edition (1981) and Pavel in the revised French (1985) and English (1996) translations. The most distinctive name change is that of Karel Gott, whom Kundera describes in the novel as 'the Idiot of Music' alongside President Husák, 'the President of Forgetting'. Both were real people, Husák the long-time Czechoslovak Communist president during the period of 'normalisation', and Gott a kitsch pop-singer who managed to stay popular throughout all the regime changes and is still popular today. In the revised French and English translations, Kundera changed his name to a fictional 'Karel Klos' (Garfinkle, 1999: 54–64). This may be because the name is too culturally specific for French and English readers or irrelevant to the book itself, the notion of such a singer being more important than the reality of fictionality of the character. As there has not been a new Czech edition, it remains to be seen whether the name is retained in any future Czech version.

The artifice of naming is underlined constantly in *The Book of Laughter and Forgetting* (1979), with the narrator calling attention to the naming of his fictional character Tamina counterpointed with the constant renaming of a certain street in Prague by the successive regimes, names which reflected their ideologies and fleeting dominance. Kundera exposes the fictional nature of political naming in his revisions, notably in the changes in reference from 'Czechoslovakia' to 'Bohemia'. In the Czech language, and in the 1981 Czech edition of *The Book of Laughter and Forgetting*, the Czech lands (not including Slovakia, but including Moravia) are referred to as 'Čechy', and this is initially translated as 'Czechoslovakia'. In Kundera's revisions of the translations, all these references are changed to 'Bohemia' (which technically refers only to a part of the Czech lands). Kundera later explains this rejection of 'Czechoslovakia':

> This composite word is too young (born in 1918), with no roots in time, no beauty, and it exposes the very nature of the thing it names: composite and too young (untested by time). It may be possible in a pinch to found a state on so frail a word, but not a novel. That is why, to designate my character's country, I always use the old word, 'Bohemia'. From the standpoint of political geography, it's not correct (my translators often bridle), but from the standpoint of poetry, it is the only possible name. (Kundera, 1988a: 126).

This questioning of political naming also resurfaces as a revision in the novel *The Joke* (1967). Jaroslav ruminates on the underestimated influence of folk music from the east of Europe on composers in comparison to the well-known influence of jazz on composers. In the passage in all of the Czech editions, he refers to the east of Europe three times. In the revised translations, Kundera changes these three references, two to simply 'Europe' and one to 'Central Europe', a revision that reflects Kundera's contemporary extra-novelistic concerns with the definition of 'Central Europe' as a distinct opposite to what he regards to be the false and purely political misnomer of 'East Europe'. The danger of this name, for Kundera, was the assumption by 'Western Europe' that the East was another separate and oppositional entity, following Cold War rhetoric, whereas Kundera has argued incessantly that Central Europe is (as reflected by the name) within the very heart of Europe (Finkielkraut, 1982: 15–29). His arguments are somewhat borne out by the first French translation of *The Joke* (1968) in which the translator, Marcel Aymonin, translates the three references three different ways: as 'l'est du continent'/'the East of the continent', 'l'est'/'the East' and, tellingly, 'l'europe orientale'/'oriental Europe' (Kundera, 1968: 162). Through the passage and his many synonyms, Aymonin serves to bolster the orientalising of the other Europe, an exotic and distant East.

In this passage in the Czech editions, Jaroslav names several composers, identifying Stravinsky, Honegger, Milhaud and Martinů as being influenced by jazz and Stravinsky, Janáček, Bartók and Enescu as being influenced by folk music. These lists of names are somewhat shortened in the revised translations, with Martinů being dropped from the first and Stravinsky and Enescu from the second. The reason may be that Martinů and Enescu are less well known and, for purposes of the passage, less important, and that the repetition of Stravinsky may appear contradictory or unwieldy. The most recent Czech edition (1991), though revised in other areas, includes all of them.

Kundera's awareness that an audience and a context for a work can change appears to be one that arose at the beginning of his literary career and was only exacerbated by translation and the ensuing obvious obstacles of cultural and linguistic differences. His Czech-language audience and the Czech context have changed both subtly and enormously since he began writing. A subtle change can be seen in his revisions in his second book of poetry, which was actually an epic poem called *Poslední máj/The Last May* (1955). The title is difficult to translate without an explanation of its cultural import, because of the meanings of 'máj', which on a superficial level refers to the month but which also refers to a certain political interpretation. May, the month, in Czech is 'květen', but 'máj' was appropriated by communist discourse to refer to a revolutionary month and the first of May, 'prvního máje'. These connotations strongly remain. *Máj* also refers to the title of one of the founding poems of modern Czech literature and modern Czech national consciousness, Karel Hynek Mácha's intensely lyrical 1836 *Máj*, a poem that most Czechs know at least partially by heart. Kundera's 1955 epic poem tells the story of the last hours of Julius Fučík, a communist martyr murdered by the Nazis and much valorised after the war both by the communist regime and by writers such as Kundera, who constructed a myth surrounding him. The poem makes constant reference to Fučík, following him on a mythical last walk in Prague with his Nazi gaoler, and uses a succession of communist motifs. Six years later, Kundera published a second edition of *The Last May* (1961) in which he altered or omitted half the lines in the book, and in which he removed the majority of the more ostentatious communist motifs. Two years after this, in 1963, he published a third edition in which he removed most references to Fučík by name, referring instead to an anonymous 'prisoner'. This aesthetic cleansing of the poem is consolidated by the appending of an epigraph from Mácha's *Máj*, which refers to 'a prisoner' and which refocuses the allegiance of the poem towards the history of Czech national literature and away from the communist tradition. It is possible that these revisions are an example of opportunistic revisionism by Kundera, but it is also very indicative of the political changes occurring in Czechoslovakia at the time – the freeing of artistic expression from the neo-Stalinist 1955 to a Kruschevian thaw in 1963 (famously the year Kafka was officially rehabilitated by the communist regime in Czech culture).

Kundera's revisions of his poetry are also not necessarily focused on removing communist elements from it. His third collection, *Monology/Monologues* (1957), is not political in the way the first two collections are, and focuses on poems about personal relationships. Kundera also completely revised this collection three times. A good example of these changes again centres on naming and relates to Kundera's fiction. The art of his fiction, Kundera argues, is one of 'themes and variations', which is another conceit of construct that Kundera has borrowed from music. In other words, his variations consistently return to themes and motifs within novels and within his body of work. In the 1957 collection, Kundera played with this notion and included three poems in this collection that are related by their titles: 'First Variation on Death', 'Second Variation on Death' and 'Third Variation on Death'. In the second edition (1964) Kundera retained the titles but removed the 'First' and 'Second Variation' poems and made the 'Third Variation' poem the new 'First Variation' poem (with some textual changes). The 1964 'Second Variation' is a new poem added to the collection and the 1964 'Third Variation' is a retitling of a poem that had appeared in the 1957 collection under the title of 'Song of a Great Runner'. In 1969 Kundera made substantial changes to this 1964 'Third Variation on Death'. The use of 'variation' in the titles perhaps suggests their own mutability but also signals the beginnings of Kundera's evolving interest in cross-pollinating the musical form of variation into writing. (These were not the only changes – Kundera removed 10 poems from the 1957 edition in 1964 and added eight new poems. He removed a further three poems in the 1965 edition and a further two in the 1969 edition, making textual changes to poems in all the editions.)

Kundera is dismissive of his poetry, but he does remind his Czech readers that it provided motivational material for his later fiction. This is true both as a meditation on the genre itself and as a return to themes in the work. He regards his decision to stop writing poetry as a real break, constantly reiterating that he came to maturity as a writer with his first prose work. This was a short story written in 1958 while he taking a break from writing his play *The Keepers of the Keys*, a story that took three days to write and which became the first of his *Laughable Loves* stories. Kundera describes the writing of it as a Road to Damascus event:

> ... in it, as they say, I found myself; that is, I found my tone, an ironic distance from the world and from my own life and I became a novelist (a potential novelist); for the first time from that moment my independent literary evolution began, which although was henceforth full of surprises, provided no change of orientation. (Kundera, 1991b: 204, my translation)

This story, called 'Já truchlivý bůh'/'I, the Mournful God', is a touchstone text for Kundera's work, but has never been published in English. Kundera revised the story several times – in 1965 and 1970, as an altered screenplay in 1967 and again twice sometime in the 1970s (under different titles) when Kussi translated one of the versions into English, although this was not published. Kundera eliminated it from his bibliography along with two other *Laughable Loves* stories, but his constant return to it suggests an uneasiness with its dismissal. Helena Kosková and Květoslav Chvatík in their monographs on Kundera both respect his order not to consider his unauthorised work, but both comment on the centrality of this story to his later work because of the manner in which it prefigures the themes and structure of his fiction. Perhaps more interesting are the revisions of the story, which show Kundera experimenting with and developing a very certain narratorial style which he eventually seems to think fails in the story but which comes to fruition in the late 1970s with *The Book of Laughter and Forgetting* (1979).

There is no original version of *Laughable Loves*: firstly because of Kundera's revisions to the individual stories and to the collection as a whole; and secondly because it exists as a different text across different languages. Kundera wrote ten *Laughable Loves* stories which were initially published in three 'notebooks': 'I, the Mournful God', 'Nurse of my Nurses' and

'Nobody Will Laugh' in *Směšné lásky: Tři melancholický anekdoty* / *Laughable Loves: Three Melancholy Anecdotes* (1963); 'The Golden Apple of Eternal Desire', 'The Messenger' and 'The Hitch-Hiking Game' in *Druhý sešit směšných lásek* / *The Second Notebook of Laughable Loves* (1965); and 'Let the Old Dead Make Room for the Young Dead', 'Symposium', 'Edward and God' and 'Doctor Havel After Ten Years' in *Třeti sešit směšných lásek* / *The Third Notebook of Laughable Loves* (1968). The first two 'notebooks' were published in revised editions: *Laughable Loves: Three Melancholy Anecdotes* in 1965 and *The Second Notebook of Laughable Loves* in 1966, and in 1970 Kundera published eight of the 10 stories (omitting 'Nurse of my Nurses' and 'The Messenger') under the title *Laughable Loves*, again with revised versions of the stories. The same year the first French translation was published, but with only seven stories – 'I, the Mournful God' was omitted. This was owing partly to Kundera but also to Gallimard, who thought the story weak, though he had second thoughts later and the story was considered for the first English translation. It was translated into Italian and all 10 stories were translated and published in Polish. However, the most recent Czech-language versions (1981, 1991) of the collection follow the French translation and contain only seven stories. Kundera published *Laughable Loves* as a novel in Germany and Spain rather than as a collection of short stories and indicated to his Czech readers in 1991 that he felt he could not do so in the Czech Republic because readers were too familiar with the book as a collection of stories. He also indicated that the stories have been altered to follow his changes made in his three revisions of the initial 1970 French translation in 1979, 1984 and 1986, but there are also changes in the text specific to the Czech-language versions, with some revisions made in 1981 and others in 1991.

'I, the Mournful God' is indicative of the evolution of the book. Following the story's initial publication in 1963, Kundera made small changes to it for the second edition in 1965. He then went on to make substantial changes in two different versions of the story: firstly, for the film version (now disowned by Kundera) for which he co-wrote the screenplay and which was directed by Antonín Kachlík in 1969 and secondly for the 1970 *Laughable Loves*. The film version, also entitled *I, the Mournful God*, diverges substantially from the plot of the initial version but the screenplay version influences the later 1970s unpublished versions of the story – two different versions entitled 'Don't Be Yourself' and 'I am Someone Else'. The 1970 *Laughable Loves* is similar in respect of plot to the initial version but Kundera revised the narrative construct of the story.

Ironically, translation is at the heart of this untranslated story. Kundera presents a melancholy satire on the Cyrano story in his native city, Brno (the only work he ever set there) and it is a simple story of failed seduction. Adolf – in later versions renamed Antonín – falls for an empty-headed opera student, Jana, who consistently rebuffs his advances. To take his revenge, Adolf/Antonín decides to play a joke on her, enlisting his Greek friend, Apostol. Apostol is a layabout who has settled in Brno, but Adolf/Antonín disguises him as the non-Czech-speaking director of the Athenian Opera and introduces him to Jana, with Adolf/Antonín playing the role of translator. The starstruck Jana is silently seduced and impregnated by Apostol, who she thinks has returned to Greece. Apostol meanwhile has fallen in love with her, but she does not recognise him when he appears in his ordinary clothes, speaking Czech. She wants to hold on to her illusions and is proud of her son's origins. At the end of the story both Adolf/Antonín and Apostol are victims of an unrequited love.

All the hallmarks of Kundera's prose are here – the joke or 'mystification' which starts the plot, the characters caught in their own illusions exposing the illusions of others, the donjuanism, mistaken identity and miscommunication. Kundera also directly returns to the Cyrano motif in his 1997 novel, *Identity*, in which the lover sends his letters under the pseudonym 'CdB' to rewoo his lover and to reignite their love. However, most distinctive in the story is the playful narrator and his self-reflection on the nature of narration and its artifice. Indeed, the mournful God referenced in the title has a twofold meaning: firstly that he is a god because he engineered the creation of Jana's son, and, secondly, because he is in control of the story of this story but not of the events. The reader is immediately brought into dialogue with Adolf/Antonín, who addresses him or her directly from the opening lines of the story and throughout the narrative, where he comments at several points on the power he has in retelling the events but his powerlessness in shaping events, a mischievous and melancholy manifesto on life and art. This self-conscious and ironic exposé of the artifice of fiction by the narrator is nothing new, and Kundera's complaint about the story that he heard 'a foreign voice' in it points to the influence of his beloved eighteenth century authors. Certainly, in the 1970 version, Kundera strips the story of the majority of the more playful examples, so that in the 1963 and 1965 versions, Adolf muses:

> Some live, others, if I could say it so, are lived. Some in life play a text of their own creation, others play a text which is not their creation. You don't think? It seems to you, that I exaggerate, but I myself think that I have the truth, and that it is a modest enough truth. So modest, that I would not only venture to say it, but that I would also venture to write it, if I was a writer of written stories, because pleasures come

from, don't you know, only truths that are very modest, or more precisely: inconspicous and common.
I am tiring you with these reflections. (Kundera, 1963: 6, my translation)

While in the 1970 edition this passage is severely shortened to:

Some live, others, if I could say it so, are lived.
I am tiring you with these reflections. (Kundera, 1970a: 9, my translation)

However, the artifice of the narrator is deliberately exploited in the 1969 film version with frequent asides to the camera, and, for instance, in the beginning of the film when Adolf walks into a theatre past the concert audience in the film and speaks to the film audience as the concert goes on around him from the stage. He leaves then through the backstage, and this image of the ropes and the wings sets a background for the artificiality of the film. To add to the narrative self-referentiality, Kundera himself appears in a cameo role in the film as one of the few unsuitable bachelors available, Pan Nebavný (Mr No-fun), who never goes out with women – an in-joke given Kundera's contrary reputation. The next versions of the story, 'Don't Be Yourself' and 'I am Someone Else', contain some of the plot changes in the film and take them further – in the film, Adolf/Antonín meets Apostol in the hospital and Apostol helps him to brush off a middle-aged woman keen on him, so Adolf/Antonín presents Jana as a gift in return (omitting to tell Apostol about the revenge). In *Don't Be Yourself* another element is added; Antonín re-discovers an ex-girlfriend and at the end of the story Antonín and Apostol, like Martin and his friend in 'The Golden Apple of Eternal Desire', drive off to meet her and her friend. In 'I am Someone Else' the plot takes a different turn in that Antonín meets his ex-girlfriend, who procures for him a younger woman and they have a threesome, which gives him the idea of finding lovers by disguising himself, as he had disguised Apostol.

What is different about the last two versions of the story is the structure of the narrative and the appearance of a narrator other than Antonín who interweaves his story with other stories, working on the variation principle described above. The stories are divided into the short chapters that become exemplified in *The Book of Laughter and Forgetting* (1979), *The Unbearable Lightness of Being* (1984) and *Immortality* (1991). In 'Don't Be Yourself', the unnamed narrator only very subtly insinuates himself in the story until the 10th chapter, when he turns to mock Antonín's assertions that he is in control of the story. The narrator points to the example of

Trotsky, who believed he was controlling the course of the revolution only to be murdered by it, and to the example of the protagonist in his novel *The Joke* (1967), who is revenged by his own revenge. This direct reference to his own work introduces a Milan Kundera as the narrator, a role he plays in *The Book of Laughter and Forgetting* (1979), *The Unbearable Lightness of Being* (1984) and *Immortality* (1991) (Clarissa Zimra makes the interesting point that the further Kundera goes into exile, the more he appears in his own novels, as if to aid their understanding (Zimra, 1991)). In Chapter Fourteen of 'Don't Be Yourself', Kundera compares Antonín's decision to wear a disguise for seduction with that of the famous King Václav, who donned a disguise to walk among his subjects and to escape his fate as king. These short essayistic peregrinations become the heart of his later fiction and are the heart of what Kundera identified in Hermann Broch's work as reflection in the novel (Kundera, 1988a: 78).

'I am Someone Else' opens with the question and artifice of naming. The narrator asks the reader what the name of the hero of the story is, and suggests the name is problematic and that one carries one's name like clothes, except you cannot change it. He names his hero Antonín – a change from the earlier Adolf. In this version, he introduces Antonín as a lecturer who has been thrown out of his job by the Party and who has to move to a provincial town. This sad history, however, has conferred upon him a glamour that is helpful for his love life, which, the narrator suggests, is plausible because it is what happens in Kafka's *The Trial*, where Lenka is attracted to the accused. The narrator adds further proof from his own experience, citing a friend of his, a scientist, who was made to work as a night watchman by the regime and who became irresistible to women. This line of thinking leads to Tomáš in *The Unbearable Lightness of Being* (1984), the surgeon who becomes a window-washer and uses his rounds and women's sympathies for his erotic adventures. The narrator opens the second short chapter of 'I am Someone Else' with irony, noting that one of the few things that is more powerful than the allure of those dissidents is forgetting. Antonín loses his lustre after a few years in the town because everyone has forgotten his past. This theme becomes central in *The Book of Laughter and Forgetting* (1979). The narrator of 'I am Someone Else' is ironic also about his own art and comments on the character of the middle-aged butcher's wife, Mrs Stenclová, who is enamoured with Antonín and whom Apostol has helped to brush off, with an aside that her character is there more for lazy humour than for his story – her point is to show the friendship between the two men, and the narrator is satirising his own two-dimensional character. The narrator mocks his character Antonín for falling into the paradox trap – for thinking he is a god who can control events when in fact they control him. As with the other version of the story, he evokes the examples of Trotsky and his own writing – this time telling the reader that the paradox trap is a theme that runs through all his writing (and not just *The Joke*). Kundera also retells the King Václav story but this time begins to add a personal anecdote about how, after falling in love with his wife, Kundera was scared of marriage because he saw it as the grave of his youth – the same wife (he adds) to whom he is dictating this story on the thirteenth floor with a view in the distance of Brittany (this image of the Breton high-rise as a place to view his past returns in *The Book of Laughter and Forgetting*).

The point about these two versions of the story (both written at the same time as he was writing what he saw as two stories, 'The Cap of Clementis' and 'Mother', both of which in fact became sections of *The Book of Laughter and Forgetting* in 1979), other than that they contain themes and images that Kundera tries out and then includes in later fiction, is that they herald a new narrative style which is borne out of the initial versions. Through his rewriting of the story, Kundera moves from the playful narration by the character immersed in the telling of the story to an ironic, distanced narrator commenting not on the action but on the existential questions arising from it: Can we escape our identities? Can we avoid the traps we ourselves create? Do we delude ourselves that we have power over our own lives? Is our struggle to be ourselves a slavery rather than a freedom, indenturing ourselves to a certain identity when we are many? These are questions that arise throughout Kundera's fiction.

Kundera rewrites the origins of his prose work by omitting this story in all its versions and by placing *The Joke* as his 'Opus 1'. *The Joke* was finished in 1965, before all the *Laughable Loves* stories were written, but, like the stories, it was not in fact finished when it was first published. Although Kundera does not overhaul the novel in the same way as he had 'I, the Mournful God', he does go through the text to alter it a year after its first publication. The novel was held up by the censors until 1967, but when it was released it proved a best-seller. Two further editions quickly followed, in 1968 and 1969. The 1968 edition contains rewrites throughout the novel, including the removal of about 30 sentences from the fifth, Jaroslav, section. The rewrites are more minimal in 1969. What is interesting is that the novel had been published in French in 1968 and then in English in 1969. Stallybrass and Macdonald removed about 300 sentences from the novel and Kundera insisted on their repatriation to the text for the paperback edition in 1970. This 1970 English-language edition, then, corresponds to the 1967 Czech edition rather than to the 1968 Czech edition. Some of the material that Kundera insisted be repatriated in the English translation of 1970, he had already removed from the Czech-language version in 1968.

An example of this can be found in another comparison by Jaroslav of musical traditions in western and eastern/central Europe. The 1970 English-language edition presents it as follows:

> All nations have their popular art. But for the most part one can imagine their cultures without it. Ours one cannot. Every western European nation has had at least since the Middle Ages an unbroken cultural development. Debussy could refer back to the rococo music of Couperin and Rameau, while Couperin and Rameau could hark back to the medieval troubadours. Max Reger could refer to Bach and Bach to the old German polyphonic school. Thomas Mann can calmly reach back through several centuries to the medieval Faust. (Kundera, 1970b: 125)

This passage more or less follows the 1967 Czech edition (though the translation does not capture the melody, which is part of its point) and is fully reinstated from an attenuated version in the 1969 English edition. In the 1968 Czech edition, Kundera had already removed the last sentence referring to Thomas Mann, showing the nascent struggle in his aesthetics between presenting the narration of the character and the imposition of another removed narratorial voice. Kundera's musical knowledge informs Jaroslav's character, but his interest in the novel does not – Jaroslav is interested only in music and specifically folk music and shows no inclination towards literature. The reference to Mann is Kundera's and not his character's, and this incongruity is possibly the reason for its removal. The paragraph *sans* Mann is in the definitive 1991 Czech-language edition (which otherwise contains a plethora of small changes from the 1969 Czech edition). However, Kundera removed the entire paragraph from the French and English translations in 1981 and 1982, and it remains omitted in the definitive French and English translations of 1985 and 1993 (both effectively translated by Kundera).

Kundera's revisions of the French translations are converted into the later Czech versions, the process of translation informing the source-language text. An example of this is the translation of the acronym 'SNB' and 'esenbák' – the post-war police in the former Czechoslovakia – the acronym and its idiomatic singular that carries connotations of regime control (1969b: 125). The initial French translator attempted to translate this connotation (though not consistently) as 'la Securité' and as 'agent de la Securité' (1968: 145), but Kundera changed this to the less threatening 'gendarme' in his revision of the translation (1985a: 195, 325). In English it is translated simply as 'the police' and 'policeman' (1993c: 126). In the 1991 Czech translation, Kundera also changes 'esenbák' and 'SNB' to 'policajt' and 'policie', effectively de-politicising the reference (1991c: 127). Because of the cultural and political changes within Czech culture, such references to the SNB may not speak as referentially to Kundera's new Czech audience, and this audience is, in some ways, as foreign as his non-Czech-language readership.

Kundera has argued that he wanted to rid his work of over-contextualisation, especially mentioning the historical references in *The Joke* (1967). He argued an aesthetic basis for such omissions, with the implication that too close a reference to actuality leads to reductive readings – so that, in his words, *The Joke* was read as a political pamphlet rather than as a novel because of the period detail as well as because of the timing of its release in the West. However, the whole novel deals with the characters' seductions by communism, and their illusions based on personal needs which the faith and ideology filled – the omission of references to the Red Army does not dilute the themes of collusion and disillusion. Kundera removes some of the references to communism, specifically in relation to Jaroslav in the translations, but he also removed them in the Czech version in 1968, and these omissions do not attenuate the examination of Jaroslav's motives for embracing communism.

Similarly, Stanger accuses Kundera of making the novel less sexist for his Western audience by removing certain reflections, for example, Čeněk's thoughts on the Czech Easter ritual in which men beat women with a symbolic stick (to profess love). Again, the problem is that these kinds of omission do not change the characters enough to make them in any way more agreeable as characters with regard to attitudes to women. In some of Kundera's own deletions in the 1968 Czech version (carried into the English and French translations), that rendered the character if anything more louche than in the initial version. Ludvík, for instance, remarks that he has slept in various beds in the definitive versions (1991c: 15; 1985a: 20), suggesting that he is a cold-hearted ladykiller, whereas in the early versions and translations of *The Joke*, this remark is slightly more innocuous; he remarks that he has slept in many different beds and sat at many different tables (1967: 11; 1968: 12). Another example occurs during Ludvík's interrogation at the university; a female student accuses him of making frivolous ('lehkovážné') remarks about women in the early editions and translations of *The Joke* (1967: 190; 1968: 224), but she accuses him of making obscene ('obscénní') remarks in the later Czech editions and the later English and French translations (1991c: 195; 1985a: 228; 1993c: 191).

Kundera removes what could be read as sexist material, but does so in the Czech versions also. In the early versions of *Life is Elsewhere* (1973: 279; 1974: 207), he includes the first of these two paragraphs in which the narrator interjects and compares the age of youth to a 'female epoch', an 'Oriental epoch', underscoring Jaromil's youth with his maternal ties:

> **Somebody once wrote that the Middle Ages can be considered the western world's Oriental epoch. Since we are fond of comparing the history of the individual with the history of humanity, we are tempted to take an analogous approach and call youth a man's female epoch.**
>
> How they resembled each other, mother and son! Both equally bewitched by nostolgia for the monistic period of unity of harmony. He wants to return to the sweet-scented night of her maternal depths, and she wants to be that sweet-scented night, now and forever.

However, this paragraph is removed from the next version of the novel, which is the first Czech-language version – the 1979 Sixty-Eight Publishers version – and is then removed in the revised English (1987c: 221) and French (1987a: 332) versions (Kundera revised the English version once again in 2000 with Aaron Asher and had already revised the French translation in 1985 – the 1987 revision was his second one).

Kundera is not as experimental with narrative voice in his next novel, *Farewell Waltz* (1976), which is narrated in the third person. However, in one passage, Kundera introduces a metafictional comment which plays with the structure of the novel. The young boyfriend of the nurse, Růžena, is waiting outside a hotel where he thinks she is with another man. In the early versions, the boyfriend walks up and down outside the hotel all night while the others sleep and right up to the 'start of the next chapter':

> He is about to walk back and forth this way all night, while everyone else is asleep, he is destined to keep marching until the break of day, until the start of the next section. (Kundera, 1976b: 157)

> Bude takto přecházet celou noc, až už všichni ostatní budou spát, bude takto přecházet až do příštího dne, až do začátku další kapitoly. (Kundera, 1979b: 163)

> Il va faire ainsi les cent pas pendant toute la nuit, jusqu'à ce que tous les autres soient endormis, il va faire ainsi les cent pas jusqu'au lendemain, jusqu'au début du chapitre suivant. (Kundera, 1976a: 212)

In his revision of the French version of the novel in 1986, Kundera removes this comment and the overt reference to the fictional construct of the novel. He also makes this alteration in his revised version in Czech in 1997, although changes the temporal reference slightly (referring to 'early' the next day, rather than just the next day). However, the alteration is *not* made in the English-language version, revised in 1998, in which the overt reference is retained although altered:

> Bude takto přecházet celou noc, až už všichni ostatní budou spát, bude takto přecházet až do rána příštího dne. (Kundera, 1997b: 175)
>
> He will walk up and down this way the whole night, until everyone else will be asleep, he will walk up and down this way until early the next day. (my translation)
>
> Il va faire ainsi les cent pas pendant toute la nuit, jusqu'à ce que tous les autres soient endormis, il va faire ainsi les cent pas jusqu'au lendemain. (Kundera, 1986c: 248)
>
> He is going to be pacing back and forth like this all night, until everyone else is asleep, he is going to pace back and forth like this until tomorrow, until the last part of this book. (Kundera, 1998a: 208)

Note that Asher (in collaboration with Kundera) changes 'until the start of the next chapter' to 'until the last part of this book' (the next chapter starts the fifth and last part of the book). This is a small example of how Kundera, in retaining the comment in just the English version, allows a deviation from the French definitive and the Czech 'original' versions and is not seeking even a content-based fidelity to either of these versions. Note also that Asher's translation (the definitive English-language translation) reintroduces the style of the Czech sentence with the repetition of 'He is going', 'pace back and forth' and 'until', which in the Czech and French has a certain lullaby effect conducive to the somnambulant sense of the content. Asher's translation is not more faithful in the sense of accurately rendering the Czech meanings – for instance, his poetic transformation of 'přecházet' as 'to pace back and forth' rather than simply 'to walk up and down' – and it is not faithful to the content. Kundera rewrites the French and the Czech versions fairly similarly (by omitting this narrative comment) and rewrites the English version by keeping it but also altering it with his translator.

Kundera's rewriting of his novels points to pathology rather than contingency, and although he deliberately produces texts across languages which differ in content (never mind in respect of necessary cultural differences), these differences do not privilege certain readerships over others but simply allow, as Kussi suggests, coexistent versions of the texts across languages. In reference to *Laughable Loves* (1970), Kundera admits that he felt less able to experiment with the collection in its Czech form than in its translation, because it was so well known in Czechoslovakia. Yet he does experiment with it, and its definitive versions (proclaimed so by Kundera) in Czech, French and English are all different – with regards to content. The freedom of the translations, and of ironically the barrier between languages, allows such experimentation to take place, and it appears to be rooted in aesthetic concerns that grow with rereading the texts and returning to them.

***

The Matrix in the Drawer

The rewriting of the Czech versions and of the translations, and the function of the French translation as a partial originating version for later Czech versions, challenges and reconceives the relationship between original and translation. Kundera replaced this duality with his concept of the definitive text. His designation of the definitive versions of his novels is both freeing and problematic. First, it is freeing in that the definitive translations are not regarded as inferior copies but as independent literary texts. However, a problem arises in that the designation of definitive requires the authority of the author. This is fair because, as Kundera argues, authors have the right to do what they want with their text, but Kundera's own intervention in the translations tended to compromise and conceal work done by translators. While there have been problems in the translations, certainly according to Kundera's criteria, the translations are regarded by him as unfaithful partially because they represent an outdated vision of the text. Also problematic is Kundera's propensity to change his mind about his definitive texts, declaring a work definitive only to retract it via the publication of a new definitive edition.

This occurred with both *The Joke* (1967) and *Life is Elsewhere* (1973). Kundera openly and decisively authenticated Heim's 1983 translation of *The Joke* by appending a laudatory author's note identifying why it was the first genuine representation of the novel in English. In 1993 Kundera produced another translation of the novel, appending a preface in which he claimed that he had barely read Heim's translation and, in dismissing Heim's efforts, authenticating this new English version of the novel. In the 1993 preface, Kundera again dwelt on the previous editions and their shortcomings, in order to authenticate the present version. Yet the authorial approval appeared suspect because of the equivocation between intense authorial control over the translations and his claim of powerlessness in controlling them previously. The preface, in other words, is not enough to sustain his claims. Two issues discussed in the previous chapter are important here: Kundera's approach to reading accuracy in the translations and the publishers' demands on the translations. Kundera's claims that he did not read Heim's translation closely appear dubious because of his close interest in his translations, but this may refer more to his ever-present consciousness of the limitations of his English in judging the translations. Heim's translation, however, represented the first real editorial freedoms Kundera had, as it was the first book published after the success of *The Book of Laughter and Forgetting* (1979). There is also evidence that Kundera did insist on changes, in that Heim had published a section of *The Joke* in 1972, which is considerably altered in Heim's 1983 translation (Woods, 2002: 96). While Kundera had the opportunity to make the translation adhere more closely to his translation wishes, it seems that this did not entirely happen, and the 1993 translation does more closely articulate the parameters of Kundera's theories – to the extent that the text and the translation are changed. In this sense his retraction of a claim to definitiveness in Heim's translation makes sense but is not entirely fair to Heim.

A similar situation occurred with Kundera's other American translator, Peter Kussi, in translating *Life is Elsewhere* (1973). Initially, the novel was translated without any substantial input from Kundera and, after leaving Knopf, he made sure that it was retranslated with his input. He attached a postscript to Kussi's revised 1987 translation, declaring Kussi the best American translator from Czech, and in doing so wholeheartedly endorsed him (at the expense of Heim). *Life is Elsewhere* was, however, retranslated from French in 1996 by Aaron Asher, and this edition was also declared definitive. One of the distinguishing features of the 1996 retranslation was the inclusion of rewrites of the novel made in the revision of the French translation. Kussi's 1987 translation had also included rewrites of *Life is Elsewhere*, and Kussi had urged Kundera to clarify this in a note preceding the text, even providing Kundera with an example of a potential note. However, the final 'Note on the Text' for the 1987 translation only declares it as the definitive edition.

The definitive text, in Kundera's *oeuvre*, is not necessarily a final one. It represents two things: firstly, Kundera's belief that it is the best version in the language at the given time, and, secondly, the degree of Kundera's own involvement in the translation process. The label of 'definitive' conceals as much as it reveals, in that the new version necessarily outmodes the previous versions and potentially reverts them to the back shelves of university libraries, doubly confined by the fact that they were produced by Kundera's previous publishers (and are therefore impossible to replicate). However, readings of these prior translations can serve only to compound Kundera's arguments in which he is already in a dialogue with these translations. The prefaces, read out of this context, come across as merely a whimsical change of mind about the translations, but a close reading of Kundera's praxis in the different definitive editions in comparison to the prior translations gives evidence of a determined policy that is almost effaced while being declared in the prefaces.

The prefaces function on several levels: firstly as a seal of authorial approval; secondly as explanations (though only partial) of the choice leading up to this approval; and, thirdly, as an exposition of Kundera's critical analysis of his work (following Borges's claim (Borges, 1977) that the preface is a lateral space of criticism). This analysis also works towards an authentication, in providing an entry from which to read the work and serving as a prime reason why Kundera attached the postscript to *Life is Elsewhere* – feeling that the work had been misunderstood. The prefaces are in fact one of the few places in which Kundera refers to his own work – although he discusses his work in *The Art of the Novel* (1986), he only refers to it obliquely in *Testaments Betrayed* (1993), choosing to discuss issues from his own experience through discussion of the work of other artists. Kundera has refused to give interviews since the mid 1980s. What is fascinating about the prefaces, however, is that they allow Kundera to address a certain audience at a certain time. This results in certain information about his work being deliberately disseminated to certain audiences and not to others, allowing a level of flexibility and elusiveness.

So, for instance, Kundera is far more candid about his body of work to his Czech readers than to his 'foreign' ones. In the first novel published after 1989, *Žert/The Joke* (1991), Kundera used his author's note as a manifesto outlining his new view of what constituted his bibliography. In this manner, he explained his wish to remove certain works from his bibliography that would have been familiar to a Czech audience and which would, potentially, have been republished. He also obliquely warns the Czech audience not to read the novel as a political one, tied to a particular era of Czech history but not directly – he does this by recounting the translation history of the novel abroad. He contrasts the reductive Western criticism of the novel with that of Czech criticism from the 1960s, which he celebrates (this seems slightly rooted in nostalgia as Kundera had appended a preface in the 1960s, to his play *The Keepers of the Keys*, refuting the efforts of Czech critics as being reductive, for similar, political, reasons). Kundera omits to mention that he had made rewrites in this edition (and in previous editions) of *The Joke* and only once mentions that there are possibly rewrites to the novel. This occurs in his preface to the 1982 English translation, in which he asserts that he made some textual alterations to the 1981 French translation, a fact he does not append to the 1981 or 1985 French translation (which included further textual changes). However, Kundera in his author's note to the 1993 Czech edition of *Immortality/Nesmrtelnost* was fully candid about rewriting his novels, locating this urge in the fact of the existence of diverse versions because of his physical situation. In the note, he claimed that there were often three originating versions to his novels: the manuscript, the Sixty-Eight Publishers version and the definitive French version. Kundera has never made such a claim in his French- or English-language prefaces.

This disjointed discourse, however, allowed Kundera to locate and relocate his work as he saw fit. For instance, he needed to define which work he regarded as being in his bibliography to a Czech audience because this audience was aware of the existence of work, or the rewriting of it, of which the majority of his readers abroad were ignorant. Should Kundera be condemned for deception? Does he privilege one audience over another? Is it possible to cope with an author who deliberately and carefully differentiates his audience according to their cultural knowledge or familiarity? The prefaces show a lateral evolution, often a response to both changing contexts and changing aesthetic ambitions, belying the perceived image of Kundera as an author whose original is set in stone. This is a less comfortable image, with readers from different times and different languages perhaps questioning whether they are indeed reading the authentic version of the novel. It is less kind to Kundera's translators, whose efforts become outmoded not only because of Kundera's increasing quest for a greater accuracy but because of his rewriting of his work and his prefaces. Yet it also represents a paradigm for the autonomy of translations as texts to be considered by their own worth. Also, it presents an argument for the comparative study of Kundera's texts, not in order to judge which is inferior or superior, but to examine the changes and the evolution of the novels. Some of this evolution is a response to translation, to the acute awareness of different languages and cultures reading the novels, and some is an evolution of Kundera's writing. The prefaces, posited and rewritten, mimic and support the translations and are a tag to this evolution.

***

Biographical Furore

Kundera's decision not to republish his early work or to allow the production of his early plays, along with the slow publication (currently at a halt) of his books in the Czech Republic, has caused a storm of controversy in his old homeland. This has been compounded by his lack of involvement in public life there since 1989 and his decision to remain in France and to write in French. Only a handful of his books have been published so far in the Czech Republic: *Žert/The Joke* (1991), *Směšné lásky/Laughable Loves* (1991), *Nesmrtelnost/Immortality* (1993), *Valčík na rozloučenou/Farewell Waltz* (1997) and the play, *Jakub a jeho pán/Jacques and His Master* (1992). His best-sellers, *The Unbearable Lightness of Being* (1984) and *The Book of Laughter and Forgetting* (1979), have not been published, nor has *Life is Elsewhere* (1973), nor the novels written in French, *La lenteur* (1995)/*Slowness*, *L'identité* (1997) /*Identity* and *L'ignorance* (2003)/*Ignorance*. Extracts from *The Art of the Novel* (1986) and *Testaments Betrayed* (1993) have been published in the Brno-based literary journal *Host*, but the books have yet to be published. In libraries it is easier to access the earlier work – the poetry and plays – than it is to access this later work, unless the Czech reader is prepared to read them in English or French.

Kundera's lack of engagement or lack of willingness to engage with contemporary Czech society or even literary circles led to a certain degree of resentment, which was often articulated in attacks on Kundera's past. To a large extent this is also a reaction to the positive reception of Kundera's work abroad, with some Czech critics deriding the gullibility of the 'West' in accepting the superficiality of Kundera's representations of the 'East', and indeed of his own past. This reckoning famously began with Milan Jungmann's *samizdat* article *Kunderovské paradoxy/Kunderian Paradoxes* (1988) in which Jungmann attacked Kundera after the publication and huge success in the West of *The Unbearable Lightness of Being* (1984). Jungmann accused Kundera of lying about his past and of deliberately simplifying Czech history for the consumption of a Western audience. Jungmann further argued that the eroticism of the novel was a product of and aimed at the Western audience. What is most interesting about the article is Jungmann's claim about Kundera's representation of himself to his new audience, in that Kundera did efface his literary past and all it entailed when interviewed in the 1970s and early 1980s in order to consolidate his identity as a novelist and as an author without allegiances.

Although Jungmann has since partially retracted the criticisms in the essay, fairly maintaining that he did not have a real sense of the context because he and his fellow *samizdat* writers were caught in a 'ghetto', alienated from the outside world, his criticism has largely defined the contemporary response to Kundera and his work in the Czech Republic. Younger Czech critics, such as Michal Bauer, question the authenticity of his work because of two matters related to his evolution as a writer: firstly, his early lip service to communist aesthetics; and, secondly, his exile and his focus on a non-Czech audience. Bauer unearthed essays and translations by Kundera that espoused the communist cant of the period; in the case of the translations, Kundera was translating poets approved by the regime and in some cases making his translations more enthusiastically bound to communist iconography and images than the originals. Bauer argued that Kundera adapted to different styles contingent to his audience, constantly rewriting himself as an author:

> When the Stalinist-Gottwald regime was consolidated, Kundera wrote poetry with this theme and translated similarly focused poetry of other authors into Czech. When the Fucik emblem was 'aestheticized', he wrote *The Last May*. When there was no question of the function of the family in socialist society, but it had been conceded that there was such a thing as a marital crisis, and that relationships were not straightforward, he wrote *Monologues* and *Laughable Loves*. When authors returned to the 1950s and reflected on their work and their life (at least to the extent of the period from around 1956 or later, the 1960s) and when the Gottwald regime was 'analysed' (as far as that time could), he wrote *The Joke* (a novel which has enough in common with the novel published a few years earlier, Jan Trefulka's *It Rained Luck on Them*). And think of the so-called postmodern Kundera. And more of the same, and so on. (Bauer, 1998a: 12–13, my translation)

Bauer dismisses Kundera's supporters' claims that Kundera was interested only in his art and that he was 'bluffing' through the communist period, arguing that Kundera was fully cognisant of his collaboration with the regime and has vacillated with every passing historical phase. The material that Bauer has unearthed is superficially an indictment of Kundera's 'guilt'. However, the main problem with it is whether this posited guilt is at all relevant, whether in fact such an archeology of guilt is more pertinent to the society and critics digging for it. Since 1989 there has been a reckoning in the Czech Republic of who collaborated with whom and when, with reference to several Czech writers and artists, for instance Ivan Klíma, Pavel Kohout, and even Bohumil Hrabal. Kohout's experience, of turning from a communist ideologue to a dissident, was mapped out in a widely publicised, serialised and popular biography *Phenomenon Kohout* (2001), and Hrabal, despite 'self-criticising' during the communist period in order to be able to write and publish, is probably still the best-loved Czech writer. Kundera has been apportioned a greater part of the guilt perhaps because he is seen as having 'run away', judged to have accepted exile as an easier option than staying in Czechoslovakia and to have shunned Czech society since then. This is in contrast, for instance, to Josef Škvorecký and his wife (and fellow writer), Zdena Salivarová, who set up an émigré press in Canada, Sixty-Eight Publishers (publishing Kundera in Czech in the 1970s, 1980s and 1990s), and have been involved in public life in the Czech Republic since 1989. This is not to say that they have escaped the reckoning – Zdena Salivarová was accused of being a secret-police informant (she won a legal case denying this and Škvorecký's most recent novel, *Two Murders in My Double Life* (1999), is based on the experience). The accusations against Kundera need to be seen within the context of Czech society of the 1950s and 1960s and Czech society today.

The constant reinvention and the sense that Kundera deliberately obscured his real self from his Western audience is seen as evidence of his lack of authenticity. Kundera, though always actively and vociferously rejecting the label of 'dissident' in the Western media, also suspected that his success with his Western readership was based on inherent misunderstanding of his work, specifically in a reductive interpretation of its supposed political intent. There is a sense in the Czech Republic that there is a complete whitewash among Western critics when it comes to Kundera's work, because he provides what they want and because they are awed by what they perceive to be his sophistication. This is a somewhat essentialist and uninformed perception, creating a homogeneous and unsophisticated Western reader and critic who are oblivious to cultural nuance, who revel in cheap eroticism and superficial philosophising. Primarily, this image serves to promote the knowing and more intelligent Czech critic making such criticisms. While there is no doubt that much truth exists in these critics' and Kundera's claims of, at best, the naïveté of 'Western' critics and, at worst, a deliberate appropriation of the novels for the Western critics' ends, this is not true of all the criticism and is not a true portrayal of his reception in the West, which has been dogged with controversy. Taking their cue from the prevailing Czech sentiment about Kundera, much of the Western media has been critical of him, especially in the last decade, in which he has constantly been compared unfavourably with Václav Havel (Woods, 2003: 31).

That Kundera has deliberately obscured part of his *oeuvre* – by not allowing it to be translated – is without contention. The fact of translation greatly aided his revisionism regarding his bibliography, giving him a natural opportunity to jettison work. It is less certain whether the publication and translation of the work would really make the difference in perception in the West that is suspected; in other words, the issue is far more pertinent to Czech society than to societies abroad. Neither Czesław Miłoscz nor Ryzsard Kapuścinski, for instance, both one-time communists, have been censured abroad either for their early convictions or for their rejection of them. The question lies, more importantly, in whether the untranslated work would facilitate any broader understanding of his work as a whole, rather than whether it would give an indication of guilt.

Kundera's poetry is cited as evidence of his ideological orthodoxy and his suppression of it, evidence of his attempt to airbrush his own past and collaboration. However, his prose work and plays of the 1960s do not subscribe to communist orthodoxy, and yet parts or the whole of them are removed by Kundera from his bibliography. He made this clear to Czech readers in 1991 (Kundera, 1991c:319–22) when he articulated and defended his re-formation of his bibliography. His argument was made specifically on an aesthetic level, and he classified the removed work in three categories: juvenalia, unsuccessful work and incidental work. His decision is based implicitly and purely on aesthetic grounds. He adopted the musical system of appelling Opus numbers to the work that remained included and sealed with his retrospective approval. He explains this in 'Sixty-Three Words':

> OPUS The excellent custom of composers. They give opus numbers only to works they see as 'valid'. They do not number works written in their immature period, or occasional pieces, or technical exercises. An unnumbered Beethoven composition – for instance, the 'Salieri' Variations – though it may be quite weak, does not disappoint us, for the composer himself has alerted us. A fundamental question for any artist: which is the first 'valid' work? Janacek found his own voice only after he was forty-five; I suffer when I hear the few compositions still extant from his previous period. Just before he died, Debussy destroyed all his sketches, everything he had left unfinished. The least an author can do for his works: sweep up around them. (Kundera, 1988a: 146)

This included all his novels, but none of his poetry and only one of his three plays. The Opus system followed the chronology of the publication of the translations of his work, even though this did not follow the chronology in which the work was written. In *Testaments Betrayed* (1993), Kundera writes about the issue of work that artists, composers and writers choose to omit from their *oeuvre* and makes a passionate and rational case for such omissions. It is also a clear attack on scholars or critics who publish or perform this inferior work or think it relevant to the whole. Kundera does not deal directly with his own work in this essay because he does not need to approach it with his readership in translation – his choice not to translate his early work has made it irrelevant to his argument. In the same book of essays, Kundera vehemently argues that the state of being a novelist does not represent an adherence to a certain genre but means the adoption of a certain outlook on the world. This is an outlook, or *Weltanschauung*, he argues, that purveys an ironic gaze on the ambiguity of the world and is a 'furious *non-identification*' (Kundera, 1996b: 158). Kundera believes that a real novelist cannot be an ideologue, cannot be didactic and cannot be *engagé* in the Sartrean sense within the novels. The removal, then, of his poetry both as a genre and as an outlook makes aesthetic and ontological sense.

Both views need to be taken into account. Kundera cannot unpublish the early work, and his refutation of the work has perhaps caused interest in it. The early work does have a relevance to his later work. However, Kundera's pleas are equally valid – while it may not be necessary to dumbly swallow either his explanation or his actions, it is imperative to understand why he perceives the work to be inferior. It is less important to know that Kundera was a communist poet than to realise the consequences of this commitment in his later work. By removing the early work from its context within his body of work, there is a danger in removing a certain path to understanding and interpreting his work.

Kundera opens his first exile novel, *The Book of Laughter and Forgetting* (1979), with an image of an airbrushed photograph. Clementis, fallen foul of the communist regime, is removed from a photograph, but the hat he has placed on the head of the first Communist president, Klement Gottwald, remains on Gottwald's head. This is no surprise to readers, but, as Kundera continues the story of the dissident writer Mirek, an opponent of this airbrushing regime, of this organised forgetting, the reader realises that Mirek too is trying to rewrite his life. Like an author rewriting the beginning of his novel, Mirek tries to airbrush out elements of his own life that do not fit into the image he and others have of himself. Mirek wants to recover love letters from an ex-girlfriend who is now a vociferous communist. It would not reflect well on his dissident status if this link were widely adverstised. Yet, at the end, it is not a link with her political stance that he wishes to erase, but a link with her ugliness. Mirek is embarrassed that his friends might discover that he slept with such an ugly woman. The metaphysical ugliness of Kundera's early poetry because of its ideological orthodoxy is innately linked to the aesthetic ugliness of the work. The interaction of the two is one of enduring themes of Kundera's later fiction.

***

The Novel Made Poetry

The concentration on Kundera's censure of the republication of his early work has limited the analysis of the influence of his early work on his later fiction. Jan Lukeš argues that Kundera is in fact one of the few Czech writers who deals with his early experiences within his art (rather than as memoir, in the vein of his contemporary, Pavel Kohout). Jungmann, for instance, points out that Kundera uses the same title for a section of *The Unbearable Lightness of Being* (1984) that he had for one of his early Stalinist poems, 'The Grand March' (1953), but he cites this as an example of how Kundera rewrites his past to forget it. There is no indication in Jungmann's supposition that Kundera's reuse of the title might be an entirely deliberate remembering. Kundera has reused titles deliberately (see his comments above on *The Art of the Novel*) and has reused material directly from his earlier work (for instance his reuse of a line in *Jacques and His Master* (1981) that originated in his earlier play *Ptákovina* (1968)). That Kundera can write a poem in 1953 (in his early 20s and under a neo-Stalinist regime) in which he urges all to join the Grand March of communism and throw dissenters from the path and 30 years later write a section of a novel in which the Grand March of freedom becomes a laughable sham, a projection of personal needs into idealism, is indicative not of Kundera's opportunism but of his experience.

Kundera baldly states that his poetry, though excised from his *oeuvre*, provides 'motivational material' for his novels (1991c: 319). Herein another form of rewriting takes place which attempts to existentially locate the initial impetus for the poetry within his fiction. There is reference in his fiction to elements of his poetry as well as to his experience as a poet blinded by and constructing ideological truth. This is conducted as an existential analysis rather than a reckoning and began with one of Kundera's very first prose works, 'Nurse of My Nurses' (1963). In this, the second *Laughable Loves* story (omitted in 1970), Kundera reappraises poetic truth and youth through prose. The protagonist is a 33-year-old – the age of Christ at his death, the age when poets die, Kundera's age when writing the story – composer who idealises a nurse, who is married to an amateur poet, Vinkler. Vinkler believes that living itself should be a poem, and that poems should be hygienic. He distributes white roses to make the world poetic. His simplistic and moralistic poems about daisies – co-written with his wife – are deeply contrasted with the composer finding his own voice, through implementing the polyphonic music of voices and songs heard while walking (again a reference to Janáček). Vinkler insists that the point of art is to convey truth, at which point the composer suggests that then he is a priest rather than a poet.

Vinkler's attitude – what Kundera defines in *Life is Elsewhere* (1973) as the 'lyric' attitude – is defined by its absolutism, its search for absolute truth, hence the equation with religious belief. Kundera later describes his personal break from poetry as akin to a religious betrayal: 'To leave poetry for prose was not for me a simple transition of genre but a real rupture', Kundera said in a 1979 interview. 'I did not leave poetry, I betrayed it. For me, lyrical poetry is not only a literary genre but above all a conception of the world, an attitude vis-à-vis the world. I left this attitude as one leaves a religion' (Biron, 1979: 17). Kundera had made such remarks already in 1967, two years *before* the final edition of his third book of poetry, *Monologues*, was published in 1969. His comments are remarkably similar to those above, made a decade later:

> I did not desert poetry. I betrayed it. For me lyric poetry is not only a literary genre, but a whole way of life, an attitude towards the world. I put away that attitude as one puts away religious faith ... An antipoetic posture grows out of the conviction that between what we think about ourselves and what we actually are there exists an infinite distance ... To apprehend this distance, this abyss, means to destroy the poetic illusion. This is also the essence of the art of irony. And irony is the perspective of the novel. (Liehm, 1976: 45)

Youth is the lyric age, according to Kundera, although he argues that the youthful lyrical attitude can persist beyond a change of years, that: "youth" does not designate a specific period of life but a *value* above age' (Kundera, 2000: 147). He contrasts Jaromil, the youthful poet, revolutionary and murderer in *Life is Elsewhere* (1973), with an unnamed man, identified only by his age – the 40-year old (also the title of the sixth section), whose compassion for Jaromil's girlfriend is rooted in a maturity about the world. In the same novel, Kundera writes:

> In immature man the longing persists for the safety and unity of the universe which he occupied alone inside his mother's body. Anxiety (or anger) persists as well – towards the adult world of relativity in which he is lost like a drop in an alien sea. That's why young people are such passionate monists, emissaries of the absolute; that's why the poet weaves his private world of verse; that's why the young revolutionary (in whom anger is stronger than anxiety) insists on an absolutely new world forged from single idea; that's why such a person can't bear compromise, either in love or politics ... The adult world knows perfectly well that the absolute is an illusion, that nothing human is either great or eternal .... (Kundera, 1987c: 220-1)

That Kundera personally identifies with the absolutism of youth is unmistakable. In a 1984 interview he was perfectly candid: 'I do not live at peace with myself at twenty. I feel myself to have been an absolute jerk from every point of view, and it likely comes from there, this suspicious attitude towards that age, especially with regard to a certain lyricizing' (Weiss, 1986: 409). In other interviews and essays, he has also indicated that the experiences of his youth in the Stalinist era have given him this 'suspicion of words' and a suspicion of man's propensity to beautify horror, having seen the results of such collusion with history. (Finkielkraut, 1982: 19). He writes about this – though not explicitly about his own involvement – in *Testaments Betrayed*:

> Lyricism, lyricization, lyrical talk, lyrical enthusiasm are an integrating part of what is called the totalitarian world; that world is not the gulag as such; it's a gulag that has poems plastering its outside walls and people dancing before them.
>
> More than the Terror, the lyricization of the Terror was a trauma for me. It immunized me for good against all lyrical temptations. The only thing I deeply, avidly, wanted was a lucid, unillusioned eye. I finally found it in the art of the novel. This is why for me being a novelist was more than just working in one 'literary genre' rather than another; it was an outlook, a wisdom, a position ... (Kundera, 1996b: 157–78)

Throughout Kundera's work these two elements keep reappearing: his obsession with youth and poetry – the markers of the lyric – and his obsession with the form of the novel as a form (as an aesthetic and as a path) of resistance. Poets populate the work – from Vinkler, through Jaromil, to the poets in the 'Litost' section of *The Book of Laughter and Forgetting* (1979), to Goethe and also Paul's love of Rimbaud in *Immortality* (1991). Kundera does not attack poetry as a genre or as a means of writing; in fact, he integrates it into his vision of the novel. For him, the novel 'has become poetry'. This may seem paradoxical at first glance, but the element of the lyric is the central issue because the difference between the poetry of poetry and the poetry of the novel is that the novel is, according to Kundera, an 'antilyrical poetry'. The poets whom Kundera keeps coming back to, both fictional and real, in his novels are espousers of the lyric attitude towards life, this attitude that Kundera believed in, had faith in, and which he betrayed – 'I, who am among the initiates' he writes in *The Book of Laughter and Forgetting* (Kundera, 1988b: 137), as he watches the fictional Lermontov impose his own absolute meanings on words. The group of poets meeting in the novel are Czech poets given the names of world-famous poets to protect their identity (for fear of real repercussions; Kundera's

Czech citizenship was taken away following the publication of this novel – Kundera notes with disgust that the letter informing him of this contained grammatical errors). Goethe, Voltaire, Lermontov, Yesenin and Boccaccio listen to Petrarch's overblown story, and it is Boccaccio – the father of the novel – who challenges the reality of Petrach's narration, making fun of his lyrical flight. All the poets are shown to be extraordinarily ordinary, all scared of Goethe's wife. Goethe is portrayed as drunk and crippled but it is an affectionate portrayal because he is only human after all, rather than a mythic literary creature. In *Immortality* (1991), Goethe in heaven is given the choice to look like himself at any period of his life and his chooses to wear 'a green eyeshade attached to his forehead by a piece of string; he had slippers on his feet; a heavy, stripy wool scarf was tied around his neck because he was afraid of catching cold'. This is his 'private look' from his old age, one that will make a mockery of young Bettina von Arnim, who makes her fame after his death from an overblown account of a sexual liaison with Goethe: 'Wherever she goes, she talks of her great love for me. So I want people to witness the object of that love. Whenever she sees me, she runs for her life. And I know she stamps her feet in fury because I parade around this way: toothless, bald and with this ridiculous gadget over my eyes' (Kundera, 1991a: 96).

Kundera is not satirising just Bettina but all of us, because of the human propensity to lyricise our lovers, our politics, our ideals and our lives. The extreme result of this is Jaromil, the young poet in *Life is Elsewhere* (1973), who is compared throughout the novel with other 'real' poets – Shelley, Rimbaud, Lermontov, Wolker, Halas – a comparison that demystifies them as much as Jaromil, as they are shown all to be distinctly under their mother's wings. Jaromil's lyricism, his narcissism and his attempt to fit into a mature world lead him to denounce his girlfriend and her brother, both of whom are imprisoned – and in the case of the brother, murdered – by the regime. Kundera underlines the connection between a personal and a public lyricism, a willingness to believe, to shout slogans and to murder for these slogans. His attempts – humorously written – to demystify the figure of the poet reach back into the depths of his own past and his own discomfort with the identity of the poet, but they also serve to demystify the human need to lyricise our lives, to create illusions and to have this 'folding screen set up to curtain off death' (Kundera, 1985c: 253). Youth is the perfect age or value for such lyricism because it is a time without memory, without experience and thereby susceptible to accepting and perpetrating illusions. Kundera is equally critical both of the communist paradigm and of the Western obsession with youth as one of the ultimate positive values. For example, in one of the most grotesque passages in his work, in *The Book of Laughter and Forgetting* (1979), Tamina finds herself on an island of children. Contrary to usual depictions of innocence, these children are horrific, unsettling and nasty – as if the castaways of *The Lord of the Flies* had met the Marquis de Sade. Tamina chooses suicide over staying on their island of no memory, experience or maturity.

This is Kundera's youth. In the same way that Bettina creates a mythic Goethe, Kundera in his mid-20s had created a mythic Julius Fučík in his version of an epic poem, *Poslední máj / The Last May* (1955). Fučík was a standard symbol in post-war communist Czechoslovakia of the courageous, righteous communist, martyred when he imprisoned and murdered Nazis. His book of prison writings, 'published after the war in a million copies, broadcast over the radio, studied in schools as required reading, was the sacred book of the era' (Kundera, 1993c: 189–90). By writing the poem, Kundera was naturally contributing to the sanctified image of the martyr, but the quote is from his first novel, *The Joke* (1967), in which Fučík makes an appearance once again. In *The Joke*, a student named Ludvík sends a joking postcard to his girlfriend, which is intercepted and used against him by the student body as an example of his anti-Party stance. In the ensuing trial, his postcard is compared to Fučík's writing and Ludvík knows at once he is lost, because no one can be compared to Fučík – the perfect communist. He looks up at a well-known portrait of Fučík hanging in the auditorium:

> The drawing of Fucik on the wall was a reproduction of the famous sketch by Max Svabinsky, the old Jugendstil painter, the virtuoso of allegories, plump women, butterflies, and everything delightful; after the war, or so the story goes, Svabinsky had a visit from the Comrades, who asked him to do a portrait of Fucik from a photograph, and Svabinsky had drawn him (in profile) in graceful lines in accord with his own taste: almost girlish, fervent, pure, and so handsome that people who had known him personally preferred Svabinsky's sublime drawing to their memories of the living face... Fucik's handsome face hung on the wall as it hung in a thousand other public places in our country, and it was so handsome, with the radiant expression of a young girl in love, that when I looked at it I felt inferior not just because of my guilt, but because of my appearance as well. (Kundera, 1993c: 190)

Here Kundera not only revisits the theme of Fučík but ironically and humorously reveals and dismantles the methods by which Fučík was constructed as a symbol (methods with which he was complicit and of which he had experience). Earlier in the novel, Ludvík as an older man reacts angrily to the appropriation of Fučík as a symbol by his old friend Jaroslav. Jaroslav, the leader of a folk band, is creating new folk songs by using new lyrics and subjects with the old tunes, following Stalin's dictum of socialist content and national form, and inserting socialist subjects into a tradition as if they *were* the tradition. Jaroslav has chosen Fučík as a subject of one of his songs and Ludvík derides this choice:

> The songs are so unnatural and false. The propaganda text sticks out from the pseudo-folk music like a badly sewn-on collar. A pseudo-Moravian song about Fucik! What nonsense! A Prague Communist journalist! What did he have in common with Moravia?
>
> I [Jaroslav] objected that Fucik belonged to us all and that we had just as much right to sing about him in our own way.
>
> In our own way? You don't sing in our own way, you sing the agit-prop way! Look at the words. And why a song about Fucik anyway? Was he the only one in the underground? The only one tortured?
>
> But he's the best known!
>
> Of course he is! The propaganda apparatus wants a hierarchy in its gallery of dead heroes. They want a chief hero among heroes.
>
> Why poke fun at that? Every age has its symbols.
>
> True, but it's interesting to know who has been chosen to serve as a symbol! There were hundreds of people just as courageous at the time, and now they are forgotten. (Kundera, 1993c: 155–56).

One can take Bauer's view here that Kundera returns to Fučík only in order to be in step with the times and to criticise communist propaganda with which he himself collaborated, when it was fashionable to do so. Kundera recants his position as one of contingency. Yet what is interesting about the way in which Kundera returns to Fučík is that he focuses on the mechanism of myth-making, whether through painting idealised portraits or by singing agitprop songs. These mechanisms are revealed through irony that does not refer directly to Kundera's own collaboration, but to the general motivations and consequences of these mechanisms. Kundera is not rewriting his past through a 'forgetting' or an airbrushing of it but is rewriting it through an investigation within art of the meaning of what he did. The Czech audience of the 1960s – 100,000 of whom bought *The Joke* when it was first published in the late 1960s – would have been well aware of Kundera's epic poem on Fučík, and the laudatory critical reception certainly regarded the novel as a reappraisal of the motivations of past actions rather than as a recanting of them.

Times change, and the figure of Fučík has been superseded by other symbols of other ideologies. Kundera reflects this also in his literal rewriting of *The Joke*. In the 1967, 1968 and 1969 Czech versions of the novel, he described Fučík's book simply as 'the most read book of its time' (1967: 188) because the Czech readership would have been aware of its cultural impact. In his revision of the 1980 French translation (1980: 273) and then in the revised 1983 English translation (1984c: 166), Kundera adds to this for further explanation, hence the quote above that it was published in a million copies. He then includes this explanation in the 1991 Czech edition (1991c: 194) because he is speaking to an altered Czech audience, one which may not be aware any longer of who exactly this communist symbol was – a Czech audience as culturally separated from their past as a foreign audience was from 1950s Czech communist culture.

The Joke as a whole investigates the ways in which the main characters create their own illusions and how other characters reveal them to be illusions through their own perspective on a partially shared past. This method of structuring the novel – as with all his novels – enables the constant revelations of various characters' illusions, giving the ironic distance that Kundera claims lyric poetry cannot, because it is structured in an entirely monologic and subjective manner. This subjectivity is both shown and revealed in Kundera's two versions of the 'Grand March': the first a poem entitled 'The Grand March', from his first book of poetry, *Člověk zahrada širá* / *Man the Broad Garden* (written in 1953, when he was in his early twenties); and the second, 'The Grand March' section of his 1984 novel *The Unbearable Lightness of Being* (written in his 50s). The poem 'The Grand March' is pure communist kitsch, an idealistic portrait of a ruined city after war, from whose ruins rise workers who lead a grand march into the future, workers heralded by the birds and the trees, who march on and on throwing those who speak against them to the side.

Kundera returns to this vision in *The Unbearable Lightness of Being* (1984), in which he exposes the Grand March as 'the political kitsch joining leftists of all times and tendencies' (Kundera, 1985c: 257). Kitsch, Kundera argues, is the aesthetic ideal of a categorical agreement with being, the mask of beauty created to cover the inadequacies and ugliness of reality. 'The Grand March is the splendid march on the road to brotherhood, equality, justice, happiness; it goes on and on, obstacles notwithstanding, for obstacles there must be if the march is to be the Grand March' (Kundera, 1985c: 257). Franz, the dreamer, goes on a march in Thailand of French and American leftists in protest against the Khmer Rouge, but he comes to realise the Grand March is coming to an end because no one is watching it any more, the world is indifferent to it:

> Yes, said Franz to himself, the Grand March goes on, the world's indifference notwithstanding, but it is growing nervous and hectic: yesterday against the American occupation of Vietnam, today against the Vietnamese occupation of Cambodia; yesterday for Israel, today for the Palestinians; yesterday for Cuba, tomorrow against Cuba – and always against America; at times against massacres and at times in support of other massacres; Europe marches on, and to keep up with events, to leave none of them out, its pace grows faster and faster, until finally the Grand March is a procession of rushing, galloping people and the platform is shrinking and shrinking until one day it will be reduced to a mere dimensionless dot. (Kundera, 1985c: 266–7)

The idealism of the March supersedes the content or the reason for it. To Sabina, this reduction of the march to its symbol is a dangerous thing. The word 'parades' is one that is misunderstood between Sabina and her lover, Franz. While he feels that partaking in such marches will lead him to a real life, articulated by protest, for Sabina parades mean something else because she has lived through the organised marches of communism. When asked by her French friends why she could not stay in a march against the Soviet occupation of her country: 'She would have liked to tell them that behind Communism, Fascism, behind all occupations and invasions lurks a more basic, pervasive evil and that the image of that evil was a parade of people marching by with raised fists and shouting identical syllables in unison. But she knew she would never be able to make them understand' (Kundera, 1985c: 100).

The Great March, which Franz is on, is one of endless misunderstandings. The French contingent in the march are upset that the Americans insist on conducting the protest in English, and protest in French. The translator is too embarrassed to translate. A French linguistics professor insults the American actress with the expletive 'Merde'; she bursts into tears, and a photographer takes her picture as one of compassion. The French raise their fists in anger at the Americans; the Americans raise their fists in answer thinking this is the symbol of leftist unity. They march to the Cambodian border, where an interpreter asks through a megaphone in Khmer to allow the doctors through to enable medical assistance. She is greeted by silence.

Franz at this point sees that the Grand March is 'laughable' but he cannot 'betray' it and imagines himself running towards the Khmer Rouge and to a glorious death in order to prove that its ideals 'weighed more than shit' (Kundera, 1985c: 269). But he does not, and meets his death in a mugging on the streets of Bangkok. Kundera's reappraisal of the Grand March, using the same title and the same words, returning to the idea of the march 'going on and on' regardless, does not refer overtly to his own poem celebrating the Grand March, which is collaborative and constructive of its myth. Yet 30 years after the poem he figuratively rewrites it, this time from the perspective not only of hindsight but also from the perspective of the 'lucid, unillusioned eye' of the novel. Franz's illusions are wrenched open only because they are seen in the light of Sabina's disillusions and illusions, as well as of those of Tomáš and Tamina. The multiple perspectives the novel allows provide layers of contradictions that prise open the tightly personally constructed worlds of the protagonists. The illusions of the characters – Franz's illusion of the Grand March, Tomáš's illusions of sex and Tamina's illusions about love – are taken apart and shown for what they are. The words 'laughable', 'melancholy' and 'betrayal' return again and again in Kundera's work and signal this novelistic move to demystify the vain constructs of mankind. The legacy of Kundera's experience with poetry, and the language of his own illusions, referred to however obliquely, is figuratively rewritten into the weave of his prose and dismantled for the world to see its motivations and its crimes.

What does Kundera mean, then, when he claims that the novel has become poetry? He writes that, 'Ever since Madame Bovary, the art of the novel has been considered equal to the art of poetry, and the novelist (any novelist worthy of the name) endows every word of his prose with the uniqueness of the word in a poem' (Kundera, 1984a: ix). He returns to Madame Bovary in his definition of the 'NOVEL (and poetry)' in 'Sixty-Three Words':

> 1857: The greatest year of the century. *Les Fleurs du mal*: lyric poetry discovers its rightful territory, its essence. *Madame Bovary*: for the first time, a novel is ready to take on the highest requirements of poetry (the determination to 'seek beauty above all'; the importance of each particular word; the intense melody of the text; the imperative of originality applied to every detail). From 1857 on, the history of the novel will be that of the 'novel become poetry'. But to *take on the requirements of poetry* is quite another thing from *lyricizing* the novel (forgoing its essential irony, turning away from the outside world, transforming the novel into personal confession, weighing it down with ornament). The greatest of the 'novelists become poets' are violently *antilyrical*: Flaubert, Joyce, Kafka, Gombrowicz. Novel = antilyrical poetry. (Kundera, 1988a: 142–43).

Kundera is of course a poet become novelist, but while he imports themes from his poetry and figuratively rewrites them in his prose, thankfully he does not import the language style, for while Kundera's poetry shows little ear for melody, his prose does. Writing on Janáček, Kundera identifies the method in which Janáček used ordinary, seemingly banal language to create melodies (Janáček, as the composer in 'Nurse of my Nurses' does, would transcribe overheard conversations on the street and incorporate phrases into his operas). Kundera suggests this discloses 'two major intentions on the part of the composer' which could equally describe Kundera's own poetics in the novel: '1. To eliminate rhythmic, melodic, metric stereotypes from music which has its origin only in music itself and to discover a new source of the musical material (of motifs, of 'melodies'). 2. To understand the enigma of musical semantics, to learn the psychological vocabulary of intonations and in that way to find a subtle instrument for picking up the most nuanced, the most hidden emotions of man' (Kundera, 1983: 374). This explanation of Janáček's poetics is also a succinct appraisal of Kundera's own. He attempts to extract beauty from rather prosaic language, through an intricately constructed placing of such language. In *Life is Elsewhere* (1973), there is a stark difference in tonality between the six sections centred on Jaromil and the section centred on the 40-year-old, which emanates a calm poetic intensity through constant repetition of phrases and words. When translating the novel, Kussi questioned the quality of Kundera's writing in the Jaromil section because it sounded like the language of a teenager, and there is real irony in the awkward language of the poet and that of the ordinary, mature man. The poetry is deliberately not that of the Grand March, marked with sweeping iconic language, but is stark and discreet. So much so, that it is often overlooked in translation, while being at the heart of Kundera's linguistic project.

In *Life is Elsewhere* (1973), Jaromil's girlfriend, when released from prison (placed there by Jaromil), goes first to her 40-year-old lover because she cannot go home (perhaps to be blamed for her brother's death). When the 40-year-old allows the girl into the room, her first remark is very plain:

'Všechno je tu, jak bylo', řekla. (Kundera, 1979c: 313)
Everything here is as it was, she said. (my translation)

And the man in his forties counterpoints this in an echoing reply:

'Ano, všechno je, jak to bylo', přisvědčil ... (Kundera, 1979c: 313)
Yes, everything is as it was, he agreed ... (my translation)

The banal statements, covering the momentous changes in the girl's life and the fact that these changes are perhaps irrelevant to the wider world, are moved to poetry by this simple repetition. In the first English translation, however, this is translated as:

'Everything here is still the same', she said.
'Yes, that's true'. (Kundera, 1987c: 273, translation by Peter Kussi)

The stark poetry of the statement is lost, along with the insight it gives into the irrelevance of personal horror within ongoing life. It also introduces flippancy rather than understanding from the man in his 40s. It is revised in the 2000 translation (following the French translation) to:

'Everything here is just the way it was', she said.
'Yes, everything is just the way it was', the man in his forties agreed ...
(Kundera, 2000: 232, translation by Aaron Asher)

The roots of Kundera's argument that the novel, since *Madame Bovary*, is poetry because each word is constructed in its place with as much importance as a word in a poem, can be seen in both the translation and the revision. What may seem to an editor like a banal statement, which may slow down the action of the novel, is in fact full of resonance and is there for a purpose – both in its sound and in its deeper significance. A similar example can be found in *Farewell Waltz* (1976), when Bertlef tells Růžena that he loves her. Růžena is a particularly unlikeable character, but Bertlef's goodness (the reader is never sure how much of a sham Bertlef's goodness is, as the reader vacillates between Jakub's cynical appraisal of Bertlef and Škréta's acceptance of him) reflects new light on her, and the scene is particularly tender because her insecurities, the bedrock of her hate, are stripped bare. It is also the last night of her life, as she will be murdered haphazardly by Jakub the next day. She cannot understand why Bertlef has pursued her, and Bertlef answers:

‚Protože vás mám rád'
Slovo ‚rád' zaznělo docela tiše, ale místnost ho bylo náhle plna.
I její hlas teď ztichl: ‚Vy mě máte rád?'
‚Ano, mám vás rád'. (Kundera, 1997b: 168)

'Because I love you'.
The word 'love' sounded quiet enough, but the room was suddenly filled with it.
And her voice now quietened: 'You love me?'
'Yes, I love you'. (my translation)

Again an editor might find the repetition awkward, especially because it surrounds the clichéd 'I love you', and indeed in the first French translation Bertlef's answer is not translated. Kundera reinstates it ('Oui je vous aime'.) in his 1986 revision (Kundera, 1986c: 240). In the first English translation it is translated as 'Yes, I do' (Kundera, 1976b: 151), which Kundera and Asher alter to 'Yes, I love you' in 1998 (Kundera, 1998a: 200). While this may seem to be splitting hairs, it is important to emphasise the function of this deceptively simple language. The cliché here is turned into something moving because of the repetition, because of where it stands in the text and with the characters. The different views of the novel, its dialogic nature, *pace* Bakhtin (Jefferson, 1991), and the different perspectives of each character on the other characters, give this kind of language a deeper resonance because it reveals a different view within the prosaic language of everyday life.

His reimagining of poetry in the form of the novel began, according to Kundera, in the 1950s when he 'wanted to solve an esthetic problem: how to write a novel which would be a "critique of poetry" and yet at the same time would itself be poetry (transmit poetic intensity and imagination)' (Kundera, 1987c: vii). This was his stated project with *Life is Elsewhere* (1973), a novel that critiques the absolutist seed in lyrical poetry while being constructed from a novelistic poetry. This extends to the wider construct and layout of his prose. When Kundera rewrote 'I the Mournful God' (1963), he reconceived it in a series of much shorter chapters (from three chapters to 16) and his fiction tends to follow the same structure because, he argues, he would like 'each chapter of my novel to be condensed, intense and expressive like a small poem' (Biron, 1979: 18). In his revisions of the translations, Kundera realigns the novels so that each small chapter begins on a new page.

Kundera's experience with poetry is figuratively rewritten on two levels: within the reappraisal of themes from his poetry and within a reconception of the novel as poetry but as anti-lyrical poetry. The importance of this in respect of translation is that each word is as intricately placed and structured within the whole as it would be in a poem, and that it has a function through sound and through a consistent reconsideration, through different characters and different contexts, of its meaning. At the beginning of the 1960s, Kundera argued that poetry was 'the inner fire of all art' and in a sense, even given his betrayal of poetry, this still seems to hold true. Kundera has not forgotten his poetry, but has radically rewritten it to expose it for what it was. This is problematic because he does not publicly repent or apologise, and this is always going to be unforgivable to some because Kundera was a poet who reigned 'hand in hand with the hangman'. Yet Kundera does address the issue constantly in his novels; indeed, it could be regarded as the driving force – the inner fire – of his novels, this constant seeking to unmask illusion and absolutism.

Kundera's renouncement ('betrayal') of poetry, enacted in his embrace of the novel form as its antithesis, can be (as it has been) seen as a flight into aesthetics rather than as a facing of his real and guilty past. The question has to be whether he does in fact enact a forgetting of it, as critics such as Jungmann and Bauer maintain. Superficially he does – removing his poetry from his bibliography – but the poetry is everywhere in his fiction. The fiction provides a platform for an analysis not of what the poetry, its absolutism and its illusions, means for him but of what it means for man, even when these illusions are perpetrated on the most personal and intimate levels. This can be read as a deflection (I am not guilty; man is), but it provides an insight into the human condition which is far more important than the confessions in a memoir (we are not guilty, he is). This is what art rather than hagiography does, what it allows, and what Kundera believes the novel allows.

Chapter 4
Writing

Writing, for Kundera, is a form of translation, and consciously so once his novels were banned and he was forced to write primarily for a non-Czech-speaking audience. This brings into question any notion of an original text: Kundera wrote in Czech, but his books from the early 1970s were first published in French and some have not to this day been published in the Czech Republic. He wrote that 'my novels lived their lives in translation; as translations they were read, criticized, judged, accepted or rejected' (Kundera, 1993b: 346, my translation). In other words, translation did not provide an afterlife for the novels; rather they were written and received as translations. Until 1989 nearly all of his readership read his novels in translation, and Kundera wrote knowingly for a foreign readership. There are, in fact, three phases in Kundera's writing career which show a development as to the awareness within the writing of writing as a form of translation. Kundera began his career writing in Czech for Czechs; once banned he wrote in Czech primarily for non-Czech-speaking readers; from the mid 1980s he began writing in a second language, French, at a time just before his Czech audience would be recovered. Through these changes in circumstance, an emerging pattern in his language style has become confluent with a self-consciousness about his language and, most importantly, his style. This style is the key not only to the constant exegesis on meaning in the novels but also to the question of what is in fact translatable when one is working in a language that few readers read and when, later, one is working in a second language.

Writing as an act is a form of translation – by making a choice in placing a word in a certain context with a certain meaning, even though it may contain the trace of other meanings and possibilities of future meanings, the writer acts as a mediator of meaning in much the same way as a translator might. This suggests an instability of original meaning in any one language even before transferring that language into another one becomes an issue. That transference, however (the interlingual translation), is a discomfiting process not only because it hints at, or openly shows up, cultural differences but because it exposes the contingency of creating meaning in any language. This instability of meaning in language is a preoccupation of Kundera's work, constantly in tension with his search for precision and constantly exposed by the translation process.

Kundera's first two exile novels, *The Book of Laughter and Forgetting* (1979) and *The Unbearable Lightness of Being* (1984), show a striking self-consciousness about language and referential meaning that coincides with his revisions of the translations of his novels. In the essay 'Sixty-Three Words' (1988), Kundera remarks on the return of the theme of 'lightness' in his novels and how this word is transformed in the context of the novels. He adds that it was only when he read the novels in translation that he realised how the word kept recurring. Aghast at first, he came to comprehend that this was an articulation of his authorial style, that these repeated words heralded the themes of his novels and that these words were 'analyzed, studied, defined, redefined' over the course of the novel 'and thus transformed into categories of existence' (Kundera, 1988a: 84). The previously more unconscious use of repetition and the contingent creation of the signature authorial style here fissures into an absolutely deliberate and self-aware promulgation of it. Translation is a lightning-rod for this for two reasons: firstly the effect of rereading his work through translation awakens him to his own style; and secondly the loss of a readership that has any referential claim to the language in which he is writing. Kundera writes in a Czech language that is shorn of the potentialities of any cultural shorthand or presumption.

Language and communication have been consistently examined and interrogated in all of Kundera's prose, but, following his exile, he explicitly addressed his readers on these issues, knowing that the vast majority would read his novels in translation (Kundera calculated that following his move to France only 1/1000 of his readers were able to read his novels in Czech). Květoslav Chvatík argues that this reality intensified his linguistic style, that his mode of expression 'reached a new level, when he was isolated from his Czech readers and was forced to write for his translators' (Chvatík, 1994: 80, my translation). He goes on to argue that Kundera deliberately chose certain words that 'were significantly easier, more precise and which avoided translatorial misunderstanding', employing 'a meditation on their etymologies in the footsteps of poets and philosophers', echoing Kundera's argument that no translator would translate and transpose Heidegger's *Das Sein* in his philosophical texts with a variety of synonyms, because the word itself is what is being investigated (Chvatík, 1994: 80–81, my translation). Helena Kosková agreed with Chvatík, but added that, besides this 'regard for the translator', his style was influenced by 'the realisation of the polysemy of words' and that both these factors made him more conscious in the text of language and of the pitfalls of synonyms (Kosková, 1998: 96–97, my translation). It is this style, a style of resistance and marker of the untranslatable in language, which becomes one significant translatable element in his French-language novels.

Certainly, in his two first exile novels, *The Book of Laughter and Forgetting* (1979) and *The Unbearable Lightness of Being* (1984), the narrator (who is specifically identified in the former as 'Milan Kundera') guides and challenges the reader to understand not only the novel but the role of the language in it (Zimra, 1991: 323). This understanding, in the case of three sections of the novels I examine here ('Litost' in *The Book of Laughter and Forgetting*, the examination of the Czech word 'soucit', and the 'Misunderstood Words' section in *The Unbearable Lightness of Being*), involves the notion of untranslatability. In the first, Kundera attempts to explain the meaning of an 'untranslatable' Czech word, *lítost*, to the reader; in the second he addresses how the differing etymologies of the same word in different languages affect the understanding of the word's referent; and in the third Kundera presents a dictionary of words used by two lovers, Sabina and Franz, to which each attaches different meanings.

With Sabina and Franz, Kundera suggests that, if each language describes a world, each individual also describes a world. Each person uses their own lexicon, including Kundera himself. Each of his characters is defined through certain theme words, and Kundera shows how these words are given meaning (or a variety of meanings) by the characters. Via this process, Kundera defines his own novelistic lexicon, which is a self-conscious definition. Rather than insisting his readers understand the meaning of his words, he insists that the readers understand the *mechanisms* of positing meaning. This is further complicated when one considers the translation of his work. Aware that he was writing in the first instance for a French translator, Kundera suggested that the language of his writing changed (Kundera, 1977: 3–4). This did not herald a hybrid Czech language in his writing; rather, it enabled Kundera to expose the Czech language in his novels to foreignness.

The coalescence of these two elements is nowhere more apparent than in the 'Litost' section of *The Book of Laughter and Forgetting* (1979). Kundera initially began the novel as a series of short stories (one of which was published as such in *The New Yorker* in 1977), a kind of 'Laughable Loves II', and this connection with Kundera's earlier book of short stories is cemented with this preoccupation with the theme of *lítost*. A problem existed, however, in that this Czech word is, according to Kundera, 'untranslatable' and had proven to be so in the translations of *Laughable Loves* in which it had been translated with a variety of synonyms – yet the repetition of the word pointed to the epistemological considerations of the stories (and provided a linkage between the stories). In this first book written in exile, Kundera knew that few of his readers would be Czech speakers so his decision to retain the Czech form is a deliberate challenge, a form of textual resistance to the elision of the word and the resonances it has for the text. That Kundera has to explain the word shows his awareness of audience (to this day *The Book of Laughter and Forgetting* has still not been published in the Czech Republic, because Kundera claims he needs to rewrite the Czech version – having made changes while revising the French translation), that he claims it as inexplicable is a provocation to his foreign audience to remember the word and its untranslatability.

The change in a single word can alter the tone of what is being conveyed, which is the very point of the section 'Litost'. It becomes clear why Kundera's act of retaining the Czech word *'lítost'* in the novel was such an act of resistance and inherently one that presumed that the text would be read in translation. It was a preventative measure against the disappearance of the word, and the Czech word was repeated through the section to consolidate its presence. This repetition served to build up a sense of the meaning of the word, even though Kundera could not finally define what the word means. *Lítost* was explicitly presented to a foreign readership as a foreign, unknown and untranslatable word. Kundera did not present his readers with a definition of it, instead giving example upon example in an attempt to define *lítost*. Unable to define it even within the Czech language, he implied that the word was foreign also in its own language, through its indefinability. By retaining the Czech word in the text and not allowing it to be translated, Kundera was explicitly making his readers aware that what they were reading was a translation, but he concomitantly revealed the foreignness of words in any given language. However, Kundera removed material from the text in his revision of the French translation and this omission occurred at the very moment when he suggested in the novel that the word *lítost* is untranslatable. In the Czech version, the second chapter, 'Co je lítost?' opened as follows in the Czech edition and in François Kérel's 1979 and Michael Henry Heim's 1980 translations:

> Lítost je české slovo nepřeložitelné do jiných jazyků. Označuje pocit nesmírný jak roztažená harmonika, pocit, který je syntézou mnoha jiných pocitů: smutku, soucitu, sebevýčitek i stesku. První slabika toho slova, pronesená s přízvukem a dlouze, zní jako nářek opuštěného psa.
>
> Za jistých okolností má však lítost význam naopak velmi zúžený, zvláštní, přesný a jemný jak ostří nože. Hledám pro něho rovněž marně obdobu v jazycích, i když si neumím představit, jak bez něho může vůbec někdo rozumět lidské duši. (Kundera 1981b: 130)

> Litost est un mot tchèque intraduisible en d'autres langues. Il désigne un sentiment infini comme un accordéon grand ouvert, un sentiment qui est la synthèse de beaucoup d'autres: la tristesse, la compassion, le remords et la nostalgie. La première syllabe, qui se prononce longue et accentuée, fait entendre la plainte d'un chien abandonné.
> Pourtant, dans certaines circonstances, le mot *lítost* a au contraire un sens très restreint, particulier, précis et effilé comme le tranchant d'un couteau. Pour ce sens-là aussi je cherche vainement un équivalent dans d'autres langues, bien que j'aie peine à imaginer qu'on puisse comprendre l'âme humaine sans lui. (Kundera, 1979a: 141–42)

> *Litost* is a Czech word with no exact translation into any other language. It designates a feeling as infinite as an open accordion, a feeling that is the synthesis of many others: grief, sympathy, remorse, and an indefinable longing. The first syllable, which is long and stressed, sounds like the wail of an abandoned dog.
> Under certain circumstances, however, it can have a very narrow meaning, a meaning as definite, precise, and sharp as a well-honed cutting edge. I have never found an equivalent in other languages for this sense of the word either, though I do not see how anyone can understand the human soul without it. (Kundera, 1988b: 121)

In his 1985 revision of the French translation, Kundera removed his own interpretation of what *lítost* was, that is, the synthesis of other feelings and the comparative analogies of a definition that was both wide-ranging and utterly precise (Crain, 1999: 40). Asher, in his fidelity to the 1985 French translation, translated the attenuated passage:

> *Litost* est un mot tchèque intraduisible en d'autres langues. Sa première syllabe, qui se prononce longue et accentuée, rappelle la plainte d'un chien abandonné. Pour le sens de ce mot je cherche vainement un équivalent dans d'autres langues, bien que j'aie peine à imaginer qu'on puisse comprendre l'âme humaine sans lui. (Kundera, 1987b: 199)

> *Litost* is an untranslatable Czech word. Its first syllable, which is long and stressed, sounds like the wail of an abandoned dog. As for the meaning of this word, I have looked in vain in other languages for an equivalent, though I find it difficult to imagine how anyone can understand the human soul without it. (Kundera, 1999b: 166)

The sound of the omitted sentences is implicit in the meaning of the passage, but the sound of the Czech words is, like *lítost*, untranslatable. Kundera's retention, then, of the Czech word did not wholly prevent some acculturation of it; it is a partial resistance that reminds the reader of a loss rather than recovering it. The sound of the very word *lítost* is also important, something which Kundera underlines in his description of it: 'První slabika toho slova, pronesená s přízvukem a dlouze, zní jako nářek opuštěného psa/The first syllable, which is long and stressed, sounds like the wail of an abandoned dog' (Kundera, 1981b: 130). For a foreign non-Czech speaking reader, the sound of the long '-í' may be impossible to reproduce, yet all of the English and French translations pre-empt this lack of awareness by reproducing the word without the long '-í'. In the translations, *lítost* lost the very sound which Kundera was at pains to underline.

In two of the omitted sentences, Kundera employs what we have seen to be a familiar poetic style, that of repetition and assonance. In the first omitted sentence 'pocit' is repeated alongside the litany of the genitive case noun endings [my use of bold]:

> Označuje **pocit** nesmírný jak roztažená harmonika, **pocit**, který je syntézou mnoha jiných **pocitů**: smutk**u**, soucit**u**, sebevýčitek i stesk**u**. (Kundera, 1981b: 130)

This assonance is mirrored in the second omitted sentence, which lulls the reader into the counterpointed sudden ending of the sentence, thus emphasising the effect of the 'sharp knife' (contrasted also with the unexpected coupling with 'jemný,' which also means 'gentle' or 'soft'):

> Za jistých okolností má však lítost význam naopak velmi zúžený, zvláštní, přesný a jemný jak ostří nože. (Kundera, 1981b: 130)

> Under certain circumstances, however, lítost has a contrary meaning that is as very narrow, particular, precise and fine as a sharp knife. (My translation.)

These examples of what Kundera contends to be the 'importance mélodique d'une répétition' are untranslatable in English and French, because neither language uses case agreements with nouns or adjectives. The use of the revised French translation as an originating text (i.e. one from which other translations are made), which cannot reproduce the sound of the text, can in some ways be regarded as a potential loss to the meaning in it. Kundera's removal of the material avoids this issue, but in itself also compromises his claim about the accuracy of the French translation in articulating the poetry of the text.

Kundera's retention of the Czech word *lítost* also did not prevent it from being acculturated, because the temptation to further explain what *lítost* was, through synonyms, led to some interpretation of the text by its translators. In several examples Heim added an explanation of what *lítost* was [my use of bold]:

> ... on se potápěl hlouběji a hlouběji do své lítosti. (Kundera, 1981b: 131)
> he would sink deeper and deeper into **his bitterness**, his *litost*. (Kundera, 1988b: 122)
> he himself would sink deeper and deeper into his *litost*. (Kundera, 1999b: 167)

> Ale pojednávala-li o lítosti ... (Kundera, 1981b: 132)
> But even if it now deals with **the emotion I call** *litost* ... (Kundera, 1988b: 123)
> But to deal with *litost*... (Kundera, 1999b: 168)

> Šel Kristýně vstříc nejistým krokem a lítost šla s ním. (Kundera, 1981b: 134)
> He wended his way insecurely over to her table, taking **his exasperation**, his *litost*, along with him. (Kundera, 1988b: 125)
> He made his way uncertainly to her, bringing his *litost* along with him. (Kundera, 1999b: 171)

> ... nepocítila to, co jsem nazýval slovem lítost... (Kundera, 1981b: 134)
> ... what she felt instead of the **delicate ineffable emotion** I have called *litost* ... (Kundera, 1988b: 125)
> ... she did not experience the feeling I have referred to as *litost* ... (Kundera, 1999b: 172)

Although the plurality of interpretations and the emphasis on the ineffability of *lítost* may have helped to convey what *lítost* was, in effect Heim prompted the reader through his own interpretation of what it meant in any one example within the text. This is exactly what Kundera was attempting to avoid through his analysis of *lítost*, that is, any reductive reading of the word whose meaning is partially located by Kundera in its plurality of meanings. Asher changed Heim's translation accordingly. In a further example, both Heim and Kérel added to the Czech [my use of bold]:

> Cítil se pokořen, odhalen ve své tělesné méněcenosti a pocítil lítost. (Kundera, 1981b: 130)

He felt humiliated, exposed for the weakling he was; he felt **the resentment, the special sorrow** which can only be called *litost*. (Kundera, 1988b: 121)

Il se sent diminué, mis à nu dans son infériorité physique, et il éprouve ce ressentiment **cette tristesse particulière** qu'on ne peut appeler autrement que *litost*. (Kundera, 1979a: 142)

In this case, considering the similarity between Heim's and Kérel's translations, it is likely that this addition was one made by Kundera. However, it was removed in the 1987 French translation and subsequently in Asher's English translation:

Il se sentit diminué, mis à nu dans son infériorité physique, et il éprouva la *litost*. (Kundera, 1987b: 199)

Feeling humbled, his physical inferiority laid bare, he felt *litost*. (Kundera, 1999b: 166)

Kundera and Asher's revisions of the French and then English translations attempted to reappropriate other theme words that populated the novel. Many of these theme words were translated by synonyms in the early translations, and their recovery may be explained partially by the fact that Kundera did not himself realise what his theme words were and how they were repeated in the text until he revised his translations. The student is described as 'lítost sama,' and Kundera thereby associates the concept of *lítost* with youth and the lyric age (lyricism is another key word), an age of immaturity defined in his previous novel *Life is Elsewhere* (1973). The narrator remarks that:

Lítost je tedy příznačná pro věk nezkušenosti. (Kundera, 1981b: 131)

This in turn relates to his next novel, *The Unbearable Lightness of Being* (1984), which, Kundera remarked, should have been called 'The Planet of Inexperience' (Kundera, 1988a: 132). Heim translated the concept, but not the literal (and also the Kunderian) meaning attached to the word:

Litost, in other words, is characteristic of immaturity. (Kundera, 1988b: 121)

Kérel translated 'věk nezkušenosti' as 'l'âge de l'inexpérience' and Asher, perhaps with the hindsight of the next novel and through following the French translations, translated this as: '*Litost*, therefore, is characteristic of the age of inexperience' (Kundera, 1999b: 168).

The connection through these words in his fiction and the problems with translating them is evidenced by Kundera's revisions. Both *lítost* and *soucit* – another Czech word that Kundera analyses – figure strongly in the *Laughable Loves* collection of stories (1970) as motivations for the characters' actions and as repeated words. Kundera, in his revision of the French and English translations, attempted to introduce some repetition of the idea through correspondingly repeated French and English terms. For instance, Kundera altered Kérel's translation of 'lítost' and 'líto' as 'pitié' to 'compassion' in 'Symposion', the emotion describing Flajšman's attitude towards women. This is problematic, however, as one reference to 'líto' is retained in the French as 'pitié' and throughout the novel most references to 'soucit' are translated into French also as 'la compassion'. *Lítost* is also translated in 'Que les vieux morts cèdent la place aux jeunes morts' as 'tristesse', 'le regret' and 'pitié' and in 'Edoaurd et Dieu' as 'triste' and 'tristesse' (1984b: 116, 117, 129; 1986d: 126, 128, 141). In English, these same examples are translated as 'sorrow', 'pity', 'pity', 'sad', 'sadness' and 'sadly'. Both *lítost* and *soucit* are translated in the English translation as 'compassion'. 'Soucit' is also translated as 'pity' (1999a: 167, 174, 208, 284). Kundera also alters both the French and the English translations in this story where both translators had translated 'lítost' as 'sa pitié et sa compassion' and 'her pity and sympathy', simply to 'compassion' (1984b: 191; 1986d: 265; 1975: 211; 1999a: 250).

In *The Unbearable Lightness of Being* (1984), Kundera halts the narrative for a digression on the etymology of this *soucit*/compassion – an emotion he has identified as key to Tomáš's and Tereza's relationship:

> All languages that derive from Latin form the word 'compassion' by combining the prefix meaning 'with' (*com-*) and the root meaning 'suffering' (Late Latin, *passio*). In other languages – Czech, Polish, German, and Swedish, for instance – this word is translated by a noun formed of an equivalent prefix combined with the word that means 'feeling' (Czech, *sou-cit*; Polish, *wspól-czucie*; German, *Mit-gefühl*; Swedish, *med-känsla*).
>
> In languages that derive from Latin, 'compassion' means: we cannot look coolly as others suffer; or, we sympathize with those who suffer. Another word with approximately the same meaning, 'pity' (French, *pitié*; Italian, *pietà*; etc.), connotes a certain condescension towards the sufferer. 'To take pity on a woman' means that we are better off than she, that we stoop to her level, lower ourselves.
>
> That is why the word 'compassion' generally inspires suspicion; it designates what is considered an inferior, second-rate sentiment that

has little to do with love. To love someone out of compassion means not really to love.

In languages that form the word 'compassion' not from the root 'suffering' but from the root 'feeling', the word is used in approximately the same way, but to contend that it designates a bad or inferior sentiment is difficult. The secret strength of its etymology floods the word with another light and gives it a broader meaning: to have compassion (co-feeling) means not only to be able to live with the other's misfortune but also to feel with him any emotion – joy, anxiety, happisness, pain. This kind of compassion (in the sense of *soucit*, *współczucie*, *Mitgefühl*, *medkänsla*) therefore signifies the maximal capacity of affective imagination, the art of emotional telepathy. In the hierarchy of sentiments, then, it is supreme. (Kundera, 1985c: 19–20)

The reason for this digression is his anticipation of a misunderstanding of what that emotion is, thanks to linguistic differences wrought by the variant etymological histories of the word and the ensuing variance in resonance and meaning. Kundera highlights the untranslatability of a word, even when there appears to be a straightforward equivalent in another language, but in a sense is offering a novelistic strategy to overcome this obstacle by including this short digression. This a form of textual resistance, allowing the trace of the Czech word and meaning to live on within the translation, but also calling the reader's attention to the fact that this is a translation. Kundera clearly is using the fact that his novel will be read almost wholly in translation as part of his writing strategy. It is also a comment on the word's elision – as in the case with *lítost* (a word, remember, which Kundera has partially defined as *soucit*) – in previous translations.

Jiří Kratochvil suggests that all of Kundera's work gravitates between *soucit* and *lítost*, words which partially overlap, but which can also be oppositional. This is clear in Kundera's earlier novel, *Life is Elsewhere* (1973), in which Jaromil the poet is, like the student in the *Lítost* section of *The Book of Laughter and Forgetting* (1979), *lítost* incarnate. He is contrasted with the 40-year-old in the sixth section of the novel, who represents a maturity that sets Jaromil in stark contrast, and his maturity is evinced in his compassion, a feeling alien to young and immature Jaromil. The 40-year-old's compassion is seen not only through his actions (his care for the redhead who has just been released from prison, sent there because her jealous and resentful boyfriend Jaromil informed on her and her brother), but also by the repetition of the words *soucit*/compassion and *sympatie*/sympathy. Kundera argues in the postscript to the novel that he had wanted to write a novel that was a critique of poetry and poetry itself, and it is this section of the book that is written in an intensely poetic way – highly ironic, given that the rest of the book surrounds the poet Jaromil but is not suffused by this intensity of language. One of the revisions that Kundera makes when he returns to the translations focuses on the translation of 'soucit' and 'sympatie' – two words that at times have been interchangeably translated. Kundera methodically changes the initial translations in French so that *soucit* is translated as 'compassion' rather than 'sympathie,' allowing it to complement, sometimes in the same sentence, his actual use of 'sympatie'. The 40-year-old's compassion is similar to that of Tomáš in *The Unbearable Lightness of Being* (1984), an emotion of co-feeling rather than of pity, which becomes clear to the reader only in translation after reading the digression in *The Unbearable Lightness of Being*. In this sense, Kundera's digression is a clear resistance which complements and enhances his actual revisions to the translations in retrospect. What his revisions do is to reinstate the repetition of the word as a method of underscoring the content of the text.

The preoccupation with misunderstanding – one which permeates all of Kundera's work – opens up into the ambiguities of cross-cultural communication in the 'Words Misunderstood' section of *The Unbearable Lightness of Being*. Kundera's point, however, is not that Sabina and Franz's misunderstandings are based solely on differences of cultural reference points but that the cultural misunderstandings are indicative of any communication. What things mean changes according to personal experience, captured in Sabina's consideration of the bowler hat as a 'semantic river':

> The bowler hat was a motif in the musical composition that was Sabina's life. It returned again and again, each time with a different meaning, and all the meanings flowed through the bowler hat like water through a riverbed. I might call it Heraclitus' ('You can't step twice into the same river') riverbed: the bowler hat was a bed through which each time Sabina saw another river flow, another semantic river: each time the same object would give rise to a new meaning, though all former meanings would resonate (like an echo, like a parade of echoes) together with the new one. Each new experience would resound, each time enriching the harmony. The reason why Tomas and Sabina were touched by the sight of the bowler hat in a Zurich hotel and made love almost in tears was that its black presence was not merely a reminder of their love games but also a memento of Sabina's father and of her grandfather, who lived in a century without airplanes or cars.

Now, perhaps, we are in a better position to understand the abyss separating Sabina and Franz: he listened eagerly to the story of her life and she was equally eager to hear the story of his, but although they had a clear understanding of the logical meaning of the words they exchanged, they failed to hear the semantic susurrus of the river flowing through them. (Kundera, 1985c: 88)

Kundera interpolates a 'Short Dictionary of Misunderstood Words' into the narrative of *The Unbearable Lightness of Being*, which is itself a narrative of their relationship. One of the words included in both is betrayal – the signature of Sabina as a character, for whom betrayal is a positive force, rather than a word loaded with its usual negative connotations. Kundera challenges the acceptance of given values implied in and by words, and suggests existential consequences. He defines 'Betrayal' in 'Sixty-Three Words' by quoting from this section: 'What is betrayal? Betrayal means breaking ranks. Betrayal means breaking ranks and going off into the unknown. Sabina knew of nothing more magnificent than going off into the unknown' (Kundera, 1985c: 91). This brings to mind Kundera's reflections in *The Book of Laughter and Forgetting* (1979) of his own decision to break out of the circle dance of his illusioned youth, and to betray the very idea of illusion and faith. If betrayal is a signature of Sabina's character, it is an equally strong signature of Kundera's, anchored in his betrayal of his past, the perceived betrayal of his country, and the perceived betrayal of his translators (Crain, 1999; Garfinkle, 1999: 54–64).

Franz, still imprisoned by illusion, believes in fidelity, thinking that Sabina will be impressed by his fidelity to his mother as a sign of his fidelity to her. He goes on the Grand March and to his death because of what he sees as his fidelity to Sabina, but his life with Sabina is based on his infidelity to his wife. Different personal inferences are connected to their disparate cultural backgrounds: Sabina's aversion to parades is based on the forced 'voluntary' participation in May Day parades, whilst Franz associates them with Paris and idealistic protest – again, Kundera returns to the circle-dance theme and his distrust of inclusive groups, of joining ranks. The highly ironic Grand March section is damning of the idea of altruistic involvement and of group understanding or purpose. One scene is telling in its comedy. The French participants protest against the American contingent enforcing English as the language of the protest and demand that all proceedings be in English *and* French. It is further complicated (and it is hard not to hear shades of self-irony here) 'since all the French had some English and kept interrupting the interpreter to correct him, disputing every word' (Kundera, 1985c: 260). One French doctor protests that the march has become an American propaganda circus and is joined by other French voices: 'The interpreter was frightened and did not dare translate what they said. So the twenty Americans on the podium looked on once more with smiles full of good will, many nodding agreement. One of them even lifted his fist in the air because he knew Europeans liked to raise their fists in times of collective euphoria' (Kundera, 1985c: 261). Sabina drops out of a march against the Soviet invasion of Czechoslovakia because it reminds her of the forced marches of her youth, of the ideology of marches, and tries to explain this to her French friends: 'But she knew she would never be able to make them understand' (Kundera, 1985c: 100).

While Franz has a nostalgia for and envy of Sabina's country because it evokes the words he associates with these marches, for Sabina the word that evokes her country is 'cemetary'. Franz refuses to understand the romance Czech cemeteries hold for Sabina, calling them 'bone and stone dumps', but she begins to understand why he has this view on going to Montparnasse with its heavy stones, rather than what she sees to be the gentler landscapes of those at home. She reflects: 'Perhaps if they had stayed together longer, Sabina and Franz would have begun to understand the words they used. Gradually, timorously, their vocabularies would have come together, like bashful lovers, and the music of one would have begun to intersect with the music of the other. But it was too late now' (Kundera, 1985c: 124). Kundera, however, scorns the idea of absolute identification through love in the 'Litost' section of *The Book of Laughter and Forgetting*, arguing that, when this illusion vanishes, 'love becomes a permanent source of the great torment we call *litost*', which he has defined (in one of his definitions of the word) a page earlier as 'a state of torment created by the sudden sight of one's own misery' (Kundera, 1999b: 167–68). The mark of maturity, of experience, renders this sight as 'ordinary and uninteresting'. The illusion of identification can be wrought through a shared vocabulary but, it seems, only on a precarious and strategic agreement that risks being unmasked when one of the agreers withdraws. While Franz searches for meaning (and finds death), Sabina realises the contingent – and betraying – nature of meaning.

The three sections, 'Litost', 'Soucit' and 'Words Misunderstood', highlight the problems of the translation of the novels by exposing the mechanics of translation and communication within the novels themselves. They represent, as much as possible, sites of resistance, a deliberate creation of distance between the signifiers and their meanings. It is within this distance, these word sites, that Kundera challenges his readers. Kundera, in both his writing and some of his revisions, faces an inevitable loss of meaning through the translations but attempts to highlight this loss and thereby make it a gain. This can be seen as his being complicit in tailoring the texts for a foreign audience, being too aware of who his audience is, but not surrendering to them and to their tastes. Kundera was translating as he wrote, but was writing in a Czech language suffused by the knowledge of its imminent foreignness. The awkwardness of this, the insistent return to meaning and making meaning, demands some reflection by the reader on the notion of meaning, loss and misunderstanding, as well as signalling an act of resistance rather than one of acculturation.

Circonflexes Renversés

'"Having to hurtle the obstacles of another language fascinates me", Kundera said in 1987, "it represents an activity I approach with almost sportive cheer. One day I suddenly realized it amused me much more to write in French than in Czech! Writing in French is linked to the discovery of an entire territory unknown to me"' (Elgrably, 1987: 19). Kundera began writing essays and articles in French in the early 1980s and wrote part of *Immortality* (1991) in French, and part in Czech. His first novel written entirely in French, *Slowness*, was published in 1995, and since then he has published a further two novels in French, *Identity* (1997) and *Ignorance* (first published in Spanish in 2000, in English in 2002, and in French in 2003). His decision to write in French has caused some consternation both in the Czech Republic and in France – his alleged 'betrayal' of the Czech language seen as yet another snub to his Czech past, and his adoption of French seen by some as an ingratiating and uninteresting endeavour. The quality of these later books has in turn been questioned, as perhaps it would not have been had he chosen to keep writing in Czech or about Czech subjects. For Kundera, however, writing in France and later writing in French seems to have been a form of release. In an interview in 1985, he argued that the loss of his Czech readership was an advantage rather than a disadvantage because he no longer had a public that had prior expectations of him, that in essence he was writing without trying to please or pander to these expectations. Kundera's strong awareness of his addressees, native and then primarily foreign, affected his writing, and the issue of translation and the dislocation of meaning became a central theme in his exile novels. Moving into French seems a natural progression – Kundera having lived in France for 20 years by the time his first novel in French was published in 1995. That same year, he told a Czech interviewer who expressed surprise that he had chosen the French language:

> People do not realize one thing. To start a completely new life at 45 in a different country takes all of a person's, listen carefully, all of his strength. In those twenty years I have barely read any Czech books. Do not be upset at me for this. No one can live fully in two countries, in two cultures. Even though I speak only Czech with my wife, I am surrounded by French books, I react to the French world, to French sentences, as you in the Czech Republic react to the Czech world and Czech sentences. One day I had to choose the language, in which I was to write. I was as surprised as you with it. Will I return again to the Czech language? I don't know. I wait to be surprised. (Sedláček, 1995: 14)

Kundera's refusal to re-embrace the Czech language and culture wholeheartedly after 1989 has been heavily criticised in the Czech Republic, but the sense that the decision was an easy one seems negated by his profound considerations of exile and the exile's art in *Testaments Betrayed* (1993). In these essays, Kundera repeatedly returns to the question of belonging and origins. Of emigration he writes:

> The adult years may be richer and more important for life and for creative activity both, but the subconscious, memory, language, all the understructure of creativity, are formed very early; for a doctor, that won't make problems, but for a novelist or composer, leaving the place to which his imagination, his obsessions, and thus his fundamental themes are bound could make for a kind of ripping apart. He must mobilize all his powers, all his artist's wiles, to turn the disadvantages of that situation to benefits.
>
> Emigration is hard from the purely personal standpoint as well: people generally think of the pain of nostalgia; but what is worse is the pain of estrangement: the process whereby what was intimate becomes foreign. We experience that estrangement not vis-à-vis the new country: there, the process is the inverse: what was foreign becomes, little by little, familiar and beloved. (Kundera, 1996b: 94–95)

He argues similarly in one of the only major interviews he has given in the Czech Republic since 1989 (in the Czech daily *Lidové noviny* in 1995):

> The relationship with a native land, in which one is no longer living, is always a question. If you are gone two, three, even five years, a return is easy. As if after a long holiday or a sickness. But twenty years, that is one quarter of a life, or half of your adult years. New ties, new friendships arise, the place of emigration becomes a new home, even a loved home. You realize that from the well-known emigrants of

former communist countries almost no one has returned to their original country? Not Czeslaw Milosz, not Leszek Kolakowski, not Kazimierz Brandys. Of the Russians, not Sinaievsky, not Zinovjev, not Brodsky [...] What makes a return difficult, are the psychological reasons. Imagine that you were used to meeting someone every day but were not allowed to seem him for twenty years. Your meeting after that long time would be fully of worries: Would you recognize each other at all? Is it possible to pick up a long-ago interrupted conversation? When a misunderstanding arises between two people who live in the same city, it is possible to explain it away that day. But when these two cannot meet, the misunderstanding remains unexplained ... (Sedláček, 1995: 14, my translation).

From his early career, Kundera had a fascination with the 'maturity' of French culture as opposed to the 'immaturity' of the young Czech culture. In his seminal 1967 speech to the Fourth Writers' Congress – a congress that in many ways heralded the arrival of the Prague Spring (his speech opened the Congress) – Kundera argued that, because of Austro-Hungarian domination and the repression of the Czech language, Czech culture was only in its youth and needed to be supported because the 'identity of a people or civilization is always reflected and concentrated in what has been created by the mind – in what is known as "culture"' (Kundera, 1984a: 97). He stressed the importance of learning from other cultures in order to develop Czech culture and identity as well as the importance of the translator in this process, a figure he described as a 'dominant figure' in this mediation of art and culture. The uninterrupted history and development of French language and culture represented a model for Kundera from which Czech culture should learn and with which it should interact.

The stroke of fate that led Kundera to France in 1975 (an invitation to lecture at the University of Rennes) resulted in an opportunity to develop such an interaction – the praxis being perhaps tougher than the theory, but the situation providing a real crucible for art. Kundera now knew the reality of working in a 'strange and scarcely accessible' language, cut off from that language. Yet, even in the late 1980s, Kundera maintained that he would not be able to write novels in French:

> I am quite capable of thinking in French; today I even prefer it to Czech. If, for instance, I am to write an essay and must choose I'll choose French. In public interviews, when given the choice between speaking in my mother tongue or my adopted one, I select the latter. And yet I do not know how to tell a single funny story in French.

When an anecdote should come out sounding laughable it is clumsy and awkward instead. So, as I was saying to develop a thought and to relate a story are two different skills. I know that I would like to write my next novel in French, but I doubt I'd be capable of it. (Elgrably, 1987: 19)

Less than two years later, however, Kundera was writing part of a novel in French, but in his correspondence with his translator (from the Czech language) Peter Kussi regarding the translation of some essays, he specifically asked Kussi to translate from French because he felt it was still inflected, the French of a Czech speaker. Kundera also said in a 1987 dialogue that he did not believe he would situate his next novel in France – which he did. This has caused considerable ire in his Czech and French critics, Angelo Rinaldi famously savaging Kundera in the *L'Express* review of *Immortality* (1991) for not staying with his exotic (in terms of French culture) native country (Rinaldi, 1990: 60–61). Kundera made the point, though, that he never attempted to strive for historical realism in the novel (if this is indeed even possible in fiction) and argued that instead he provides a 'geographical décor' for the novels. His move west began as early as *Life is Elsewhere* (1973), which (he argued) has a 'European' décor (with its considerations of Shelley in Dublin and Rimbaud in France), and with *The Book of Laughter and Forgetting* (1979), which was set two-thirds in Czechoslovakia and one-third in the 'Occident' (Elgrably, 1987: 10).

In many ways, the influence of France was evident when he was writing in Czech before 1970, not only with regard to the writers he quoted (his analyses of Balzac in *Umění románu*, the 1960 *The Art of the Novel*, for instance, or his use of the Cyrano story for his first short story, 'I, the Mournful God' (1963)), but also in his writing style. What distinguished Kundera from many of his contemporaries on the Czech scene was his neutral style. The flowering of Czech prose in the 1960s, with writers such as Hrabal and Škvorecký at the fore, was deeply based in a playful bastardisation of standard Czech. In the Czech language, there is a real division between spoken and standard written Czech, and writers such as Hrabal and Škvorecký challenged this division by making spoken Czech literary, playing with language, inventing neologisms, and mixing registers. In contrast, Kundera's prose always had an apparently neutral and cerebral style which again denotes a French influence, consolidated by the abstract and existential thought in the prose. This texture of his prose has undoubtedly aided his acceptance in France, though it has been regarded as particularly 'Czech'.

If French writing influenced Kundera's writing even before he became reliant on a French and a wider foreign readership, then to what extent has any 'Czech' style influenced his French prose? Once again, the issue of what is translatable comes to the fore. While Kundera's voice is, on the surface, neutral, he does have this signature author's style that became more apparent because of translation. His adamance in maintaining that this style is a translatable element of his language, and his subsequent fight against the 'synonymising reflex' of translators and editors, is to some extent justified in his translation of this style into his French-language novels. This style was, of course, developed within the Czech langauge and borne from the language. While Kundera created sites of resistance in his novels when writing in Czech for a primarily foreign readership, which opened up the question of untranslability because of cultural and referential differences, he also affected another way of writing translation by taking a style initiated in one language and translating it into another.

The first question that arises when an author adopts, and writes in, a second language, however, is usually 'what changes?' With Kundera, some changes are immediately obvious; his first two books written in French are much shorter than his previous novels, and they do not obviously conform to the precise polyphonic and variational structure of his previous three novels. Kundera mentions the importance of this structure in its mathematical precision in *The Art of the Novel* (1986) and critics have noted (in reference to the Czech-language novels) the importance of the number seven – most of his novels being divided into seven parts (apart from *Farewell Waltz* (1976)). Guy Scarpetta contends that Kundera's linguistic style has also changed in French, the brevity of the novels being paralleled by a new brevity in the sentences (Le Grand, 1999: xi).

Yet what is more striking in Kundera's case is what has not changed, given the upheaval of adopting a new language within which to write, and that is his linguistic project. The translatability of this style is here in evidence, and it is apparent from the opening pages of his first novel written in French, *La lenteur* (1995)/*Slowness* (1996). One of the central themes of the novel is indicated exactly by its title: the lack of slowness in the modern world and its existential consequences. For Kundera, the speed, and the exaltation of speed, in the modern world is essentially nihilistic and an agency of forgetting. This is embodied by the contrast between the young Vincent on his motorcycle (whose seduction of a young woman is a pretence and a parody of the sexual act) and Madame de T.'s seduction of the young chevalier (a langourous seductive act which he has the time to mull over on the slow carriage ride back to Paris). Kundera compares these two remembrances – the reflective remembering and the speedy forgetting – on a larger historical scale, with the rapidity of world events placed before us in such quick succession that none of them hold any meaning or resonance.

On the second page of *La lenteur* this thesis is presented in Kundera's characteristic 'Czech' writing style. As Kundera and Véra watch a motorcyclist speed past them, Kundera remarks:

> …il est dans un état d'extase; dans cet état, il ne sait rien de son âge, rien de sa femme, rien de ses enfants, rien de ses soucis et, partant, il n'a pas peur, car la source de la peur est dans l'avenir, et qui est libéré de l'avenir n'a rien à craindre.
>
> La vitesse est la forme d'extase don't la révolution technique a fait cadeau à l'homme … Tout change quand l'homme délègue la faculté de vitesse à une machine: dès lors, son propre corps se trouve hors du jeu et il s'adonne à une vitesse qui est incorporelle, immatérielle, vitesse pure, vitesse en elle-même, vitesse extase. (Kundera, 1995: 10)

> … he is in a state of ecstasy. In that state he is unaware of his age, his wife, his children, his worries, and so he has no fear, because the source of that fear is in the future, and a person freed of the future has nothing to fear.
>
> Speed is the form of ecstasy the technical revolution has bestowed on man … all changes when man delegates the faculty of speed to a machine: from then on, his own body is outside the process, and he gives over to a speed that is non-corporeal, non-material, pure speed, speed itself, ecstasy speed. (Kundera, 1996a: 3–4)

The two paragraphs not only state the thesis that sits at the core of the novel but do this through the intricate repetition of terms within the paragraphs. The first paragraph echoes the nihilism of the act of speed with the repetition of 'rien' (which in itself also echoes the 'point de lendemain' of the title of Denon's novella and echoes the playful negativity of Madame de T. – 'point de questions, point de résistance'). The second paragraph then opens with a thud, 'La vitesse …', which is the first appearance of the word and which precedes any mention of, and acts in stark contrast to, 'la lenteur' – the title of the novel. The word is repeated through the paragraph in conjunction with the 'extase' with which the paragraphs opened, and ends with 'extase', an ecstasy supported by the repetition itself, Kundera deliberately following the syntax of ecstasy to ironically support his point. This syntax is supported by other resonances in the paragraphs: 'dès lors, son propre corps se trouve hors'; 'incorporelle, immatérielle'.

There is a real self-reflexive irony in this, as Kundera goes on to recall a young American woman, 'sorte d'apparatchik de l'érotisme/a kind of apparatchik of eroticism', who informs him about her idea of sexual liberation: 'le mot qui revenait le plus souvent dans son discours était le mot "orgasme"; j'ai compté: quarante-trois fois/the word that came up most often in her talk was "orgasm"; I counted; forty-three times.' (Kundera, 1995: 11/1996a: 4) His preoccupation with the return of words is evident, alongside his thesis of the clinicisation of sex (and its connection with youth and the modern world), which strongly recalls Kundera's critique of the ideology of *jouissance* in *The Book of Laughter and Forgetting* (1980). The next paragraph opens plaintively in the light of the preceding paragraphs: 'Pourquoi le plaisir de la lenteur a-t-il disparu?/Why has the pleasure of slowness disappeared?', and this is how the key word is introduced (and, again in this paragraph, Kundera echoes Denon as he engages with 'désoeuvrement/having nothing to do'). In the second chapter, Kundera introduces and describes Denon's novel and emphasises the lack of names given in the novel; neither the chevalier, nor Madame de T., nor her real lover, the Marquis, are named, which is further reflected in the anonymity of the text, printed under an anagrammatic pseudonym.

Another Kunderian theme that arises in *La lenteur* (1995) is the false polarity of 'les enfants' and 'les adultes' because of what Kundera regards as the infantilisation of adulthood. His recollection of the famine children and 'les mouches qui se promènent sur leur visages' and the French politician Duberques's visit to Africa and his photo opportunity with 'une fillette noire mourante, au visage couverte de mouches/a little dying black girl whose face was covered in flies' (Kundera, 1995: 20/1996a: 16) is contrasted with the opulence of French society not only in its description but also in the grotesque recurrence of the image of 'la bouche'. Kundera contrasts these dying African children with 'les mouches' and the six-year-old children on French television who 's'embarrassent sur la bouche/kiss on the mouth' in fake imitation of adults and the sensual kissing in a washing powder and baby ad: 'une belle femme s'approche, entrouvre la bouche et en fait sortir une langue terriblement sensuelle qui se met à pénétrer la bouche terriblement bonasse du porteur de nourisson/a beautiful woman approaches, opens her mouth, and sticks out a terrifically sexy tongue, which then penetrates the terrifically good-natured mouth of the baby-carrying fellow' (Kundera, 1995: 21/1996a: 13–14).

This image of the mouth anchors the next chapter, in which the politician Duberques and his rival, Berck, put on a dinner for AIDS sufferers to show their solidarity. Duberques, aware of the photo opportunity, kisses one of them 'sur la bouche encore pleine de mousse au chocolat/on the mouth which was still full of chocolate mousse' (Kundera, 1995: 22–23/1996a: 15). Berck wants to emulate this but is scared to have contact with 'la bouche malade/the sick mouth' and 'la bouche séropositive/the seropositive mouth', and his hesitation is caught on camera. This brings Kundera on to a reflection of the 'danseurs', those people enamoured with fame rather than power. The words, the contrast of *mouche* and *bouche*, shuttle through the text interweaving in this part of the novel and not only are indicative of Kundera's use of his style in the French language but also herald something of an untranslatable element of it, as the French sounds cannot be translated. The two words permeate the text: the Czech entomologist at the chateau is famous for his rather melancholy discovery of the *musca pragensis*. The mouth features again in Vincent's desire for Julie – or rather her mouth – to say (in reference to another orifice) 'le trou de cul/the hole of her ass', causing the narrator Kundera to recollect Apollinaire and his designation of the nine portals of the body in a poem that exists in two versions, sent to two lovers – one in which the celebrated ninth portal is the vulva and the other in which it is the anus. The mouth is associated with love – not only with embraces but with the lack of them. Immaculata rejects her lover because of his 'mauvaise haleine/bad breath', but in fact it is the lover she covets, Berck, who has bad breath, which signifies to her that he has no lovers who might cure him of it.

These visceral images, of life and decay, embodied in the same word, are echoed in the insults traded between Immaculata and her lover when she protests against his repetition of vulgarities, 'baiser/to fuck' (again a slang term with its roots in the mouth and kissing) and 'poufiasse/slut'. The strength of words and their association is clinically examined by Kundera, in an echo of his comparison of the etymology of words in different languages, in a chapter devoted to the results of a poll. This is a poll from *Le Monde* in which *gauchistes* were asked what the most resonant words were for the left. Unsurprisingly, Kundera reports after lamenting the paucity of words agreed upon, the words 'révolte/revolt' and 'rouge/red' appeared in the top three, but with a surprising addition – 'la nudité/nudity' – as if this encapsulates a still subversive connotation (Kundera, 1995: 114/1996a: 96). Yet this is tested in the desultory way in which Vincent and Julie undress by the swimming pool and in Immaculata undressing in protest in front of her lover, as if to say 'Tu es un non-oeil, une non-oreille, une non-tête/You are a non-eye, a non-ear, a non-head' (Kundera, 1995: 108/1996a: 91).

This is a different language, French and not Czech, but Kundera has 'translated' his signature style, using the aesthetic of repetition but also with a local flavour, in his use of the specific resonance of the sound of the

French language and in his subtle referencing of the sounds of Vivant Denon's novella. On another level, Kundera does effect a translation in his revisiting of a classic 18th-century French text, Vivant Denon's *Point de Lendemain*, within the text of *La lenteur*. As with the three chambers, through which the lovers move in their partitioned night of love, Kundera constructs *La lenteur* as a complimentary chamber around Denon's novel. This can be seen as a move to embrace the French heritage or to construct a French pedigree for his own novel. The choice of *Point de lendemain*, however, is interesting not only for its themes, which Kundera explores, but in its style. In the 1980s, Kundera had already referenced the novel in 'Sixty-Three Words' under the definition 'Repetition'. In this entry, he writes about the importance of repetition, quoting Nabokov on the opening of Anna Karenina and Hemingway's use. He goes on to quote the opening of *Point de lendemain*:

> Nabokov points out that at the beginning of the Russian text of Anna Karenina the word 'house' occurs eight times in six sentences and that the repetition is a deliberate tactic on the author's part. Yet the word 'house' appears only once in the French translation of the passage, and no more than twice in the Czech. In that same book: where Tolstoy repeatedly writes skazal ('said'), the French translation uses 'remarked', 'retorted', 'responded', 'cried', 'stated', etc. Translators are crazy about synonyms. (I reject the very notion of synonym: each word has its own meaning and is semantically irreplaceable.) Pascal: 'When words are repeated in a text, they should be left in, they are the benchmark of a piece'. The playful elegance of repetition in the first paragraph of one of the loveliest pieces of French prose, the eighteenth-century novel *Point de lendemain* ('No tomorrow') by Vivant Denon: '*J'amais éperdument la Comtesse de …; j'avais vingt ans, et j'étais ingénu; elle me trompa, je me fâchai, elle me quitta. J'étais ingénu, je la regrettai; j'avais vingt ans, elle me pardonna: et comme j'avais vingt ans, que j'étais ingénu, toujours trompé, mais plus quitté, je me croyais l'amant le mieux aimé, partant le plus heureux des hommes …*'. (Kundera, 1988a: 146–47)

The repetition of 'j'avais vingt ans/I was twenty' serves to highlight the theme of youth in the novel and the novel as an exploration of a certain coming of age or induction into mature sexuality. Kundera's attraction to the novel, given his own exploration of youth and illusion that suffuses his work, is unsurprising, largely because of this stylistic identification. It is interesting to note also that this opening to the novel was rewritten: in fact it is the opening to the 1812 version of the novel that had been rewritten once and possibly twice by Denon.

Other French works are thematically and formally referenced in *La lenteur*. Especially interesting is Kundera's consideration of the form of Choderlos de Laclos's *Les liaisons dangereuses* (1782). He argues that the epistolary form is not simply a technique that could be replaced but that it enables a form that is in a way a theme of the novel. It functions as 'une coquille résonnante': 'tout le monde semble se trouver à l'intérieur d'une immense coquille sonore où chaque mot soufflé résonne, amplifié, en de multiples et interminables échos/everyone seems to love inside an enormous resonating seashell where every whispered word reverberates, swells, into multiple and unending echoes' (Kundera, 1995: 17–18/1996a: 10). This could be as eloquent a description of Kundera's own narrative project, his use of polyphonic structure and his use of language and repetition. He returns to the question of form and repetition in consideration of *Point de lendemain* and Madame de T.'s carefully structured night of seduction and the importance of that structure:

> Imprimer la forme à une durée, c'est l'exigence de la beauté mais aussi celle de la mémoire. Car ce qui est informe est insaisissable, immémorisable. Concevoir leur rencontre comme une forme fut tout particulièrement précieux pour eux vu que leur nuit devait rester sans lendemain et ne pourrait se répéter que dans le souvenir.
>
> Il y a un lien secret entre la lenteur et la mémoire, entre la vitesse et l'oubli ... le degré de la vitesse est directement proportionnel à l'intensité de l'oubli. (Kundera, 1995: 44-45)
>
> Imposing form on a period of time is what beauty demands, but so does memory. For what is formless cannot be grasped, or committed to memory. Conceiving their encounter as a form was especially precious for them, since their night was to have no tomorrow and could be repeated only through recollection.
>
> There is a secret bond between slowness and memory, between speed and forgetting ... the degree of speed is directly proportioned to the intensity of forgetting. (Kundera, 1996a: 34-35)

Not only is the Nietzschean question of eternal return grappled with in *The Unbearable Lightness of Being* (1984) as a theme, alongside that of forgetting, seen most notably in *The Book of Laughter and Forgetting* (1979), but these themes are investigated also through structure. Kundera argues that repetition enables memory, that a polyphonic or multi-chambered narrative can sustain memory, that the constant return of words can recalibrate thought. In many ways, *La lenteur* (1995), while anchoring in an adopted harbour of French classics, has sailed from the ports of a Kunderian intertextuality.

Setting *La lenteur* in the quintessential French château and embedding it in the embrace of a French novel would seem to be a strategy of relocation – Kundera creating a French territory in and through the novel not only through his use of French but also in his use of Frenchness. Kundera, however, appears as himself, 'Kundera', in the novel, with his wife, 'Véra', (his wife's actual name) arriving at the chateau *as a guest*. Detached from events and able to see the second story, the events at the chateau in the 18th century as told by Denon and retold by Kundera, the narrator is not explicitly foreign but neither does he present himself as an insider. Already, in the opening pages, Kundera quotes a Czech metaphor and refers also to the Czech King Václav and his adoption of disguise as an antidote to the search for fame of the 'dancers'. This reference to Václav is reused from his first story 'I, the Mournful God' (1963), with which Antonín's wish to disguise himself is connected. These Czech references appear alongside something of a satire of contemporary French culture, albeit mostly from the point of its embrace of the modern disease of forgetting – Kundera's adopted homeland seems to be the 18th century rather than France – but also from its lack of understanding of the outside.

In this first French-language novel, *La lenteur* (1995), Kundera chooses to introduce a Czech character (there were no Czechs in his previous Czech-language novel, *Immortality* (1991)): the entomologist 'Cechoripsky'. Rather than Beckett's *Innommable* we have here Kundera's *Inprononcable* ('ce monsieur avec le nom inprononcable/this gentleman with the unpronounceable name') – the lack of comprehension between the French and Czech experience is summed up in the problems with which the French secretary has in coming to grips with Čechořipský's name.

> Près de la porte il y a une petite table avec la liste des invités et une demoiselle qui paraît aussi délaissée que lui. Il se penche vers elle et lui dit son nom. Elle l'oblige à le prononcer encore deux fois. La troisième fois elle n'ose plus et, au hasard, cherche dans sa liste un nom qui ressemblerait au son qu'elle a entendu.
>
> Pleine d'amabilité paternelle, le savant tchèque se penche au-dessus de la liste et y trouve son nom: il y pose l'index: CECHORIPSKY.
> 'Ah, monsieur Sechoripi?, dit-elle.
> – Il faut le prononcer Tché-kho-rjips-qui.
> – Oh, ce n'est pas facile du tout!
> – D'ailleurs ce n'est pas correctement écrit non plus', dit le savant. Il prend le stylo qu'il voit sur la table et trace au-dessus du C et du R de petits signes qui ont l'air d'un accent circonflexe renversé. (Kundera, 1995: 58–59)

By the door is a small table with the list of the participants and a young woman who looks as left behind as he. He leans towards her and tells her his name. She has him pronounce it again, twice. Not daring to ask him a third time, she leafs vaguely through her list for a name that might resemble the sound she has heard.

Full of fatherly goodwill, the Czech scientist leans over the list and finds his name: he puts his finger on it: CECHORIPSKY.

'Ah, Monsieur Sechoripi?' says she.

'It's pronounced "Tché-kho-rjips-qui".'

'Oh, that's a tough one!'

'And incidentally, it's not written correctly, either,' says the scientist. He takes up the pen he sees on the table, and above the C and the R he draws the little marks that look like inverted circumflexes. (Kundera, 1996a: 47)

Čechořipský kindly pronounces the name for her and tells her the history of the Czech diacritics, the Hus reforms which changed 'tch' to 'č,' but the secretary confuses Hus with Luther despite being reminded about Hus. He tells her how important these diacritics are to Czechs, and a certain degree of self-irony on the part of Kundera is apparent, heralded in part by the orthographic joke – the colon and the bracket reinforcing the notion of the smile (again, the masked humour of Kundera's texts):

> Vous comprenez maintenant pourquoi nous autres Tchèques sommes si fiers de ces petits signes au-dessus des lettres. (Avec un sourire :) Nous sommes prêts à tout trahir. Mais pour ces signes, nous nous battons jusqu' à la dernière goutte de notre sang. (Kundera, 1995: 61)

> So now you see why we Czechs are so proud of those little marks over letters [with a smile:] We would willingly give up anything else. But we will fight for those marks to the last drop of our blood. (Kundera, 1996a: 49)

She still cannot pronounce the name, 'monsieur Chipiqui!', 'monsieur Chenipiqui,' and when she informs him she has added the 'circonflexes', he discovers that she has indeed added them but in the wrong places and as French circumflexes, 'Cêchôripsky' (Kundera, 1995: 61/1996a: 50). This appropriation of his name by its familiarisation through French orthographic marks succinctly satirises both the will to understand the foreign and also tight retention of this will within the borders of domestic understanding, that Čechořipský's name is accompanied by 'inverted circumflexes'. The secretary is left unable to pronounce his name, but it is an entomological explanation that comes the nearest to some form of explanation – Čechořipský explains that the Czech háčeks look like 'des papillons' (butterflies) and the secretary watches him walk away with 'un accent circonflexe renversé qui, en guise de papillon, voltige autour du savant et, à la fin, s'assoit sur sa crinière blanche/an inverted circumflex in the form of a butterfly fluttering around the scientist and finally settling on his white mane' (Kundera, 1995: 61–62/1996a: 50).

In *La lenteur*, Čechořipský has been invited to the entomology conference, not because his knowledge is new or challenging but as an act of solidarity with his past, Čechořipský having been forced to work as a labourer under the communists. Berck heralds his 'témoinage/testimony', adding that 'Nous sommes enclins à oublier trop vite/We are inclined to forget too quickly', and, wanting to add 'une touche de familiarité', remarks on what a magnificent city Budapest is. Timidly corrected by the Czech entomologist, Berck realises his mistake: '... je veux dire Prague, mais je veux dire aussi Cracovie, je veux dire Sofia, je veux dire Saint-Pétersbourg, je pense à toutes ces villes de l'Est qui viennent de sortir d'un énorme camp de concentration/... I mean Prague, but I also mean Cracow, I mean Sofia, I mean Saint Petersburg, I have in mind all those cities of the East that have just emerged from an enormous concentration camp' (Kundera, 1995: 77–78/1996a: 64). Čechořipský protests that they weren't concentration camps and that they were not the East, that Prague is 'une ville aussi occidentale que Paris/as Western a city as Paris.' Berck tells him not to be embarrassed about being from the East when the Czechs have such artists as Mickiewicz, and repeats this on camera, oblivious to Čechořipský's protestations that Mickiewicz is in fact Polish. The humour is placed not only in French benevolent but appropriative misunderstandings of this 'pédant exotique/exotic pedant' but also in Čechořipský's later admission that 'il ne connait pas encore bien la vie en Occident/he is not yet familiar with life in the West', when he sees Vincent and Julie apparently making love openly by the pool (Kundera, 1995: 122/1996a: 104). Čechořipský is himself a laughable melancholic character who had been thrust onto the stage of history through his own indecision rather than his bravery and who, now in the limelight because of the Western misunderstanding, forgets his lines, his scientific speech, in lieu of an emotional recap of the historical situation. This is symbolic in that he is not there in the first place because of interest in the speech and in that he is defined by his past. It also reverberates with the sense of the novel in that Čechořipský is a character that Kundera could have easily become and that there is a sense in his portrayal of him of Kundera's escape. Čechořipský's unsaid speech, his lost letters, are written in Kundera's new language.

L'identité (1997), Kundera's second novel written in French, uses a French literary character – this time Cyrano de Bergerac. As we have seen, Kundera had used this as a basis for the premise of his very first prose work, 'I the Mournful God' (1963), in which Adolf/Antonín sets himself up and compares himself to Cyrano with a twist in the premise that his proxy has to be mute because he has to pretend he does not speak Czech. In *Identity*, Jean-Marc sends letters signed CdB (Cyrano de Bergerac) to give his lover Chantal confidence again, because she feels that men no longer perceive her sexually. Chantal believes the letters are from a stranger and keeps them hidden from Jean-Marc. Her discovery of who it is leads to a fissure in their relationship, ending in reconciliation in a dream-like sequence at the end of the novel. The theme of mistaken or half-disclosed identity returns again and again in Kundera's novels, perhaps more inventively and with more brio than in this one. Again, however, he uses his signature style, with theme words recurring through the novel, notably his use of colours, which is a kind of language for both Chantal and Jean-Marc.

The signature colour of her sexuality for Jean-Marc is red and emanates from the way she blushes. This is how he knew she had fallen for him at the ski lodge, and it is something he wishes to resurrect to dispel her fear of no longer being looked at by men. Her returned blushes become a language that engages with the colour of sexuality in the book – the red necklace and red mantle, and the red curtains and carpet of the orgy house in London. The colours are repeated throughout the book and in a kind of melody in certain paragraphs:

> L'apercevant, elle rougit. Elle fut rouge non seulement sur ses joues, mais sur son cou, et encore plus bas, sur tout son décolleté, elle fut magnifiquement rouge aux yeux de tous, rouge à cause de lui et pour lui. Cette rougeur fut sa déclaration d'amour, cette rougeur décida de tout ... Le fait qu'ensuite, pendant des années, il ne l'ait plus vue rougir lui avait confirmé le caractère exceptionnel de cette rougeur d'alors qui, dans le lointain de leur passé, brillait comme un rubis d'ineffable prix. Puis, un jour, elle lui a dit que les hommes ne se retournaient plus sur elle. Les mots en eux-mêmes insignifiants sont devenus importants à cause de la rougeur qui les a accompagnés. Il n'a pas pu rester sourd au langage des couleurs qui était celui de leur amour et qui, lié à la phrase qu'elle avait prononcée, lui a semblé parler du chagrin de vieillir. (Kundera, 1997a: 120–21)

> Spotting him, she flushed. She was red not only on her cheeks, but on her neck, and lower still, down to the low neckline of her dress, she turned magnificently red for all to see, red because of him and for him.

That flush was her declaration of love, that flush decided everything … The fact that thereafter, for years, he never saw her flush again was to him proof of the extraordinary nature of that flush back then, which glowed in their faraway past like a priceless ruby. Then, one day, she told him that men no longer turned to look at her. The words, in themselves insignificant, became important because of the flush that accompanied them. He could not be deaf to the language of colours, which was part of their love and which, linked to her phrase, seemed to him to speak of the distress of ageing. (Kundera, 1998b: 87–88)

For Chantal, however, this colour does not capture the essence of their relationship, which she identifies with whiteness. For her, in her youth the 'Parfum expansif de rose' was a 'métaphore de l'aventure' (Kundera, 1997a: 54), but that this rose smell faded into whiteness, into a pleasing absence of adventure. The fragrance comes back after she wears the red nightgown against her body when she feels she 'never had skin so white' (Kundera, 1998b: 67–68):

> … elle en garde un intense souvenir de blancheur; les planches, les tables, les chaises, les nappes, tout était blanc, les réverbères étaient peints en blanc et les lampes irradiaient une lumière blanche contre le ciel estival, pas encore sombre, où la lune, elle aussi blanche, blanchissait tout alentour. Et, dans ce bain de blanc, elle éprouvait une insoutenable nostalgie de Jean-Marc [...] Elle savourait l'absence totale d'aventures. Aventure: façon d'embrasser le monde. Elle ne voulait plus embrasser le monde. Elle ne voulait plus le monde.
>
> Elle savourait le bonheur d'être sans aventures et sans désir d'aventures … la rose diluée dans la blancheur. (Kundera, 1997a: 55–56)

> … she retains an intense memory of whiteness : the deck, the tables, the chairs, the tablecloths, everything was white, the lampposts were painted white and the bulbs beamed a white light agínst the summer sky, not yet dark, where the moon, itself white too, was whitening everything around them. And in this bath of white she was struck by a feeling of unbearable nostalgia for Jean-Marc … She relished the utter absence of adventures. Adventure: a means of embracing the world. She no longer wanted to embrace the world. She no longer wanted the world. She relished the happiness of being adventureless and without desire for adventures … the rose diluted in the whiteness. (Kundera, 1998b: 37–39)

Two key words – 'insoutenable nostalgie' – appear in this passage above, and together they recall *The Unbearable Lightness of Being* (1984) and its repetition of the 'unbearable' nature of lightness, of living once, which suffuses *L'identité* (1997), as well as his next novel *L'ignorance* (2000/2003), which is centred on an investigation of nostalgia. Another theme, shared by *L'identité* and *The Unbearable Lightness of Being*, is that of the polarity of soul and body, examined here with similarities also to *Immortality* (1991). The weakness in *L'identité* is, to some extent, the lack of an inventive premise that often grounds Kundera's novels: here Kundera returns to the themes without really producing an inventive variation on them. The use of the Cyrano story has a staleness in this novel, which it does not have in his first story 'I, the Mournful God' (now expunged from his bibliography). There, Kundera worked on a ruse that was playful and which considered the issue of misplaced identity with considerable profundity. In *L'identité*, the premise is that Jean-Marc mistakes an older woman for his wife and muses on the shock of not being able to recognise those you love. He then hides his identity through the letters, at least for a while. This does not grab the reader in the way in which, for instance, Antonín's co-option of his Greek friend in 'I, the Mournful God', or Agnes's wish for an afterlife where everyone is faceless, or Tereza's dreams of the naked women at the poolside, do. In each of these instances, Kundera turns his back on the current obsession with individuality and how to express it, returning again and again to the notion of our inherent sameness, betrayed by our bodies and our human likeness. Antonín's rebellion against the 'Be yourself' culture, his need to be someone else, at least knowingly at an artificial level, encourages the reader to think. The most striking elements of *Identity*, then, do not revolve around these letters, but around Jean-Marc's relationship with the body.

Doctors and hospitals populate Kundera's fiction from the start – the three stories removed from *Laughable Loves* in 1970 all take place partially in hospitals, and two of the remaining stories revolve around Dr Havel. Nurses are the prey in 'The Golden Apple of Eternal Desire' (1965). Kostka in *The Joke* (1967) works in a hospital; Ludvík's revenge takes place in the accommodation there. *Farewell Waltz* (1976) takes place in the sanatorium, with Dr Škréta the master of proceedings. Tomáš in *The Unbearable Lightness of Being* (1984) is a surgeon. This is no simple preoccupation with the medical sector but points to a preoccupation with the materiality of the body and how it engages with or betrays the soul. The viscerality of the body and its non-identity is a fear that permeates the fiction – from the name of the young Dr. Flajšman (the Czech derivitave of the German 'Fleischmann'), to Tamina's sense of the 'unbearable insult' of becoming a corpse:

One moment you are a human being protected by modesty, by the sacrosanctity of nakedness and intimacy, and then the instant of death is enough to put your body suddenly at anyone's disposal – to undress it, to rip it open, to scrutinize its entrails, to hold one's nose against its stench, to shove it into the freezer or the into fire. (Kundera, 1999b: 236)

In *Identity* (1997), the turning point of Jean-Marc's professional life is when he walks out of medical school, having 'suffered a shock from which he never recovered: he was incapable of looking squarely at death; shortly thereafter he acknowledged that the truth was even worse: he was incapable of looking squarely at the body' (Kundera, 1998b: 62–63). The distaste for bodily functions – Jean-Marc's youthful obsession with the eyelid, the images of tongues and saliva – returns through the novel, epilogued by Leroy's comment 'Why are we living? To provide God with human flesh. Because the Bible, my dear lady, does not ask us to seek the meaning of life. It asks us to procreate' (Kundera, 1998b: 130). The body is a traitor to individual identity, when Jean-Marc can mistake another woman for Chantal, when Chantal cannot remember her name, naked at the end in the nightmare orgy. Ageing, with the decomposition of the body, is the treachery of life, the loss of control over one's dead body, the final insult (echoing Tamina in *The Book of Laughter and Forgetting* (1979)).

These elements in *Identity* strongly recall 'The Border' section of *The Book of Laughter and Forgetting* (1979), in which Jan, walking on the nudist beach, thinks of the Jews walking into the gas chambers: 'Maybe it meant that at that moment the Jews had also been on *the other side of the border* and thus that nakedness is the uniform worn by men and women on the other side. That nakedness is a shroud' (Kundera, 1999b: 310). In this section too, a friend is dying in hospital, bringing up reflections on the decay of the body, and here, too, the paradox of the gaze; in *Identity* (1997), Chantal worries that she is no longer the object of men's gazes, here Jan realises that his 'sovereign gaze' has lost any meaning in its repetition, 'that all repetition was mere imitation and all imitation was worthless' (Kundera, 1999b: 284). Jan thinks that the border between meaning and non-meaning in life is 'the maximum acceptable dose of repetitions' ('Where was the border?' Chantal asks, 'Where is the border?' (Kundera, 1998b: 152)), but the narrator disagrees with him: 'The border is not a product of repetition. Repetition is only one of the ways of making the border visible. The borderline is covered with dust, and repetition is like a hand whisking away dust' (Kundera, 1999b: 297–98). This is a coda to Kundera's aesthetics (his repetitions of words and of themes through all his novels) – how to find meaning when the referent is potentially lost – a condition not limited to a writer in exile but one suffered by modern humanity in an age of *Göttverlasserung*.

This profound alienation, the homelessness of the new world in which Jean-Marc finally understands his real identity as 'a marginal person, homeless, a bum' (Kundera, 1998b: 138) is the homeland of the novel as a genre – as Lukács and Kundera argue, when God left the world, Don Quixote left his house to go on his travels. The melancholy picaresque of Cervantes's *Quixote*, its satire and that of Denis Diderot's *Jacques Le Fataliste*, is the *point de départ* for Kundera's play *Jakub a jeho pán / Jacques and His Master*, written just after the Soviet invasion of Czechoslovakia in 1968 (though not published until 1981). Kundera chose to base the play on Diderot's work rather than work on, as had been suggested, a theatre adaptation of Dostoyevsky's *The Idiot*, expressly to turn his back on any notion of pan-Slavism and to face west: 'from the Renaissance, Western sensibility has been balanced by a complementary spirit: that of reason and of doubt, of play, and of the relativity of human things. Thus the West came to its full self. When the heavy Russian irrationality fell on my country, I felt an instinctive need to breathe deeply of that spirit' (Kundera, 1986a: 11). The 'variation-homage' to Diderot was a pledge of allegiance not merely to the West but to the novel tradition and to the aesthetic capabilities of the genre. For Kundera, the play is also an 'homage to variation form', the return of themes and the polyphonic unity of form created by this. These variations are made not only on Diderot's work, but also on Kundera's own:

> I wrote *Jacques and his Master* for my private pleasure and perhaps with the vague notion that one day it might be allowed to play in a Czech theatre under an assumed name. As a signature, I spread through the text (another game, another variation!) memories of my earlier work: the Jacques and his master evoke the couple from *The Golden Apple of Eternal Desire* (*Laughable Loves*): a few phrases are quotations from my farce (*Ptakovina*) put on in Prague in 1968 and 1969 and then banned; there's an allusion to *Life is Elsewhere* and another to *The Farewell Party*. Yes, they were memories; the whole play was a farewell to my life as a writer, 'farewell in the form of an entertainment'. (Kundera, 1986a: 18)

Jacques and His Master plays with the theme of rewriting, with the characters talking to the audience about the rewriting the author has done, rubbishing the idea that they could walk the whole way through France as they are made to do in the play: 'Death to people who rewrite what's already been rewritten!' the Master cries. 'I'd like to see them skewered and barbecued. They should have their balls and their ears cut off!' He is incredulous that the audience won't look up the original text, but is comforted by Jacques, who tells him that you can make the audience believe anything (Kundera, 1986a: 67). Certain elements are repetitions from his other work: the discussion of Simon Stylites (which appears again in *Farewell Waltz* (1976)); the ridicule of the young poet (*Life is Elsewhere* (1973)), and Jacques's suspicion that the one who wrote them is the 'worst bad poet ever, the king, the emperor of bad poets' (Kundera's early career); the 'forward is everywhere' line originally in *Ptákovina* (1968); addressing the audience like *I, the Mournful God* (1963) (and the equation with fiction writing and fictional god-like power) and so on (Kundera, 1986a: 82). Jacques wonders whether, like the Bible, 'the one who does all the writing up there hasn't repeated himself an incredible amount and whether he, too, doesn't take us for imbeciles …' and certainly the play is built up on repetitive phrases and devices (Kundera, 1986a: 78). This is especially apparent, for instance, in Act One, Scene Four, when Saint Ouen is trying to tell the Master that he has slept with the Master's love, Agathe, and several words are incessantly repeated: 'friend', 'friendship', 'most friendly' ('přítel', 'přátelství', 'nejpřátelštější'), the verb 'to know' ('znát') interspersed with 'bad' ('špatný') and 'blot' ('skvrna') – all indicating the theme of the revelation. Regarding the one blot on his character, the Master dismisses it (before finding out what the blot is) as 'Einmal ist keinmal', once is nothing, which not only acts as a refrain to all the repetition in the short scene, but reappears as a motif (of Beethoven's) in *The Unbearable Lightness of Being* (1984) and profoundly resonates as a reflection on the lack of eternal return in life (Kundera, 1992: 42). Unfortunately, this 'Einmal ist keinmal' is changed (by Kundera) in the French version to 'Une hirondelle ne fait pas le printemps' and is translated in this vein in both English translations (Michael Heim's and Simon Callow's): 'One swallow doesn't make a summer' (Kundera, 1981a: 51/Kundera, 1986a: 37).

In his postscript to the French translation of the play, Kundera reflects on the productions of *Jacques and His Master* (which had been produced under an assumed name in Czechoslovakia in 1975) in the Czech Republic and Slovakia since 1989, claiming that these productions were the ones that fully understood the melancholic humour of the piece: 'Étrange: inspiré directment par la littérature française, peut-être ai-je écrit, à mon insu, mon texte le plus profondément tchèque' (Kundera, 1981a: 138)/'Strange: directly inspired by French literature, perhaps I had unconsciously written my most profoundly Czech text' (my translation).

Kundera returns to Prague in his latest novel, *L'ignorance* (2000), but once again bases the novel on a Western text, this time not a French text, but one at the heart of Western culture, Homer's *The Odyssey*. Yet he overturns the premise of the epic, challenging the myth of the 'Great Return', the nostalgia for the past and for the homeland. The key term that the book is hinged on is that of nostalgia and to argue his point, Kundera makes an etymological connection between 'nostalgia' and 'ignorance', once again providing a digression on the way in which a word is made to mean different things in different languages and how this affects the cultural usage and sentiment:

> Le retour en grec, se dit *nostos*. *Algos* signifie souffrance ... Pour cette notion fondamentale, la majorité des Européens peuvent utiliser un mot d'origine grecque *nostalgia, nostalgie*) ... Dans chaque langue, ces mots possèdent une nuance semantique différente. Souvent, ils signifient seulement la tristesse cause par l'impossibilité du retour au pays. Mal du pays. Mal du chez-soi. Ce qui, en anglais, se dit: *homesickness*. Ou en allemande: *Heimweh*. En hollandais: *heimwee*. Mais c'est une reduction spatiale de cette grande notion. L'une des plus anciennes language européennes, l'islandais, distingue bien deux termes: *söknuður*: nostalgie dans son sens general; et *heimfra*: mal du pays. Les Tchèques, à côté du mot *nostalgie* pris du grec, ont pour cette notion leur propre substantive, *stesk*, et leur propre verbe; la phrase d'amour tchèque la plus émouvante: *stýská se mi po tobě*: j'ai la nostalgie pour toi; je ne peux supporter la douleur de ton absence. En espagnol, *añoranza* vient du verbe *añorar* (avoir de la nostalgie) qui vient du catalan *enyorar*, derive, lui, du mot latin *ignorare* (ignorer). Sous cet éclairage, étymologique, la nostalgie apparaît comme la souffrance de l'ignorance. Tu est loin, et je ne sais pas ce que tu deviens. Mon pays est loin, et je ne sais pas ce qui s'y passé. Certaines langues ont quelques difficultés avec la nostalgie: les Français ne peuvent l'exprimer que par le substantive d'origine greque et n'ont pas de verbe; ils peuvent dire: *je m'ennuie de toi* mais le mot *s'ennuyer* est faible, froid, en tout cas trop léger pour un sentiment si grave. (Kundera, 2003: 11–12)

> The Greek word for 'return' is *nostos*. *Algos* means 'suffering'...To express that fundamental notion most Europeans can utilize a word derived from the Greek (*nostalgia, nostalgie*) ... In each language these words have a different semantic nuance. Often they mean only the sadness caused by the impossibility of returning to one's country: a longing for the country, for home. What in English is called 'homesickness'. Or in German: *Heimweh*. In Dutch: *heimwee*. But this reduces that great notion

to just its spatial element. One of the oldest European languages, Icelandic (like English) makes a distinction between the two terms: *söknuður*: nostalgia in its general sense; and *heimprá*: longing for the homeland. Czechs have the Greek-derived *nostalgie* as well as their own noun, *stesk*, and their own verb; the most moving Czech expression of love: *styska se mi po tobe* ('I yearn for you', 'I'm nostalgic for you'; 'I cannot bear the pain of your absence'). In Spanish *añoranza* comes from the verb *añorar* (to feel nostalgia), which comes from the Catalan *enyorar*, itself derived from the Latin word *ignorare* (to be unaware of, not know, not experience; to lack or miss). In that etymological light nostalgia seems something like the pain of ignorance, of not knowing. You are far away, and I don't know what has become of you. My country is far away, and I don't know what is happening there. Certain languages have a problem with nostalgia: the French can only express it by the noun from the Greek root, and have no verb for it; they can say *Je m'ennuie de toi* (I miss you), but the word *s'ennuyer* is weak, cold – anyhow too light for so grave a feeling. (Kundera, 2002: 5–7)

As with his essayistic digression on 'soucit' in *The Unbearable Lightness of Being* (1984), Kundera defines his terms by questioning the historical and cultural differences in their meaning. This sets the tone for *L'ignorance* (2000), which centres on the notion that nostalgia is entwined with ignorance. *The Odyssey*, Kundera writes, is the 'epic of nostalgia', but he questions its viability, its existential truthfulness as a founding text of what he regards to be the myth of the Great Return. He cannot believe that going home to Penelope is an inevitable and preferable choice over staying with Calypso, or that for his protagonists – two Czech emigrants Irena and Josef – going home to Prague after 1989 is a preferable or inevitable choice over staying in their adopted homelands. If the Grand March was the illusion of progress that Kundera tried to shatter, then the Great Return is the illusion of the past regained that needs to be shattered. The parallels with Kundera's own experience are obvious, with his decision not to return to the Czech Republic, but it is more than that. This is an unwanted observation, that infidelity to the homeland, the past as another country, may be a positive and even necessary act, because in the modern world, the world of forgetting, Ithaca will always be an illusory paradise.

There are striking paragraphs in this novel – written in French, first published in Spanish and unpublished in Czech – in which one of the protagonists, Josef, reflects on his native language and on his native past. Sitting in a restaurant on his first trip back to Prague, he listens to the waiters speak:

> C'était la musique d'une langue inconnue. Que s'était-il passé avec le tchèque pendant ces deux pauvres décennies? Était-ce l'accent qui avait changé? Apparemment. Jadis fermement pose sur la première syllable, il s'était affaibli; l'intonation en était comme désossée. La mélodie paraissait plus monotone qu'autrefois, traînante. Et le timbre! Il était devenu nasal, ce qui donnait à la parole quelque chose de désagréablement blasé. Probablement, au cours des siècles, la musique de toutes les langues se transforme-t-elle imperceptiblement, mais celui qui revient après une longue absence en est déconcerté: penché au-dessus de son assiette, Josef écoutait une langue inconnue dont il comprenait chaque mot. (Kundera, 2003: 55–56)

> It was the music of some unknown language. What had happened to Czech during those two sorry decades? Was it the stresses that had changed? Apparently. Hitherto set firmly on the first syllable, they had grown weaker; the intonation seemed boneless. The melody sounded more monotone than before – drawling. And the timbre! It had turned nasal, which gave the speech an unpleasantly blasé quality. Over the centuries the music of any language probably does change imperceptibly, but to a person returning after an absence it can be disconcerting: bent over his plate, Josef was listening to an unknown language whose every word he understood. (Kundera, 2002: 54–55)

That Kundera would focus on the changing melody of the language is perhaps predictable given his writerly preoccupations, and this ties in with the theme of nostalgia – the retention of the idyll of one's native language as compared to the reality when one returns to it. It will perpetually be 'une langue inconnue/an unknown language' because of the illusions of how it sounds, of its melodies reconstituted in an authorial signature style but, in doing so, removed from the moorings of its quotidian use. When Josef goes to see his friend N. and realises that they are not going to have the conversation he expected – one weighted down with the tumult of history and changes – he suddenly rediscovers his language ('Il parlait comme s'il volait …/Talking was like flying …') and feels suddenly at home (Kundera, 2003: 147/2002: 158). While speaking Danish with his wife had been straightforward, their own 'sabir intime/private jargon', he had found that speaking it with others had emphasised his own outsiderness: 'avec les autres, il était toujours conscient de choisir des mots, de construire une phrase, de surveiller son accent. Il lui semblait qu'en parlant les Danois couraient lestement, tandis que lui trottait derrière, chargé d'un poids de vingt kilos. Maintenant, les mots sortaient tout seuls de sa bouche, sans qu'il ait besoin de les chercher, de les contrôler' (Kundera, 2003:

147)/'with other people he was always conscious of choosing his words, constructing a sentence, watching his accent. It seemed to him that when Danes talked they were running nimbly, while he was trudging along behind, lugging a twenty-kilo load. Now, though, the words leaped from his mouth on their own, without having to hunt for them, monitor them' (Kundera, 2002: 157). Yet on the final page of the novel, as Josef leaves Prague, he once again feels alienated from his native language; again it seems 'monotone et désagréablement blasée, une langue inconnue' (Kundera, 2003: 181)/'flat and unpleasantly blasé, an unknown language' (Kundera, 2002: 195). The monitoring of language, a pastime for Kundera, is considered here in his second language. French is also Irena's second language and the one that has so far defined her relationship with Gustaf, the Swede. French, 'auquel elle se sentait de plus en plus attachée/to which she felt ever more attached', gives her some dominance in their relationship because she speaks it more fluently: 'dans leurs conversations, elle le dominait et l'entraînait dans son monde à elle' (Kundera, 2003: 92–93)/'in their conversation she ruled, and she drew him into her own world' (Kundera, 2002: 96). What begins to draw them apart in Prague (apart from Gustaf's enthusiasm for the city) is his reversion to English, which Kundera argues has become the *lingua franca* of Prague which 'impatiente de se faire applaudir sur l'estrade du monde, elle s'exhiba aux passants parée d'inscriptions anglaises: skateboarding, snowboarding, streetwear, publishing house, National Gallery, cars for hire, pomonamarkets et ainsi de suite. Dans les bureaux de sa firme, le personnel, les partenaires commerciaux, les clients riches, tous s'addressaient à Gustaf en anglais, si bien que le tchèque n'était qu'un murmure impersonnel, un décor sonore d'où seules phonemes anglo-saxons se détachaient en tant que les paroles humaines' (Kundera, 2003: 91–92)/'eager for applause on the world's proscenium, displayed to the visitors its new attire of English-language signs and labels. In Gustaf's company offices, the staff, the trading associates and the rich customers all addressed him in English, so Czech was no more than an impersonal murmur, a background of sound against which only Anglo-American phonemes stood forth as human words' (Kundera, 2002: 95). The demotion of the Czech language in its capital city makes the language inhuman and irrelevant and this is a double alienation for Irena, who can no longer speak French with Gustav, who has become 'une étrangère qui se taisait (Kundera, 2003: 93)/a silent foreigner' in her own relationship (Kundera, 2002: 97). Prague has become 'la Prague de Gustaf. Elle se dit qu'il n'existe pas pour elle de lieu plus étranger que cette Prague-là. Gustaftown. Gustafville. Gustavstadt. Gustafgrad (Kundera, 2003: 128)/Gustaf's Prague. She reflects that there is no place more alien to her than Prague. Gustaftown. Gustafville. Gustavstadt. Gustafgrad' (Kundera, 2002: 136). Kundera spits out the suffixes of colonisation and dominance. The truth of Irena and Gustaf's relationship, however, is finally revealed and parallels that of some of Kundera's other Czech/'West' European relationships (Jan and Edwige, Sabina and Franz, Tamina and Hugo – though not Josef and his Danish wife): 'elle le voit, les traits estompés derrière la vitre mate d'une langue qu'elle connaît mal, et elle se dit, presque réjouie, que c'est bien ainsi car la vérité s'est enfin révélée: elle n'éprouve aucun besoin de le comprendre ni de se faire comprendre de lui (Kundera, 2003: 128)/she sees him, his features blurred through the clouded windowpane of a language she barely knows, and she thinks, almost joyfully, that it's fine this way because the truth is finally revealed: she feels no need to understand him or to have him understand her' (Kundera, 2002: 136–37).

The complexity of adopting a second language and culture is tied up with a key notion in *L'ignorance* (2000): death and the brevity of life, 'qui nous procure trop peu de temps pour que nous nous attachions à un autre pays, à d'autres pays, à d'autres langues (Kundera, 2003: 114)/which allows us too little time to become attached to some other country, to other countries, to other languages' (Kundera, 2002: 121). Irena and Josef have both lost their spouses, but the key figure is Milada, the tenous connection between them. Milada lost her ear through frostbite when attempting suicide as a result of Josef and his youthful insistence on loneliness and, as a result, gave up her sexual life, embarrassed by this perceived defect. She has a moment of happiness just before the suicide attempt, 'un sentiment bref, tout bref, de bonheur, qui lui fait oublier le but de sa marche. Sentiment bref, tout bref, trop bref (Kundera, 2003: 102)/a brief, very brief, sensation of happiness, which makes her forget the purpose of her walk. A brief, very brief, too brief sensation' (Kundera, 2002: 107). Her life thereafter is caught up in visceral images of disembodiment and decay: her inability to eat meat because she sees her own flesh on the plate, the final image of her looking at her fading beauty and realising she is looking at it in the reflection of a butcher's shop. This sense of disembodiment follows Josef also, again a character who turned his back on medicine to treat animals, with the giant hands on the poster reaching from earth to sky outside his hotel and the fir tree back in his home in Denmark, like an arm stuck in the ground. The weight of flesh, of death, is contrasted with the lightness of life, Kundera once again returning to the theme of no return. Irena too confronts this visceral weight – meeting her friends, she feels as if they 'l'amputaient de son avant-bras et fixaient la main directement au coude; comme si elles l'amputaient des mollets et joignaient ses pieds aux genoux (Kundera, 2003: 45)/were amputating her forearm and attaching the hand directly to the elbow; as if they were amputating her calves and joining her feet to her knees' (Kundera, 2002: 43). For both Irena and Josef, exile has presented them with freedom, with lightness, from the tethers of the past. Irena acknowledges that the forces that took her freedom made her free; Josef does not look back at the border. This lightness is present in an image that suffuses Kundera's exile fiction: Irena and Josef both reflect on their lives from the height of buildings. Irena lives on the top floor in Paris and under the eaves of Gustaf's office in Prague; Josef stays on the top floor of the hotel in his home town. In *The Book of Laughter and Forgetting* (1979), Kundera announces his presence in the novel from his new home in France, 'the top floor of the tallest high-rise tower' (Kundera, 1999b: 176) where he has moved from the top floor in a building in Prague where 'down below unfolded the history of reknowned prisoners' (Kundera, 1999b: 96). The *terra perditae* of the 'shredded identity' haunts these habitats, neither here nor there, habitats of the lightness of exile and the weight of death (Kundera, 1996b: 14).

In *L'ignorance* (2000), Josef has to face 'masochistic memory' when he rediscovers his diary in Prague, written when he was a young man. Again, the image of the lost letters comes through as well as the sense of the difference within writing. Josef cannot see or comprehend the same person behind the same handwriting:

> Il contemple longuement les deux écritures: l'ancienne est un peu maladroite, mais les letters ont la meme forme que celles d'aujourd'hui. Cette resemblance lui est désagréable, elle l'agace, elle le choque. Comment deux êtres si étrangers, si opposes, peuvent-ils avoir la meme écriture? En quoi consiste cette essence commune qui fait une seule personne de lui et de ce morveaux? (Kundera, 2003: 81)

> He contemplates the two handwritings for a long time: the one from long ago is a little clumsy, but the letters are the same shape as today's. The resemblance is upsetting, it irritates him, it shocks him. How can two such alien, such opposite beings have the same handwriting? What common essence is it that makes a single person of him and this little snot? (Kundera, 2002: 83)

Josef contemplates himself back in that lyric age when his attitude towards his girlfriend as presented in the diary is encapsulated in a dual desire to feel compassion towards her and to make her suffer, the 'sentimentality mixed with sadism' of *lítost*. His reaction to re-encountering himself is to destroy the evidence that his young self existed (again the parallels to Kundera are striking):

> Il se met à déchirer les pages du journal en petits morceaux. Geste sans doute exagéré, inutile; mais il éprouve le besoin de laisser libre cours à son aversion; le besoin d'anéantir le morveux afin qu'un jour (ne serait-ce que dans un mauvais rêve) il ne soit pas confondu avec lui, hué à sa place, tenu pour responsible de ses paroles et de ses actes! (Kundera, 2003: 84)

> Josef sets about ripping the diary pages into tiny scraps. The gesture is probably excessive and useless; but he feels the need to give free rein to his aversion; the need to annihilate the little snot so that never (even if only in a bad dream) would he be mistaken for him, be vilified in his stead, be held responsible for his words and his acts! (Kundera, 2002: 87)

As Gombrowicz wrote in his diary, sailing back to Europe after many years' exile in Argentina, Argentina was not a country but a past, and so it is that the geographical distance, the borders and the exile, measure the break from the idyll of youth. Except that the youth and the country can never disappear, however much Kundera wishes that Athena could not clear the mist and let Ithaca reappear before Odysseus. To revisit youth is not quite the same as never having left it – the latter a state of illusion which Kundera warns his readers that modern society fosters; a Penelope consistently unravelling Laertes's shroud. There are parallels with Kundera's own instinct to destroy the testaments of his youth, but the fact that he revisits that instinct here as elsewhere in his *oeuvre* points to a constant *analysis* of this instinct: remembering, in a way, the motivation for forgetting. The alienation of the exile returned home, more familiar with the new country than the old, articulates in a sense the alienation inherent in life and the inescapable realisation that one can never go back. Nor, he argues, would one want to, because 'La vie que nous avons laissée derrière nous a la mauvaise habitude de sortir de l'ombre, de se plaindre de nous, de nous faire des process (Kundera, 2003: 87)/The life we've left behind us has a bad habit of stepping out of the shadows, of bringing complaints against us, of taking us to court' (Kundera, 2002: 90). The problem with returning home is returning to surveillance from a vantage point of lost history: 'le passé est là, l'attendait, l'observait ... à quoi peut penser un homme venu voir le pays de son passé, sinon à son passé? (Kundera, 2003: 87)/... the past was there, waiting for him, watching him ... when a man has come to look at the land of his past, what can he think about if not his past?' (Kundera, 2002: 90).

In *L'ignorance*, Irena dreams of her native land by day and has nightmares about it by night, of the women with their mugs of beer haranguing her, uninterested in her. Her native land is at once a 'paradise' and a 'hell'. The lack of interest in her experience is mirrored in the loss of her exoticism in her new native land. Irena loses her best French friend, Sylvie, who had been so keen for her to return home: 'je n'était plus une émigrée. Je n'était plus intéressante (Kundera, 2003: 158)/I wasn't an émigré any more. I wasn't interesting any more' (Kundera, 2002: 170).

Kundera, like Antonín/Adolf in his first story, becomes Cyrano, narrating an elegy, a 'Great Farewell' (another one, *pace Farewell Waltz* (1976) and *Jacques and His Master* (1981)) in a borrowed voice, but it is as if he could write his return only in another language. Kundera argued in *Testaments Betrayed* (1993) that Gombrowicz's reluctance to return to Poland was inexplicable, *incommunicable* because 'too intimate', 'too wounding for others': 'Some things we can only leave unsaid,' he wrote (Kundera, 1996b: 95). Unsaid, at least, in the Czech language, which across the borders still 'makes a noise as trivial as the twittering of birds' (Kundera, 1999b: 297). Czech, for Josef and for Kundera, is the 'gros mots de son Ithaque' (Kundera, 2003: 168)/language of Ithaca' (Kundera, 2002: 178).

Yet it is not forgotten: the incommunicability of Czech becomes, in the writing of the novels and in the novels, indicative of the incommunicability of meaning between two people unless an agreement, a 'private jargon', has been constructed. The donkey of misunderstanding, which Kundera rode out on into exile, is his mount upon return because it is the underpinning of his language and his novels. From his first piece of fiction, misunderstanding and estranged language motor the text and the humour of the writing. This is intensified by exile, which consistently highlights the border between meaning and misunderstanding that exists in any writing or communication. In *The Book of Laughter and Forgetting* (1979), Jan finds some melancholy reconciliation in the humorous recognition of miscommunication with his foreign lover:

> They never understood each other, Edwige and he, yet they always agreed. Each interpreted the other's words in his or her own way, and there was wonderful harmony between them. Wonderful solidarity based on a lack of understanding. He was well aware of it and almost took pleasure in it. (Kundera, 1999b: 310–11)

It is the *modus operandi* of human life, and he finds it at the border.

Chapter 5
Reception

Kundera has no doubt about the relation between an author and his critics: 'By insisting on decoding him', he writes, 'the Kafkologists killed Kafka' (Kundera, 1988a: 132). The scene of literary interpretation is set as a battleground whose prize is the possession not so much of the text but of its meaning. For Kundera the danger is this: while the novels are carefully constructed to open up meaning, to cultivate a polysemy of meaning where different characters and different situations provide a multitude of views and possibilities, the job of the literary critic is antithetical to this aim. Kundera, however, is also an interpreter of his own texts, writing at length explicitly or implicitly about them in critical essays, prefaces and interviews. The tension that has arisen is that his interpreters under attack – critics, reviewers, journalists – have questioned to what extent Kundera has fallen foul of his own accusations, providing readers and influencing literary critics with his own 'correct' interpretation of his texts.

The ambivalence in this reading however, is in whether Kundera is asserting his own authority over his texts and demanding that his interpretation of his own work is the only legitimate interpretation, or whether he is critiquing the dangers of interpretation as a process. Opinion tends to be polarised between the two, but most of the criticism, journalistic or otherwise, is not particularly self-reflective – there is no questioning of the critics' own motives or awareness of the cultural context of their own criticism. This is understandable to some extent, as otherwise there would be no end to the analysis, but it creates the problem of a criticism focused on deciphering Kundera – often at the expense of his work – in the light of contemporary cultural needs rather than in terms of trying to understand the work. That Kundera consistently attacks literary critics and the mediators of his work, however, has tended to exacerbate the polemics; the more he claims to be misunderstood, the more misunderstanding surrounds his character and his work.

If one examines the interpretation of his work in two different cultures, the role that cultural agendas play in the reception of Kundera's work is clear. This division mirrors a contentious division in the world of Kundera criticism in order to examine the contention: that is, literary critics and journalists have claimed that Kundera is treated and interpreted differently in the Czech Republic and abroad, especially in English-language criticism. The accepted opinion is that while in the Czech Republic he is interpreted with thoroughness and knowledge and with a sceptism towards his self-presentation and self-interpretation – in other words, that he is interpreted 'correctly' – in the West he is interpreted superficially, benevolently and gullibly – critics swallowing whole Kundera's interpretation of his life and work because they are ignorant of the 'true' story. Translation has played a part in this, both in Kundera's translation of himself and lack of translation of some of his work abroad, and also in the lack of translation of Czech criticism in the West, which, as Caleb Crain argues, might change the wholesale positive image of him in the West.

To some extent, Kundera makes a similar claim, though with a slightly different interpretation: certainly in the past, Czech critics, he proposes, have had a more profound engagement with his work, interpreting it with a depth of understanding not only of the cultural context but also of the literary one. In contrast, critics in the West, he argues, have succumbed to 'journalistic thinking', making 'fast' and reductive interpretations of work which serve to uphold preconceived notions and, in doing so, uphold cultural and ideological stereotypes. Kundera cites the experience of *The Joke* (1967) being reduced to its political content, received in 'the most clichéd way imaginable, the most schematic way' (Elgrably, 1987: 14), judged only as 'a denunciation of Stalin' (Finkielkraut, 1982: 27), and valued primarily as part of 'a literature of opposition to the Soviet regime' (Elgrably, 1987: 14). The move in the West towards journalistic rather than literary interpretation is for Kundera an indication of the future annihilation of artistic culture: 'literary criticism is almost non-existent these days, and novels are at the mercy of the journalists and the minor ideologues of the day – at the mercy of those workers of reduction' (Finkielkraut, 1982: 27).

The interpretation of Kundera's return – or rather non-return – to the Czech cultural and literary context post-1989 has occurred not only in lengthy literary exegesis on his work, but also in the highbrow, literary and tabloid media. The interest in Kundera as a personality has been ignited by his public and print invisibility, and this interest in his personality and personal motives has in turn tended to overshadow and affect the literary reception of his work. Kundera argues that his retreat into privacy is necessary in order to prevent exactly this, and, in one of his only interviews in the Czech Republic, he defended this position. When challenged by the interviewer as to how he can justify his retreat when the writer is a public personality, he replied 'His books are a public thing. But he isn't' (Sedláček, 1995: 14). When asked if this contradicted his very public involvement in Czech cultural life in the 1960s, Kundera simply argued that he does not recognise the man he once was, suggesting that his embrace of the identity of novelist has made such public involvement redundant because it is his novels, not he, that engage with cultural debate. However, this apparent negation of his past involvement in Czech cultural life is often read as a convenient way in which he prevents dealing with the ambiguities a consideration of this past might involve, which is, on a general level, a central preoccupation of Czech culture post-1989.

Of the inadequacy, on an epistemological level, of interviewers, Kundera writes, '(1) the interviewer asks questions of interest to him, of no interest to you; (2) of your responses, he uses only those that suit him; (3) he translates them into his own vocabulary, his own manner of thought' (Kundera, 1988a: 133). This revelation of agenda runs through to different levels on the chain of interpretation, Kundera going on to argue that literary critics 'no longer distinguish between the words a writer has written and signed, and his remarks as reported'. This leads to 'the disappearance of the writer: he who is responsible for every one of his words'. Kundera enacts a policy of damage limitation, refusing since 1985 to conduct interviews, providing clarifications of his mode of writing in critical essays, or appending prefaces and author's notes to his work. In all of this paratextual work, he broaches the issues of interpretation – who is interpreting, why and when, the consequences of such interpretation, and ways of recognising its invidiousness. Each reading, he argues, carries with it a value-judgment, an agenda that must be unravelled or at least recognised. This consideration coincides with a major preoccupation in his novelistic and literary work: misunderstanding, misinterpretation and miscommunication as a central trope in all his work, one that has been exacerbated by the fact of translation. Thus, Květoslav Chvatík's analysis of misinterpretation in *Farewell Waltz* (1976) could be as telling a reading of Kundera criticism:

> The characters speak continually to each other, but seldom really communicate and never understand one another. They do not perceive the other person as a true partner in an authentic dialogue, but only as a sign, a cipher, as a function of their own interest. (Chvatík, 1989: 31)

Can going back to Kundera's texts be in any way revelatory of the interpretation of them? This question is perhaps at the heart of any consideration of his work. From some of his earliest work Kundera's preoccupation with the subjective imposition of meaning and the miscommunication this creates is clear, from the 'Monologues' of his third book of poetry directed to an absent listener, to the sign on the blackboard that sets in motion investigation and retribution in *Ptákovina* (1968) or the question of who has the right to the keys in *The Keepers of the Keys* (1962). Kundera's writing is about reading misreading. To what extent, then, has, does or should literary or journalistic criticism take this into account when considering Kundera's work?

This is not merely a playful question or a whimsical observation on the irony of a writer who writes in his novels about misinterpretation and feels the work itself is misinterpreted, or who writes about this misinterpretation in paratextual writing that is in itself potentially misinterpreted. It is a question of the scope and degree of mediation under way in any interpretation and the deflection of such interpretations on work which requires the reader to consider such mechanisms of mediation. The novels and indeed elements of the work that preceded them resonate with the questions that acts of interpretation should, but often do not, ask. Reading Kundera has replaced reading his work. While some Czech journalists and literary critics are incensed by Kundera's rewriting of his past or his bibliography or by his re-presentation in the West by himself and by Western critics, there has been little self-reflexive criticism of how Kundera and his work are being received in an altered and changing Czech culture with issues of its own about its past. Similarly, in English-language criticism, there is little reflection on what meaning Kundera and his work have in an English-language setting, and there is not much interest in a sustained analysis of the Czech context.

Kundera's often oblique readings of his own work seem to contribute to these critical misunderstandings, referring foremost to the work and experience of other artists – such as dealing with issues about Kafka's translators or Janáček's musical interpreters – that directly correlate with his own experience but do not explicitly reference them. When he talks or writes about his own work, it is almost always about its construction or its betrayal (by translators, publishers or critics). These two elements are innately linked for Kundera – the novels are intricately constructed to allow dissonant viewpoints while, he argues, the interpreters of the novels want to present only one. Kundera's interpretation of his work is predicated not on explaining it but on explaining how it functions and why this is antagonistic to criticism of the journalistic type.

Still, detractors believe that Kundera is imprisoned by his need for control and authority over the text, that he belligerently and condescendingly does not trust others to make an educated reading of his novels or indeed of his persona. They have a point – Kundera is in many ways the 'melancholy god' he writes of, or the writer 'chasing after hordes of words like a shepherd after a flock of wild sheep – a sorry figure to himself, a laughable one to others' (Kundera, 1988a: 121–22). However much he tries, he cannot control others' views or interpretations, and he is evidently aware of this, to the point of self-deprecation. On the other hand, he continues to point out and emphasise the inadequacies and reductive agendas of those reading him.

In this chapter, I focus on readings of his work at two periods and in two cultures to see whether Kundera's claims can be validated or not, whether the interpretation of his work has been educated and informed, and how these readings affect how we see and understand him. Firstly, I look at the Czech reception of his work post-1989, which is vital because there has never been an assessment of this reaction in English before and because the issue of how to interpret Kundera post-1989 has been so contentious. Secondly, I view the British reception of his work from 1968 to the present, which is an interesting case because the interpretation of his work changes as the world political context changes and reflects central issues pertaining to changes in British culture. It is also an interesting case because while there has been barely any sustained literary criticism published on Kundera, there has been substantial media coverage. This discrepancy presents fertile ground in which to analyse Kundera's claim that journalism has replaced criticism, and to explore how the recognition of an author or his work may not necessarily lead to an understanding of either.

Czech Criticism and Literary Reception Post-1989

I took a strangely wicked pleasure at seeing myself riding back into my native land on a donkey of misunderstanding. (Sedláček, 1995: 14)

The issue of reception back in his native country was approached immediately by Kundera. Refusing interviews, one of his first public platforms after 1989 was his afterword to *The Joke* in 1991. This was the first of his books to be published since 1970 in the Czech lands and it was still remembered as a novel that had a huge impact in its time. This afterword was an attempt at a reintroduction into Czech literary life and focused on the issue of his bibliography – Kundera laid out a manifesto on which works were to be considered as part of his work – and on the issue of interpretation, or the lack thereof, abroad. He gave a detailed history of the translation of the novel, which may seem odd at first glance because it might be asked what relevance the translations have to an audience that speaks the language the novel was written in. However, it leads up to Kundera's arguing that the mistranslation of the novel was indicative of the misunderstanding of it abroad. Here, he deliberately differentiates between the quality of criticism the book received from Czech critics when it first came out in 1967 and the inadequate reductive criticism of the Western critics, who perceived the book as simply a 'political pamphlet':

It was not only the translation which infuriated me, but also the critical interpretations. That is a chapter which is probably unknown in the Czech Republic, so a few words in explanation: I remember today several really profound critiques, written on *The Joke* in 1967, for instance Opelík, Pohorský, Václav Černý or Kožmín. My novel was examined not as some political pamphlet but as a 'novel of existence' ... For literary critics in the Czech Republic of the second half of the sixties (at that time the Czech literary critic did not have an equal perhaps anywhere else in the world, as I realised later abroad) this position was a given. In Western Europe, however ... cultural reviews disappeared and with them a platform for the serious reflection on literature; the authority of culture has stepped aside for the authority of journalism and the media; the terror of the news has even penetrated what was literary criticism ... everything that was written at that time about *The Joke* was just shallow political commentary and lyrical exclamations. This was not only my fate but the fate of art coming from our part of Europe, the fate of Vaculík and Havel, Brandys and Milosz, Konwicky and Hrabal or Kiš ... (art that did not have a political dimension remained quite unnoticed). Nothing worse could have happened to Central European art. Nothing worse could have happened to the novel. From the beginning of my time in France, I defended myself and others against this kind of journalistic reduction, systematically and sometimes frantically, and I am proudly satisfied that this was not completely without success. (Kundera, 1991c: 326, my translation)

While this is no doubt what Kundera believes, and it has a definite element of truth in it – the Czech critics' acceptance of the context, their knowledge of Kundera's literary development, and their involvement in what was a flowering literary community cannot be compared to the initial superficial analyses given to the novel abroad, where it was read in the light of 1968 – Kundera is also effecting a base for what he wants from his new Czech critics. This flattery, the suggestion of a profundity here in 'our part of Europe' as opposed to the West seems also to be a signal to the critics to focus on the work and not the politics, to differentiate themselves from the crass West. It must also be added that Kundera's nostalgia for the criticism of the 1960s elides some of his own criticism of the 1960s of Czech critics then. In 1962, Kundera's play *The Keepers of the Keys* was published after a very successful run. Kundera wrote an afterword to the play, admonishing the reviewers for seeing the play as only political, as only an 'occupation drama':

> It is the end of June, it is already two months since the play was performed, the reviewers have reviewed it and in the reviews the majority did not fail to mention the plot ... But is this the plot of my play? I can tell its story quite differently ... Both stories, as is evident, have a quite different tenor. While the first story, told by the reviewers, recalls the common occupation drama, the second story, which I am telling now, recalls the maybe distant dramaturgy of the Ionescu anti-drama or pseudo-drama.
>
> Nevertheless, *The Keepers of the Keys* is neither a common occupation drama nor a drama of the Ionesco type. That is to say, both plots run concurrently through the 100 minutes of the play ... (Kundera, 1962: 83, my translation)

Despite his professed high esteem for the Czech critics of the 1960s, there have been problems within Czech critical reception of his work. Kundera's 1991 afterword indicates three such problems which arose when his work returned to the Czech context after 1989: firstly, in his insistence on categorising his work and demanding that parts of it not be published or performed; secondly, in his choice of an afterword as a public platform rather than an interview; and, thirdly, in the fact that it is appended to only one of five books by Kundera that have so far been published in the Czech Republic. The first issue has been regarded by many, as has been discussed, as a move to disregard his compromised past, which Czech critics argue that only the Czechs really know about. The second has caused a sense of betrayal, because Kundera has refused to actively engage in public life in Czech society, even though he is so famous abroad. The third has fed into this, with a sense that Kundera does not really care about his Czech readership enough to publish his work there; that he values his foreign readerships more.

Because of his world wide fame and his refusal to engage in public life, Kundera's story has been well reported in the popular press, with its speculation on why he rejects Czech public life. He made the front cover of the weekend magazine supplement to the Czech daily *Dnes* in 2001 with the front-page headline, 'The Phantom Kundera: Why is he hiding?'. The article opens: 'Already twice nominated for the Nobel Prize for literature, Milan Kundera, Czech, now living in France and a French-language author. One of the greatest that we ever had. And yet in the Czech Republic he is barely thought of. Even the author himself is happy about this. The last thing he wants is publicity' (Verecký, 2001: 6). The section of the article entitled 'French writer' continues:

A new order arrived [1989], exiled authors began to return home or at least appear on Czech television. Only Milan Kundera had nothing to do with this.

On the contrary: in 1986 there was another injury. *L'art du roman* was published – the first book Kundera had written in French. He concurrently proclaimed himself a French writer. He hurt a lot of people with this. Turncoat. (The Polish have similar individuals, but they seem to love them more for it.)

Even before this, his jealous appraisers pointed out that the Czech in Kundera's novels written in exile was poor, elementary, because it was above all important for the author that his work could be translated more smoothly into French and other world languages. (Verecký, 2001: 10, my translation)

The journalist recounts how Kundera had urged his students (when teaching literature at the film academy in Prague) to learn a foreign language, and ends his article by suggesting to readers who want to read Kundera, because he refuses to publish all his work in Czech, that they should do the same.

Kundera's story is clearly fodder for the popular media because they can create a scandal from it, working on the complex feelings in Czech society about any emigrants and about national identity (which is why the polarising comment about the Polish is so interesting). In a popular weekly magazine in 1996, *Týden*, the journalist Jan Lukeš (though this time also an academic) opens his article on Kundera:

> In the seven post-November (1989) years, only four of Milan Kundera's books have been published in the Czech Republic, of which only one is among those that were written after he left for abroad and among those which, above all, established his worldwide success. The delay in Kundera's return home as an author collides with the understandable impatience of readers, producing a variety of conjectures, furthered by the even stricter decision of the author to communicate with the public only through his work, carefully composed, revised and commented on. (Lukeš, 1997: 80, my translation)

In 1999, in *Lidové noviny*, another daily, Petr Fantys asserts that: 'the relationship between Milan Kundera and his native land and on the other hand the relationship between Czech critics and readers and Kundera is one of the most problematic in contemporary literary life'. He adds that Kundera is partly to blame for this: 'To a certain extent, Kundera's "alienation" and his lack of interest in our daily life in the nineties contribute to this' (Fantys, 1999: 21, my translation). In 2000, the paper returns to the scandal of Kundera in relation to Czech society. Jaromír Slomek compares Kundera's attitude in the 1960s towards the importance of cultivating a defined Czech culture and language to his new attitude of abandoning it: 'Towards the close of the sixties, at the height of his native popularity, Milan Kundera wrote, "I believe in the great historical mission of the small nation ..." And proclaimed: "What is important is whether Czech will be a European language, or only a dialect". Today, ten years after the fall of European communism, the worldwide feted novelist travels incognito to the Czech Republic and writes his prose in French'. Slomek also comments on Kundera's delay in publishing his work and the effect this might have on his Czech audience: 'Part of the Kunderian paradox is that out of his last eight prose works, only two have appeared in Czech. Kundera is not rushing with his Czech editions. Will his readers also have such patience?' (Slomek, 2000: 32, my translation).

Journalists have also liked to comment on any negative reception Kundera receives abroad, at times as if it were a punishment for his seeking approbation there. Writing in *Dnes*, Verecký quotes a French article that criticised Kundera's novel *Identity* (1997) for trying to be too French: 'Maybe we are more fascinated by dissidents – especially in communist regimes ... Today Milan Kundera, as he wishes, is a French writer ... And what he writes has a strange appearance for us. He is French, to the point where he bores us' (Verecký, 2001: 12, my translation). However, Aleš Knapp in *Respekt*, an intellectual weekly, points to this 'bewildered, harsh reception' in France as a symptom of French ideological and cultural assumptions:

> 'Kundera, go home!' With this arrogant title, an article appeared in the French magazine *L'Express* in 1990. The reviewer, Angelo Rinaldi (also a belle-lettriste, who has met with less success than Kundera), challenged the writer to withdraw from the country and to kindly not write books with a 'non-Czech' theme at a time when Czechoslovakia was undergoing such an epochal political reversal ... For Communists it was the Great Betrayal, in the West he was the Great Sufferer, who should return home at the first opportunity, from which arose 'Kundera, go home!' (Knapp, 2000: 19, my translation)

The complexity of Kundera's position as not quite French and no longer quite Czech, and how this affects the reception of his work, is well articulated by Knapp as he is quite direct about the barrier at home: 'From the moment he started writing in French, a language barrier was raised between him and the majority of readers in his former Czech homeland'

(Knapp, 2000: 19, my translation). Milan Jungmann, writing in *Týden*, also comments on the barriers that Kundera has set up because he adopted the French language:

> In the world [abroad], Milan Kundera is unarguably the best-known Czech writer and has an extraordinary artistic authority there. At home he is the most secretive writer: he does not arrange autograph sessions; no one has met him at readings; he does not speak out from our television sets. It is as if he were hiding from his readers, who do not know his novels *Life is Elsewhere* and *Farewell Waltz*, nor his essays *The Art of the Novel* and *Testaments Betrayed*, all written in French. People with no knowledge of gallic culture are cut off from his latest novel, *Slowness*, because the author has not authorised its translation. We can accept the review by Růžena Gřebeníčková as an individual interpretation by a literary specialist, but [not speaking French] we cannot persuade ourselves of the quality or problems of the novel. (Jungmann, 1997: 74, my translation)

Jungmann has a point here in the odd situation in which the Czech literary community find themselves – analysing a writer who has published only a handful of his books in his home country. This results, for instance, in reviews of Kundera's novels being printed in literary journals or papers when the novels themselves are not published in Czech. For example, Růžena Gřebeníčková's review of *Slowness*, when it was published in France in 1995, or Aleš Knapp's review of *Ignorance* after it was published in Spanish in 2000. While monographs have been published in the Czech Republic on Kundera's work – Květoslav Chvatík's *The World of Milan Kundera's Novels* (1994), Helena Kosková's *Milan Kundera* (1998) and Eva Le Grand's *Kundera or the Memory of Desire* (1999) – many of the books they analyse have not (Le Grand, of Czech origin, first published her book in French in 1995, then in Czech in 1998, translated by Zdeněk Hrbata).

Literary reviews are also compromised by the need to acknowledge the wider debate about Kundera the personality within Czech society. In his 1998 review of the Atlantis Czech-language edition of *Farewell Waltz*, Martin Hybler feels he has to analyse how to review Kundera before he begins his review of the novel:

> In interpreting, it seems to me that here, more than with other writers, it is necessary to be wary on two accounts: in part there is perhaps an extreme circumspection with regard to being tempted by the author's self-intepretation – Milan Kundera offers reviewers his own hallmark illumination on a plate, which feeds on their laziness and inclination

to make their work easier. In writing 'a review' it suffices to quote the proper pages, slightly alter the word order and there you have it. On the part of the author, who likes to manipulate not only his characters (and his authorial narration) but also his readers and reviewers, it is not so hard to fall into the set trap. And partly there is a wariness with regard to the easy moralising or anti-emigrant 'patriotic' anti-Kunderaism of some Czech critics, which can be found in writing on Kundera from the 1980s on. Their claims are based on what they see as Kundera's amorality, libertinism, contingent patriotic indifference, and by what the author has cut out. His writing is of superfluous concern. (Hybler, 1998: 79, my translation)

There is a strong sense in Czech criticism that Kundera has an overarching need to control the interpretation of his work and that he has in many ways (as Hybler suggests) succeeded – especially with Western critics. As Kundera polarises Czech and Western critics in his 1991 afterword, this polarisation can be seen in Czech criticism as a criticism of Kundera and as a way of placing Czech criticism in relation to the world. Michal Bauer, in a long review of Peter Petro's (ed.) *Critical Essays on Milan Kundera* (1999), published in one of the main literary papers, presents the arguments of all the Western critics in each of the essays but concludes that the reception is 'uncritical' and based on 'emotional reactions' to the work. The problem, he suggests, is that Western critics have no sense of from where Kundera came or the literary development of his work, and that this feeds into Kundera's re-presentation of his past:

> The disadvantage of French, Canadian and American critics is their lack of knowledge about the Czech literary context. The crushing majority know only Kundera's books written in French or, at the most, those translated into French or Czech, and so their knowledge of Kundera's art begins with *The Joke* and most of the stories of *Laughable Loves*, which answer to Kundera's own view of his work. (Bauer, 2000: 5, my translation)

Bauer goes on to criticise foreign critics who have a Czech background and know the language because they have the ability to reveal the 'real' Kundera and the real context, but they rarely do so, which he attributes to the strength of Kundera's personality and his insistence that his work be presented in a certain way. The problem with Bauer is that the polemics serve to create an empty hegemony of Czech critics over foreign ones, in which foreign critics simply cannot understand or are somehow too weak to challenge what Kundera says, while Czech critics (such as himself) can reveal the truth of the matter – although he suggests they do not, because they focus only on his texts.

This is quite the opposite to what Petr Bílek argues in a similar presentation of Western criticism to Czech readers in an article reviewing anglophone criticism to date: '...Czech literary critics still solve the question of Kundera's "position" on this or that and the way in which the author refers to what surely we all know well, because we lived, fought and suffered it, while he left for his career and fame ...', though Bílek also argues that 'today English-language critics are concerned above all with his texts, with the self-referential text ...' (Bílek, 1996: 17, my translation). Bílek and Bauer share a wariness about the tendency in Anglo-American criticism, in focusing just on the text, to impose theoretical readings on it which give less a sense of work than a sense of justifying the theory. In a sense, Kundera's rise to prominence in the wider world with the success of *The Unbearable Lightness of Being* (1984) carried with it the irony of coinciding with the height in the academy of the belief in the 'death of the author' – that the text is what matters and not the author – his/her psychology or past. This, in Bauer's view, has led to an escape for Kundera because no theorist has probed his past, taking into account also his own stringent views on misallying an author's past or present with a reading of the work that author has produced.

Bauer suggests the flight into theory is not just a Western contrivance but also a characteristic of some Czech criticism, creating another kind of 'tyranny' which has allowed Kundera to escape the spotlight of his own past. It is true that the bulk of sustained literary criticism on Kundera does have a theoretical background: Chvatík's *The World of Milan Kundera's Novels* (1994) is heavily influenced by structuralist thought; Sylvie Richterová's essays 'Three Novels of Milan Kundera' (1986), 'The Identity of Man in the World of Signs' (1986) and 'Laughter in Novels, and Novels of Laughter' (1997) take a strong semiotic approach, as does Eva Le Grand's *Kundera or the Memory of Desire* (1999) and to some extent Kosková's *Milan Kundera* (1998). Jiří Kratochvil's *Príběhy příběhů* (1995) takes a post-modern approach to analysing the narrative structures of Kundera's novels (something Kratochvil practises in his own novels). Despite theoretical excesses at times, however, the real value of the meeting of theory and Czech-speaking critics has been an incisive analysis of the role of language in Kundera's work. This analysis of language has everything to do with interpretation.

All the above critics focus on the repetition and return of words and their polysemic force in the text. 'A word is often in Kundera's work an ideogram of a theme', writes Kosková. As each word returns in a text, its polysemic meanings are revealed (Kosková, 1998: 97, my translation). 'Through continual excursions into the semantic crossroads of each one of his words', Le Grand writes, 'Kundera reinvests his language with a little of its forgotten polysemy, relativity and laughter' (Le Grand, 1999: 50). This carefully constructed polysemy, the investigation of one word and its different meanings in different contexts, is a construction which, as Chvatík writes, is carefully overseen by Kundera; 'for Kundera the art of the novel is the *art of the word* ... I do not know of another novelist who would be so directly obsessively dutiful to the precision of each word, to the removal of unwanted connotations and to the rhythm, intonation and tempo of a sentence. This goes for the care of elements of the text of a novel in individual sections, chapters and paragraphs. It would be difficult to define Kundera's style better than as a *fanaticism of precision* ...' (Chvatík, 1994: 80–81, my translation). Kosková and Chvatík also point to how the tone of the language also constructs the tone of the characters, both commenting on Jaroslav in *The Joke*:

> Jaroslav's myth begins with a dream, from which he moves to a confrontation with reality. From this he soon escapes to the idealised world of traditional folk music. His language is drawn from this environment: the poeticness is linked to simple, folk language. This is especially palpable in the syntax ... (Kosková, 1998: 55, my translation)

> The tone of Jaroslav begins with a dream ... The style of his narration is the direct opposite of the rational, intellectual and analytic tone of Ludvík or the confused, emotional, precipitous soliloquy of Helena. The short sentences are emotionally stirring, but in the homogenous minor key of the dream. (Chvatík, 1994: 49, my translation)

Such analysis is rarely found in English-language criticism, partially because of semantic reduction in the translations and a sense that Kundera's style is simple and lucid, without a poetics. 'Kundera's linguistic style has been called intellectual, rational, even "colourless"; it is natural to differentiate it for instance from the emotional, poetic, subjective language of Hrabal or the slang, spontaneous narrative style of Škvorecký' (Chvatík, 1994: 80, my translation), Chvatík writes, but he then goes on to argue that this does not mean it does not have a thoroughly preconceived style.

Chvatík, Kosková and Le Grand all point to the intrusive problematic of translation and how, in a sense, this intrusion highlights Kundera's linguistic project. Chvatík argues that Kundera's fanaticism of precision reached new heights in exile and in translation: 'It is natural that Kundera's effort towards a precise linguistic expression reached a new height when he was isolated from his Czech readers and was forced to write for his translator' (Chvatík, 1994: 81, my translation). This precision is threatened by translation, for if Kundera's words are 'ideograms' of a theme, Kosková suggests that any alteration by a translator 'disturbs the ingenious compositional construction of intertextual bonds' (Kosková, 1998: 97, my translation). Le Grand discusses this with a concrete example of such intervention:

> The development of the theme in a phenomenological (existential) metaphor through variational repetition can even be manifested by the recurrence of a single word, of which the 'joke' remains the best example: at the moment when Ludvík thinks of the subjugation of his own joke to a 'system of jokes', that of history itself, the word is repeated up to seven times in a single paragraph. In the name of such repetition, the 'joke' can claim the status of a quite particular 'phenomenological' category, that of a synthesis of knowledge which is specific to the novel and acquired throughout the textual journey. The new translation of *The Joke* was therefore all the more necessary since, unlike the first one, it does not replace the keyword with equivalents: trick, fun, prank, hoax, game ... The 'synonymising reflex' of many a translator, proclaims Kundera in *Testaments Betrayed* on the subject of Kafka's work, before exclaiming with him: 'O ye translators, do not sodonymize us!' (Le Grand, 1999: 73)

Such an analysis of the function of language in Kundera's prose is extremely useful not only in reading his response to the translations but in reading all his work. The concentration on textual readings alone, following Kundera's exhortations, however, tends to allay the questions of historical, literary and political contexts brought up by his Czech opponents, echoing Kundera's retreat into the text, as Bauer would have it. This retreat is not a wholesale one, however, and both Chvatík and Kosková deal to some extent with Kundera's work beyond pure textual analysis. Given his theoretical affiliations, Chvatík, analysing the relationship between Kundera's life experience and his writing, in many ways takes a predictable if interesting path, arguing that 'there is no difference of poetry and truth between the texts of the artistic and the texts of biographies, for both are *literary* texts, but texts of *different genres*' (Chvatík, 1994: 22, my translation). Kosková ultimately takes perhaps a more persuasive route, arguing that the critics who take such a polemical stance on Kundera's work make the mistake of identifying the author with the characters and thus initiate a system of judgment, a move she describes as 'the tragicomic residue of the past'. She adds, 'Our problem, rather, is an opposite one: we pose the question of whether the events of Kundera's life, hidden from many dedicated Western interpreters, can influence an understanding of his work' (Kosková, 1998: 28, my translation). Her answer is a tentative yes, pointing to the influence of Kundera's musical background on his novels, and to his experience as a lyric poet, including his presentation of Jaromil in *Life is Elsewhere* (1973). She questions whether Kundera should be judged without consideration of his early work, arguing that this has been the reflex of many prose writers and that Kundera is the rule rather than the exception. 'For the literary historian, however', she adds, 'it is an unarguably important source for an understanding of Kundera's anti-lyricism, which critics often mistakenly regard as cynical rationalism ... The experience of the communist left, to which his father also belonged, and his later break with it, is possibly also one of the roots of the motifs of betrayal, flight from circles of people united by their same views and aims, the feeling of guilt with regard to the collective' (Kosková, 1998: 30, my translation).

Chvatík also proposes that some of the work that Kundera has omitted from his bibliography is symptomatic or indicative of his later work, showing the development of his writing style. He argues that, while respecting Kundera's taxonomy of the Opus work, he would add that the first *The Art of the Novel* (1960) is important because it shows Kundera's first articulation of the poetics of the novel, and that 'I, the Mournful God' (1963) is important because it is indicative of Kundera's later use of narrative. The former also shows the influence of Vančura; Chvatík writes, in 'the fascination with language; the work of Vladislav Vančura was not only a theme of Kundera's first *The Art of the Novel*, but was also an inspiration for his prose debut at its most fundamental level: in the game with the language of narration and in the game with narrative strategies and masks ...' (Chvatík, 1994: 36, my translation). Kosková also points to the latter story as being something of an Ur-narrative for his later prose. She argues that while his play *The Keepers of the Keys* (1962) 'had many of the fundamental features of his later novelistic poetics ... in contrast to *The Keepers of the Keys* (1962), here ['I, the Mournful God'] clearly, as in the rest of Kundera's prose work, is the palpable ironic authorial distance from the characters, and it is left up to the reader to look for the deeper meaning of the story, which is intentionally polysemic' (Kosková, 1998: 31–36, my translation). Jiří Kratochvil also points to the portent of the story within the context of Kundera's previous and later work, describing 'I, the Mournful God' as:

... the only one of his prose works which shares with Vančura his fascination with language as the primary motivator of a story ... And when we read the story today, that is in the context of Kundera's seven prose works, we come to realise how here for the first time and in an anecdotal variation, he lays before us the majority of his fundamental themes ... (Kratochvil, 1995: 174, my translation)

Though Kundera's presence is visible as the narrator in his novels, both Chvatík and Kosková explicitly support his assertion that the author is irrelevant within the arena of literary criticism. Chvatík compares Kundera's decision to post-structuralist literary theory, arguing that Kundera's decision is a more radical position on the 'death of the author'; he writes: 'The author as a private person is negated more radically than in the most rigorous theories of the structuralists and post-structuralists' (Chvatík, 1994: 26, my translation). Kosková points to Kundera's experience of living under a totalitarian regime as a factor of his insistence on privacy, something exacerbated by his success in the West, the media invasion of his privacy, and the resultant reduction of his personality to that of dissident (Kosková, 1998: 27). Neither critic writes in any depth about either Kundera's past or the debates surrounding his personality and past in the Czech Republic. Both critics are Czech émigrés – Chvatík's book was written originally in German – which shows in their analysis of the effect of Kundera's exile on his language and their distance from his past.

These critics show that the import of Kundera's attitude to his Czech past can be interpreted in different ways, all valuable in understanding his work. Czech critical interpretation has attracted little notice in Anglo-American circles. Indeed, the only recent analysis of Czech criticism – Caleb Crain's 1999 article 'Infidelity' – chose to ignore critics such as Kosková, Chvatík and Kratochvil, and concluded that 'Kundera-twitting is something of a national sport' in the Czech Republic (Crain, 1999: 43). Crain in fact argues that Czech criticism has been ignored because it is critical of Kundera: 'These fierce disputes about Kundera's artistic and political past have been little reported in the West, and here, too, one senses the power of translation's almost invisible hand ... Defensibly enough, he has quarantined his early, socialism-tinged work. Hard as it is for Czechs to read Kundera's late, capitalist novels, it is much harder for Westerners to read his early, communist poetry and essays. The Czechs, as a result, know a Kundera even more muddied, human, and self-contradictory than the rest of the world knows' (Crain, 1999: 47).

Crain's analysis is presented as a window onto the Czech scene, but it also reveals its own agenda – the reduction of Kundera's exile work to the throwaway sobriquet of 'capitalist novels' (as if there is such a thing as a capitalist novel, or that the Czechs are immune to capitalism). The danger is, though, that this is a less-considered portrayal of the Czech literary reception of Kundera's work. Crain echoes critics such as Bauer and Jungmann, who defer to the Czechs as the only true arbiters of Kundera because they know all about him. Yet at the same time Crain's article is something of a negation of such criticism. The contention that only Czech critics are cognisant of the 'real' Kundera is contradicted immediately by Crain and his own 'knowledge' of the 'real' Kundera. The dismissal of foreign and notably anglophone critics, because of their gullibility and lack of knowledge about the Czech context, is argued alongside a delight (as Crain points out) in printing negative foreign portrayals of Kundera – for instance *Literární noviny*'s translation of the flawed Allison Stanger article, 'In Search of *The Joke*: An Open Letter to Milan Kundera', published as 'Hledání žertu' (1997). The ultimate question is what this knowledge of a 'muddied, human and self-contradictory' Kundera tells us about the work, and why it is indeed even an issue.

The Czech reception of Kundera's work post-1989 has not been as one-sided and as critical as Crain suggests. Literary critics such as Bauer and Jungmann have critiqued Kundera's work based on their disagreement with his personal actions, and this has been appropriated to some extent by the popular press, eager for a story and eager to reflect cultural trends in Czech society, especially in the not wholly positive consideration of exile and Czech identity. On the other hand, sustained literary criticism of Kundera's work published in the Czech Republic has been incisive and deals with Kundera's language style, the tropes of miscommunication and the effects of translation. They do not, as Bauer suggests, retreat into purely textual analysis to ignore what he regards to be Kundera's compromised past, but rather suggest, quite constructively, that his past is, in Kundera words, 'motivational material' for existential enquiry within his work.

The British Reception

> The Czech Republic became one of the most popular lands in Europe. But please, take that statement with all of your healthy Czech skepticism. It was shortly after November 1989. In Paris they put on a twenty-year old Menzel film, which had just been released from the censor's vault: Hrabal's *Lark on a String*. A wonderful film, unique, modern, I was there with my wife, and some tears flowed. But imagine: we two were entirely alone in that cinema! Naively, we thought that the response to the Prague revolution would attract a large audience

to that film. It attracted no one. Instead mobs charged into buses and planes in order to gawp at the Old Town Hall clock in Prague. I then read in a book by one Englishman, who visited the Czech Republic at this time, that Prague, a city built by Germans and Italians, had nothing to do with those who live there. By which I want to say that interest in a Menzel film is a thousand times more important for Czech culture and its place in the world, than these millions of tourists who trample across Charles Bridge and make Prague an uninhabitable city. (Sedláček, 1995: 14, my translation)

Among Kundera's first words to his British readership was an invective for them *not* to read *The Joke* (1967), because he felt it had been compromised by its translation. This introduction by suspicion has set the tone for the reception of his work in Britain ever since. Kundera is recognised as a famous author in Britain; his books are prominently reviewed in the British media and his books (or rather, book, *The Unbearable Lightness of Being* (1984)) – are prominently displayed in bookshops. Yet this acknowledgement of Kundera and his work is not predicated on the basis of a profound literary discussion of his ideas, work or portent for British culture. The term 'British culture' is complex. In this section, I refer to British culture as a construct, one forged partially through English media discourse, and the effects this discourse has on narrow views of otherness and foreignness. Susan Bassnett in *Studying British Cultures* (2003) makes this point in her introduction to a set of essays that mark the ethnic, social and religious diversity of British cultures:

> The study of British cultures can be undertaken from an infinite number of starting points ... Traditional (British) Cultural Studies looked primarily, almost exclusively at *English* culture, accepting without question the old imperial equation of British with English, because attention was centred on other more pressing issues of the moment such as class or gender. But in recent years, the use of 'British' as a synonym for 'English' has been called into question from many different sources ... Nor is the uneasiness with the term 'British' linked only to the aboriginal peoples of the British Isles. The transition of society to multiculturalism and multi-ethnicity, which has happened more visibly in England than elsewhere in the British Isles, has also contributed to anxiety about the ideological implications of the terminology and to the debates about national identity. For any sense of a *national* identity is also implicitly concerned with otherness, with what is *not* part of the national heritage (Bassnett, 2003: xxi–xxii).

Kundera is barely taught in Britain, in schools or in universities, and this is reflected in the paucity of scholarly work on him – the single book on Kundera by a British academic was published in 1981 in Denmark (Porter, 1981) and there have been only a handful of scholarly articles on his work by academics working in Britain (Eagleton, 1987, 1989; Kuhiwczak, 1990; Lodge, 1984b; Porter, 1975; Woods, 2001). One of them, Piotr Kuhiwczak, analyses the case of the first British translation of Kundera's work, the 1969 Hamblyn–Stallybrass translation of *The Joke*, for which Hamblyn and Stallybrass removed a large amount of material from the novel and rearranged its chronological structure because they and the publisher (Macdonald) regarded it to be aesthetically deficient; this is the translation that provoked Kundera into asking his British readers not to read his novel. Kuhiwczak argues that this 'first English version of the novel is not simply an inadequate translation of the Czech text, but an appropriation of the original, resulting from the translators' and publisher's untested assumptions about Eastern Europe, East European writing, and the ability of the Western reader to decode complex cultural messages' (Kuhiwczak 1990: 124). He further argues that these untested assumptions about Eastern Europe led to the fashioning of an East European canon in English that reflected ideological needs in the West:

> The East European writers who began to be discovered in the 1970s are occasionally discussed in the columns of review periodicals; it is, however, difficult to get rid of the impression that they are not perceived as writers with something vital to communicate about the human condition, but as political animals, who bring a grim message from 'faraway countries of which we know ...' only a little more than we did, and whose experience is strictly tangential to that of the 'free world'. (Kuhiwczak, 1990: 122)

Kuhiwczak emphasises the discrepancy between Kundera's position (and that of Central European writers) as a best-selling author and the lack of scholarly and critical writing on his work, arguing that the criticism that does exist often underlines the political element, referencing Terry Eagleton's work on Kundera (Eagleton, 1987). He concludes that the reason for this may be because Central European writing is 'regarded as elitist or over-intellectual' (Kuhiwczak, 1990: 121) and that it is 'the "dangerous" character of Kundera's writing that either frightens some critics or makes them confine their analyses to the realm of Kundera's dissidence ...' (Kuhiwczak, 1990: 129). What is important about Kuhiwczak's analysis is his emphasis on the role of translation – the belief on the part of the translators and publisher that the novel's value lay in its political content, and how this affected their approach to its translation. Kundera claims that, as Kuhiwczak puts it, he was 'misinterpreted, mistranslated, and misunderstood' (Kuhiwczak, 1990: 122). Despite such so-called 'mistranslation', Kundera has had a great deal of media exposure in Britain, which may reflect some of the concerns Kuhiwczak raises and the reasons why Kundera is little taught or commented on in academia (Kuhiwczak, 1990: 122).

Kundera has been simultaneously canonised and rejected by the British media, which has played a central role (as opposed to education) in presenting him to the British reading public. The British media has constructed what appears to be a very definite image of Kundera, and this stereotype has exerted untold influence on how his writing is understood within British culture. This stereotyping mechanism familiarises the foreign and serves to uphold British assumptions about its own culture and foreign cultures. Though apparently fixed, this stereotype has in fact changed to cope with changing times. Kundera, initially represented as an East European dissident during the Cold War, has, since the end of the Cold War and the media's concomitant realisation that he had moved to France, been represented as a member of the French and European *literati*. Both foreign identities are treated with ambivalence when interpreted and mediated by the British media – the first seen as impressively but suspiciously intellectual and politicised, and the second as intellectual but inauthentic and pretentious.

This paradoxical acceptance of Kundera as an intellectual, and rejection of him because he is one, reverberates within British media discourse. What lies behind it is rarely questioned, rather Kundera has been commodified and simplified – his name being used in reviews and articles as a symbol and gauge of both intellectuality and pretension. This avoids the question of whether his work is relevant or understandable to British culture, with its emphasis solely on what Kundera represents for British culture as it is seen, or even created, by the British media discourse. It is partly a result of the changing face of the British media, which have begun to focus less on sustained literary analysis and more on reviews of newly published material, that has led to less discussion of Kundera but more references to him. The references reflect another change in media presentation of writers – the tendency towards a mixing of low and high culture – so that Kundera, for example, is deemed to be an apposite reference for an article on Manga cartoons (see below, Smith, 2001: 6). The anxiety of intellectualism is again revealed here: hip to quote a difficult writer but hip to deflate the difficulty.

Considerations relevant to a discussion of Kundera's reception in the British media include, firstly, issues of class and education and how widespread within British society Kundera's readership is (discussed briefly below); and, secondly, the notion of what is considered 'British'. I would suggest in this book that part of the foregrounding of Kundera as 'foreign' results from an increasing discomfort in Britain about how to define the British identity. Two of the most discussed domestic issues in recent years have been immigration and European integration in London-based newspapers. An assimilated Kundera, repackaged as a symbol of containable intellectualism, is far less threatening than a difficult-to-categorise foreign writer who raises issues of foreign and exile identity, hyphenised identity and language as being ultimately and always foreign to itself.

Kundera's refusal to give interviews or to become a personage in order to avoid reductive interpretation of his work has, paradoxically, left a space that has been appropriated by some British journalists in order to do exactly that. Kundera had addressed his British audience in the early and mid 1980s via what he later described as 'incidental' essays whose function was to 'explain to a non-Czech public the basics of the Czech situation' in *Granta* (Kundera, 1991c: 320–21; 1985d; 1984a). These essays dealt with the possibilities and doom of Central Europe and its culture, which led to greater debate on the issue of Central Europe and certainly aided the resurrection of the term 'Central Europe' in Anglo-American literary and political circles. However, it also led to a consolidation of the politicised image of Kundera, which has not been helped by his lack of communication with a wider British audience. (Kundera can attempt to control the mediation of his image to some extent through his insistence on the retranslation of the English-language versions of his novels, but this depends also to some extent on the reception of the retranslations.)

During the Cold War, Kundera's identity and appeal to a British audience was much more fixed. From the very first reviews in Britain, Kundera was equated with his country's situation and his books were read primarily as responses to the context of world affairs. In 1984, Peter Kemp reviewed two television interviews with Kundera for the *Times Literary Supplement* (Kemp, 1984: 614). The article particularly praised the BBC's *Arena* programme for its visuals during the interview: 'The motif *Arena* chose to amplify was Kundera's fictional response to Czechoslovakia's political history. Invasions, show-trials, Party rallies flickered greyly across the screen, with particularly full coverage of the events of 1968; jeaned and sweatered students attempting to reason with gun-turrets, bedroom-slippered citizens in dressing-gowns incredulous as tanks lurched past their homes. As in previous *Arena* programmes directed by Nigel Williams, the visual material was not just powerfully atmospheric, but also precisely informative' (Kemp, 1984: 614). Yet the visuals were not particularly informative about Kundera or his work; rather, they consolidated images of what Czechoslovakia must be like and why this might be relevant to Kundera's work. This pigeon-holing had been satirised by Kundera in *The Unbearable Lightness of Being* (1984), the very novel that precipitated the interview. When the artist Sabina picks up the catalogue from one of her exhibitions in Germany, Kundera writes, 'the first thing she saw was a picture of herself with a drawing of barbed wire superimposed on it. Inside she found a biography that read like the life of a saint or a martyr: she had suffered, struggled against injustice, been forced to abandon her bleeding homeland, yet was carrying on the struggle ... She protested but they did not understand her' (Kundera, 1985c: 254). Sabina feels that she is being used for an ideological agenda, when her own agenda is to escape the reductive terms of ideology.

Two reviews in *The Times* in the 1970s state that *The Farewell Party* (1976) was written by 'a supporter of the Dubcek [sic] regime', with a central character who is a 'political dissident' who sees in the nurse 'all he hates about his native country' (*Times*, 1973: 9). One review concludes that '*The Farewell Party* is banned in Czechoslovakia: all the more reason for its being widely read elsewhere' (Lewis, 1977: 12). Kundera passionately argued against his books being read as political pamphlets, famously writing in his preface to Michael Henry Heim's 1983 translation of *The Joke* (1967) that *The Joke* was not political but a love story. However, Clive Sinclair in the 1983 *TLS* review of this new translation responded directly to Kundera's admonition by both accepting it and dismissing it – Kundera should not be seen as simply a political writer, Sinclair argued, but 'like it or not, those writers ... have become the true historians of modern Czechoslovakia'. He adds: 'Poor Czechoslovakia to have such a history, lucky country to have such writers!' (Sinclair, 1983: 149). What follows is a review in which Sinclair talked as much about censors, and invasions, banned books, Czech culture and the Soviets as evil oppressors, as about the book itself. Sinclair ends, however, by giving the book his thumbs-up – he concludes, 'It is so good it almost persuades you to forgive the Russians' (Sinclair, 1983: 149).

Europe's 'East' provided critics with an exotic place that could be inscribed within their own longings and fears: the attraction of and identification with a dissident writer outweighing what lay beyond the political and ideological context. David Lodge touched on this in the *TLS* in 1984 when he described 'the sentimental attitude, which sometimes takes the form of a perverse envy, that persecution automatically confers a special value and authenticity on writing from Eastern Europe' (Lodge, 1984a: 567–68). The sympathy that Kundera elicited held the danger that his work would be read only in one dominant context. Even a decade after the end of the Cold War, Kundera was still described, despite his protestations, as a 'dissident' unable to escape the label even though the world has moved on (Plummer & Holloway, 1992; Rabinovitch, 1999: 11).

The legacy of the stereotypes continues in how Kundera and Czech identity and literary identity is portrayed in the media today. The well-known media commentator on Central Europe, Timothy Garton-Ash, suggests that it is only the stereotypes that have changed. He summed up what the British know about the Czech Republic in 1998: 'Prague, beer and Skoda cars,' he writes, conceding that readers of the broadsheet he was writing in might have heard of Švejk and Kafka and might 'have read a novel or two by Milan Kundera and seen the marvellous recent Czech film *Kolya*' (Garton-Ash, 1998: 5). The paucity of translation of Czech writers into English has effected a narrow conception of Czech literature, one limited to within the parameters of 'the four major writers it has produced since the Second World War' – Havel, Kundera, Klima and Škvorecký (Curtis, 1991: 18). The fallacy that these are the only major Czech writers since World War II and that only Kafka and *The Good Soldier Švejk* (1921–2) are what came before is perpetuated by the lack of translation. The four mentioned above are the only widely translated Czech authors currently in print in British editions (there is a wider publication history of Czech literature in the United States); the availability of translations, rather than the quality of Czech post-war prose, is the creating factor in the canon as seen by British eyes. In almost every article related to one of the four, the other three are mentioned, consolidating this canon (Pizzichini, 1998: 13; Rabinovitch, 1999: 11; Rees, 1994; Wullschlager, 1992: 17). In the 1990s, Hrabal began to be mentioned as some of his novels were reissued. His place in Czech literary history is summed up by Ian Samson in *The Guardian*: 'Milan Kundera writes philosophy. Skvorecky does satire. Hrabal tells stories' (Samson, 1998: 11). Jasper Rees in a 1992 article in *The Daily Telegraph* suggests that Czech literature had achieved greater prominence in 'British publishing' in the previous decade and that this was 'thanks not least to Kundera' and the success of *The Unbearable Lightness of Being* (1984). However, Rees goes on to add that the Czech language is a handicap to popular acceptance, along with the long novel titles chosen by Czech authors – never mind, he adds, their own unpronounceable names: 'Even press officers at Faber, his publishers, do not know how to pronounce Skvorecky' (Rees, 1992).

The British media caught up with Kundera's 1975 move to France only in the early 1990s, when the move came to represent a division in the British view of a Czech canon between those who fled and those who stayed. As a result, Kundera's courage and integrity (values placed upon him by the British media during the Cold War) began to be questioned not only because he chose exile but because he chose France. In a 1994 article entitled 'Cold War Divides the Authors of Prague's New Spring', Tom Gross invoked the 'two grand old men of the Czech cultural resistance', Kundera and Havel, and wrote that 'as Kundera was being fêted by the glitterati in Paris, Havel and his fellow dissidents were languishing in Czech jails or under house arrest'. The moral result, he argued, is that 'today Havel is president. Meanwhile, Kundera, the best-known Czech writer since Kafka ... continues to sit, brooding alone, in his adopted home of Paris' (Gross, 1994). Gross's comments reflect the kind of stereotypes present in British culture, working on a portrayal of Czech culture and Czech dissident culture through three of a handful of Czech authors translated into English, and through a shorthand description of what life must be like both in exile and back at home. The moral equation is rooted in the assumption that a political end is what the point of these two writers' *oeuvre* is, that Havel's struggle was vindicated by his election and that therefore Kundera must be jealous. The portrayal also of France and its 'glitterati' perhaps suggests more about the British perception of French high culture than about Kundera. Kate Connelly echoed Gross in an article on Bohumil Hrabal, underlining Hrabal's authenticity as the right kind of Czech writer because he stayed in Czechoslovakia in the pub, which is more authentic, she implies, than Kundera's elitist Prague and Parisian cafes: 'Whilst other writers such as Milan Kundera and Ivan Klima exchanged their tables in Prague's Café Slavia for café tables in Paris, Vienna or London, Hrabal retreated to the Golden Tiger. Only he and Havel stayed' (Connelly, 1998: 10). Connelly implies that the only two people left in the country were Hrabal and Havel, again underlining the assumption that Czech life and culture can be represented by a limited synecdoche of names, invariably from the limited numbers of Czech writers who have been translated into English.

In the 1990s, then, there appears to be a moral division of the stereotype of the Czech writer into those who authentically suffered and were courageous and those who took the route of exile, as if this could be judged to be an opportunist and easy option. In this vein, in 1995, Paul Bailey from the renowned annual British literary festival in Cheltenham announced that while 'a few important poets and novelists managed to escape to America or Western Europe (one thinks of Czeslaw Milosz or Milan Kundera) ... the majority stayed to face the enemy'. He added, 'It is the writers who have stayed put whom we have invited to Cheltenham' (Bailey, 1995).

Kundera is also accused of not responding to contemporary Czech life, and seen as having turned his back on it in order, as one journalist wrote, to enjoy 'truffling through 18th century France' (Rees, 1996: 6–7). Kundera's embrace of France and French culture has in some reviewers' eyes rendered his work somehow less authentic than if he were still occupied entirely with the Czech culture. In a series in *The Observer* entitled 'Classicwatch', an unnamed critic heralds the reissue of the 'classic' novel *The Joke* (1967) while comparing it to Kundera's later works, which are apparently compromised by their Frenchness: '[*The Joke*] was written while Kundera was still resident in what was then Czechoslovakia ... His later work – *Immortality, Slowness, Identity* and *The Art of the Novel* – has largely been written in France and betrays the influence of the Parisian literary scene. *The Joke*, however, is vintage Kundera ...' (*Observer*, 2000: 14). Jasper Rees remarks on the curiosity of Kundera's embrace of France: 'It's his Frenchness that makes him so enigmatic to readers in this country where, among living authors, the Czechs sell much better than the French' (Rees, 1996: 6–7). For these critics, the perception of French writers is burdened with its own associations of pretension. An unnamed critic in *The Independent* on writing a positive review of *Slowness* (1995) adds: 'Read it wearing dark glasses at the boulevard café' (*Independent*, 1996: 28–29).

Thus the intellectual quality of Kundera's work is both outlined and derided, perhaps signalling an ambivalent attitude towards intellectualism in British culture, in which it is to be at once admired and satirised. British critics constantly emphasise the intelligence of Kundera's work and this intelligence is connected to his foreignness. In *The Financial Times*, Rogaly writes that *Immortality* (1991), 'wrestle[s] the intellect to the ground ... the product of a coruscating Central European intelligence' (Rogaly, 1991: 20). This is contrasted with British writing, which is seen as being less intellectually challenging. In the *Independent* Keates writes that *Identity* (1997) 'represents a fictional strain certain British novelists would love to affect if only they knew how' (Keates, 1998: 15). In an article on literacy, the *Guardian* critic bemoans the lack of intellectual leaders like Kundera and Havel in British society, suggesting that such leaders would bring intellectual intelligence into the British culture (Hoggart, 1991: 21). A *Daily Telegraph* writer argues that the Czechs outclass British artists because they can 'cross-pollinate' in the arts, specifically mentioning Kundera's wide knowledge of classical music as well as his literary abilities. In contrast, the same writer derides English writers such as Graham Greene who boast that they do not even listen to music and British composers 'who have not read a book since leaving school' (Lebrecht, 1995). Both camps, he argues, could learn from Czech exiles. Geoff Dyer in an article entitled 'No ideas please, we're British' goes further and argues – using a particularly apt British metaphor – that the intellectual punch of 'exotic foreign imports' has actually damaged the quality of British writing: 'We have tended to rely on exotic foreign imports (Borges, Calvino, Kundera and, most recently, Sebald) to do the idea stuff for us, thereby – the parallel with football is irresistible – impoverishing the domestic game' (Dyer, 2000: 9).

The intellectual exoticism of Kundera as a francophone writer and as 'one of Europe's greatest living writers', canonised alongside Calvino, Grass and Proust, is extremely ambivalent (*Observer*, 2000: 14). These 'faintly intimidating figures with heavyweight reputations' are suspicious as well as admirable (Hoffman, 1996: 17). Max Davidson in *The Daily Telegraph*, known for its anti-European and anti-anything-foreign stance, derided the cachet accorded to foreign writers, suggesting that any book which is 'fat and foreign' – using as examples Umberto Eco, Georges Perec and Milan Kundera – becomes immediately trendy because of its exoticism to a British reading public. Davidson goes on to remark, 'Foreign, not quite so fat, but fiendishly clever, was Milan Kundera's *The Unbearable Lightness of Being*, which was made into a film every bit as pretentious as the original' (Davidson, 1992). Thus the reviewers of *Immortality* (1991), reviewed earlier the same year in the same paper, declared that the novel is 'at times brilliant and, rather less often, impossibly pretentious' (Plummer & Holloway, 1992). The suspicion of pretension appears in earlier reviews. In 1984 Christopher Hawtree declared that *The Unbearable Lightness of Being* 'could easily have become a hideously pseudish con-trick', 'but', he concedes, finally 'everything does take its place' in the novel (Hawtree, 1984: 29). Kundera has even become a gauge for pretension, with reviewers criticising other novelists trying to be too 'Kunderian' – the majority view being that while Kundera somehow gets away with it, others do not.

Yet the accusation of pretension is not centred only on the novels themselves but also on what they have come to represent within the terms of British society. A review of the West-End run of an Irish theatre company's production that satirised the pretensions of the trendy Irish middle class with 'nothing Irish left' in it notes how the props enhance the meaning of the play, including some prominently displayed books which underline these pretensions – 'Kundera, of course', the theatre reviewer adds (Murray, 1992: 17). The popularity of Kundera's novels is thus innately linked with their dubious *zeitgeist*, what cultural value they represent rather than what the novels themselves say.

The suspect nature of perceived intellectualism is demonstrated in several instances by the juxtaposition of Kundera as, in effect, a symbol of intellectualism with so-called 'low culture', producing a humorous effect that serves to declaw the intellectual element. Kundera is invoked as a cultural reference for a completely diverse range of subjects, from Cowes yachting week, to food, wine and healthy-eating reviews, to DJs and dogs, easy listening and pop music, supermodels and soccer, through to (perhaps more obviously) articles on and reviews of art and theatre and classical music. A review of Japanese *manga* cartoons, for instance, gently ridicules the dialogue in them as 'existential and every bit as opaque as Kundera' (Smith, 2001: 6). Gossip columnist Dillie Keane satirises supermodel Christy Turlington's claims to be reading Hemingway and adds, 'Now if she'd said Milan Kundera in the original Czech, I might be impressed' (Keane, 1994: 33). Kundera is invoked in discussions of two bastion elements of British culture, football and cricket, in which players and managers are lampooned for admitting to reading Kundera. Ex-England cricket captain Mike Atherton took 'a long time to live down the few seconds in which he entered the name of Milan Kundera on the dotted line marked 'Favourite Authors' in the *Cricketer's Who's Who* a few years ago' (Williams, 1996: 22). A reference *The Daily Telegraph* added in its own pro-British way was 'lost on his team-mates, the majority of whom would imagine Kundera was the chap who owned the Tandoori in the Harleyford Road' (Heffer, 1993). In *The Observer* in 2001, a reviewer noting the cultural difference of the French manager of the famous British football club Liverpool, Gérard Houllier, commented as follows: 'Stories, not all of them apocryphal, abounded about bewildered looks among the senior players as he quoted Marcel Proust or Milan Kundera in team-talks' (Whittell, 2001: 9). In British society, then, these comments suggest a division between the kind of impressive but distinctly odd and even foreign characters who read Kundera and those – perhaps of a different class or education – who do not. Certainly, Kundera is again regarded as a symbol invested with domestic culture perceptions rather than as simply a writer.

The quality of Kundera's writing is questioned on other levels than its intellectualism. Sex, one of these levels, is reductively read as the *raison d'être* of Kundera's novels, the reason for his popularity but also a site of dubiousness and, again, a thing that is foreign to the British make-up. Readers, Max Davidson sneers, are 'even more excited at the thought of ideas rubbing shoulders with sex and mittel Europe' (Davidson, 1992). Reviewers of *Identity* (1997), roll their eyes at this 'miniature version of the familiar Kundera mix of sex and existential analysis' (Tonkin & Miller, 1997: 7). Peter Walker, in a review of Hong Ying's *Summer of Betrayal* (1997), suggests that the sex in it perhaps reflects the private freedom in the oppressive public sphere of modern-day Beijing as it had in cold-war Prague or Budapest: 'Ying's version of sexual liberation recalls the endless copulations of an early Kundera hero' (Walker, 1997: 26). This contains all sorts of cultural and politicising assumptions and suggests that there is a flaw in foreign writing that allows this endless copulation to be printed. The 'sexism' noted in Kundera's writing is directly attributed as being a flaw in Czech writing by Jonathan Coe in *The Guardian*, arguing that *Immortality*'s (1991) 'voyeuristic objectifying version of masculinity is not unique to Kundera (it seems to be bane of much Czech writing in fact – Skvorecky and Hrabal spring to mind)' (Coe, 1991: 24).

Another fault found with Kundera's fiction is its lack of 'real' characters, which appears to reflect the demands of domestic notions of what a novel is supposed to be rather than reading anything innovative into what Kundera is attempting. 'In his novels it is not Kundera's characters that stick in the mind', Geoff Dyer writes, ' – one is left with an oddly Benny Hill-ish memory of women in their underwear, men chasing after them – but the essayistic digressions woven around them' (Dyer, 1995). In 1984, David Lodge complains that anyone reading *The Unbearable Lightness of Being* 'can't help hankering after ... fuller characters' (Lodge, 1984a: 567–68). Alan Bold complains in similar terms about *The Book of Laughter and Forgetting* (1979), declaring it 'a provocative, unsettling and wholly admirable book', but also one in which 'the complexity has everything to do with cogitation and very little to do with character' (Bold, 1982: 131). Christopher Hawtree writes in *The Spectator* that '*The Farewell Party* is little more than a game ... and the stories in *Laughable Loves* rehearse similar themes and settings, in particular the sexual one with which Mr Kundera appears to be obsessed, without creating any characters that remain in the mind' (Hawtree, 1984: 29). No commentator or reviewer suggests that what Kundera does with his characters might be worth further thought; rather, his style is dismissed as qualitatively suspect, read within the norms of the British literary scene.

Hawtree, however, goes on to argue that the intelligence of Kundera's novels encourages reviewers 'for fear of looking stupid' to reach out for superficial analyses of the books as a 'substitute for real thinking' (Hawtree, 1984: 29). It is difficult to judge to what extent British culture has engaged in real thinking about Kundera's ideas. Ideas and themes from the novels are certainly referenced to a limited extent. For instance, the quote from *The Book of Laughter and Forgetting* (1979), 'The struggle of man against power is the struggle of memory against forgetting' (1999b: 4), is referenced in discussions on apartheid in South Africa, on Kosovo, on Russian theatre and on Nicaragua (Billington, 1991: 30; Gilbey, 1996: 6–7; Neely, 1999: 13; Pilger, 1998: 14). Yet the paucity of any profound consideration of his work is striking, and while such profundity may be impossible to achieve in newspaper articles, there is little attempt beyond the media in Britain to consider his work.

In literary terms, Kundera has most evidently made an impact on one of the most successful contemporary British novelists, Salman Rushdie. The connection between Kundera and Rushdie is clear – Rushdie quotes Kundera in two of his novels, in *Shame* (Rushdie, 1984: 88) and in *The Ground Beneath Her Feet* (Rushdie, 1999: 380). Kundera provides a laudatory analysis of *The Satanic Verses* (1988) in *Testaments Betrayed* (1993). What has not been commented on is the similarity between Kundera's *The Book of Laughter and Forgetting* (1979) and Rushdie's *Shame* (1984). *Shame* was published a year after *The Book of Laughter and Forgetting* had been published in Britain (though the latter was published two years earlier in the United States) and this proximity may preclude evidence that Kundera's novel influenced Rushdie's. However, both the narrative style and the structure of the novels are strikingly similar – Rushdie interweaving thematic essays and the biography of a fictionalised narrator with the narrative of Omar Khayyam. Rushdie names the character Omar Khayyam, just as Kundera named his Czech poets with pseudonyms of great poets, and notes how the real Omar Khayyam has been reworked into Western languages rather than translated. The narrator provides a clue to resistance of such assimilation: 'To unlock a society', he says, 'look at its untranslatable words', (Rushdie, 1984: 29), just as Kundera had provided a chapter on the untranslatable Czech word *lítost*. Rushdie considers the nature of exile and translation of the self in his essays: 'We have floated upwards from history, from memory, from Time', he writes, echoing the recurring theme of lightness in Kundera's novel (Rushdie, 1984: 104). Migrancy, Rushdie writes, is like Kundera's expulsion from the dancing circle, an 'antibelonging' (Rushdie, 1984: 87). *Shame* deals with Pakistan's secession as Kundera deals with the former Czechoslovakia under normalisation, through exposing the processes of power in fiction and its consequences, through naming and renaming. 'The country in my story is not Pakistan, or not quite', it becomes 'the bilingual pun ... Peccavistan', (Rushdie, 1984: 86), as Kundera's Czechoslovakia becomes 'Bohemia'. Both novels are a 'leavetaking' (Rushdie, 1984: 88), apparently their 'last words on the East' (Rushdie, 1984: 28).

The similarity between Rushdie's and Kundera's novels perhaps arises because of their responses to similar cultural situations in their homelands, to their conditions of exile and to their dual identities. The hard-to-pin-down foreignness causes difficulty in defining either Kundera or Rushdie in relation to British culture. Jasper Rees criticises Kundera's adoption of France and bemoans the fact that 'Kundera gives no sign of having read anyone English', and then adds, 'apart from Sterne and Rushdie, hardly our most characteristic novelists' (Rees, 1996: 6–7). The question here lies in what constitutes a characteristic British novelist and whether Sterne's and Rushdie's hyphenised Anglo-identities have anything to do with not being characteristically British. Kundera's threat again is that his presence may inadvertently point out the foreignness in British culture. A way of avoiding this is to adopt Kundera as a British writer, which is an approach taken by Margaret Drabble, who includes him – but not (as a more usual appropriation) James Joyce – in the *Oxford Guide to English Literature* (Hawkins, 1999: 23).

Measuring Kundera's impact on the English language, George Steiner noted that 'the title of one of his fictions, *The Unbearable Lightness of Being*, has entered the language' (Steiner, 1998: 15). The statement reveals a paradox in the impact of Kundera's work in Britain: while the novel's title and Kundera himself have become common references in the British media and the particular novel remains a best-seller, it could be argued that both names have become a synecdoche for the entirety of his work. The constructed and temporarily accepted perceptions of who Kundera was, or is, and why he and his work are important, have evolved into self-referential symbols. The familiarity of the symbol, however, is not an innocent familiarity – it serves to belie the foreignness of the work.

What marks foreignness, and at the same time conceals it, is language. Although reviewers and critics refer to the novels as translations usually by commenting on the quality of the translations, the cultural differences between languages exposed by the translation process are ignored. If Kundera is received as 'almost another brilliant English writer' (Steiner, 1998: 15), and if even the pre-eminent translation scholar George Steiner eschews the relevance of examining the question of translation when reviewing Kundera's novels, then what is going to be overlooked is what has been concealed in the translation process – Kundera's linguistic project.

By dismissing the importance of translation, critics are also dismissing the primary mechanics of mediation from one culture to another. This facilitates a denial of any potential resistance in the work to its assimilation by focusing only on the assimilated text, which is seen as familiar rather than as having been made familiar. Kundera, in his first-ever contact with his British readers, as noted above, exposed the deliberate and admitted acculturation of *The Joke* through the translators' removal of material that they regarded to be culturally irrelevant to a British readership (Stallybrass, 1969a, 1969b). Later translations, when commented upon at all, are assumed to be in order because they read fluently in English (except for instances in which the translations are seen as too American). This reflects how the critics gauge the translations, ready to see the problematic of translation resolved because of the restrictions of not knowing Czech, and simply judging the English. In a review of *Identity* (1997) entitled 'Foreign but familiar', Victoria Moore writes that 'Kundera is the sort of foreign writer that anyone ought to be able to get to grips with. He may be a Czech but, fortunately for him, his writing isn't as impenetrable as his mother tongue ... Kundera's prose is as lucid and straightforward to the point of childlike simplicity' (Moore, 1998: 39). How it got to be that way, and what it means aesthetically, is seldom questioned (nor is there any mention that the novel was actually written in French). What is important is that the text is conveniently and readably familiar in English, even though it is by a foreign writer.

Kundera needs to be read as a translated writer not only because translation is pivotal in understanding his work, but because the concerns arising from any analysis of the resistance of translation question any use of language. The ultimate danger and beauty of seeing the work as foreign is that it unearths a foreignness in the familiar language itself (such as, for instance, in questioning the accepted uses of punctuation in any language). That the ambiguities of language harbour the ambiguities of interpretation should be an entry point for reading Kundera's work, or any work: Kundera's deliberate stylisation of this ambiguity through narrative or lyrical drive within his work is an open invitation to the reader to consider ways of unfamiliar reading that move beyond a certain text.

Kundera's reception in Britain has been extremely ambivalent, a result of several layers of mediation that have tended to assimilate the work by imposing domestic tropes of understanding. The inadequacy of this imposition and the subsequent overflow of what does not fit into accepted parameters challenge the existing readings, specifically the mechanism of stereotyping that makes the foreign familiar. While Kundera has received a great deal of exposure, most of it has involved only superficial and contingent interpretations that consolidate stereotypes. Kundera's complaint that his books, as best-sellers, are treated as 'current events' to be quickly consumed and forgotten seems to be supported by this kind of reception in Britain. Kundera writing on the perception of Aleksandr Dubček in the West could have been writing about himself: 'Western intellectuals ... often take an interest in events not in order to know them but so as to incorporate them into their own theoretical speculations ... In that way Alexander Dubcek [sic] may in some circumstances merge with Allende or Trotsky, in others with Lumumba or Che Guevara. [He] has been accepted, labelled – but remains unknown' (Saunders, 1993).

***

> *Every evil comes from the moment a false word is accepted. Capitulation begins there. One can make compromises with people, but never with words.* (Finkielkraut, 1982: 20)

Ironically, Kundera gives his readers and critics a path for the interpretation of his work. In the French version of *The Art of the Novel / L'art du roman* (1986) Kundera defines a word that appears constantly in his own literary criticism – mystification. He tells a story of Diderot, who at the age of 47 convinced a Marquis de Croismare that a young religious woman was seeking his protection. Diderot for months sent the Marquis letters full of emotion and signed by a woman who never existed. To a degree, this could be a metaphor for Kundera's own predicament; some critics insist on reading his interpretations as the letters from a religious signee rather than as from Diderot. This is not to say that Kundera is entirely playful in his assertions about his own work, but that his assertions are also not necessarily ones that purvey an orthodoxy of thought that insists on one reading of his own work, one imposed by Kundera himself.

Jungmann articulates well the kind of reading that places Kundera as the auto-didact of his own prose, within the prose as well as within his interviews regarding that prose:

> ... his analytical intellect forces him consistently to explain what is indicated in the plot, to articulate *verbis expresis* his thought, as if it was too enciphered in the picture ... Some situations are constructed so consciously, that the author assumes misunderstanding and rushes to help the reader by laying his thought in front of him ... All the time in Kundera's texts we meet the following phrases: 'Have you worked out this word?', 'Are you noting well this subtle difference?', 'We return again to the bowler hat!' or with the occasional questions, which are in no time answered with the definitiveness of an instruction: 'What is betrayal? Betrayal means, leaving the ranks ...', 'Why is ... idyll such an important word? ... the idyll is a picture, which stays in us like the memory of paradise ...' etc. These definitions of course are fit to the measurements of the situation and can be ceaselessly altered, as it is perhaps with the concept of kitsch: 'kitsch is the absolute denial of shit', 'kitsch is the cross-over stop between being and forgetting', 'the source of kitsch is the absolute agreement with being' and so on.
>
> Not satisfied however with narrative explanations, Kundera himself additionally develops the thought of his stories in many interviews, so the explanation is gone over for a second time, which proves that he realizes to what extent the fabula itself is not self-sufficient. (Jungmann, 1988: 220)

This reading is in direct opposition to the reading of, for example, Eva Le Grand, who argues that the constant questioning and the heteronomy of answers points to Kundera's construct of variation, allowing a heterogeneous voice that refuses to give one definition, one answer, and that this is the core of Kundera's novelistic poetics. Kundera's definition of 'DEFINITION' points to this: 'The novel's mediative texture is supported by the armature of a few abstract terms. If I hope to avoid falling into the slough where everyone thinks he understands everything without understanding anything, not only must I select those terms with utter precision, but I must define and redefine them ... A novel is often, it seems to me, nothing but a long quest for some elusive definitions' (Kundera, 1988a: 127). The question, then, as Jungmann poses it, is why does Kundera feel he needs to provide further exegesis in his dialogues, prefaces or critical essays? Or rather, what kind of answer does he give in this paratextual work? Is there a paradox between Kundera's asserting that the novel is a distinctive form because it is one that asks questions and refuses to answer them, and Kundera's informing his readers how to read these novels?

The crux is really this question of how to read the novels, or rather the manner in which Kundera suggests we read them. The issue is whether Kundera's instructions point to an explication of the meaning of the answers he purveys in the narrative writing or whether they point to a epistemological questioning of meaning itself. Kundera is perhaps most democratic in his 1962 postface to *The Keepers of the Keys*, in which, while dismissing the political interpretation of the play as the only one, he suggests that this interpretation is a possible one that lies alongside his own. Or, when he writes about *Farewell Waltz* (1976) in both *The Art of the Novel* (Kundera, 1988a: 139) and *Testaments Betrayed* (Kundera, 1996b: 6), discussing the oddity of other interpretations of the novel – a Scandinavian translator's and publisher's assumption that the novel's point is to convey an anti-abortion message and a medical professor's assumption that the novel was a celebration of artificial insemination that didn't go far enough – he does not suggest that they are wrong because there is a 'right' (i.e. Kundera's own) interpretation of the novel. Kundera's point in both these cases is that the translator and the professor have missed the 'moral ambiguity', the irony and humour, which are the signatures of any novel as a form. That they have interpreted the novel in such a way, Kundera argues, is a signal both of the success of the novel – it allows for a heterogeneity of interpretations – and also of the dangers of reduction; the novel is not just one moral justification for a single position but allows different characters to espouse different positions that are presented but not judged by the novelist.

This is reminiscent of Gyorgy Lukács' theory that irony is the mode in which the novel articulates itself, that the distance between what is said and what is meant by the author is self-reflexive to the extent that the reader can find that any truths posed are immediately to be questioned. Kundera writes, 'As God slowly departed from the seat whence he had directed the universe and its order of values, distinguished good from evil, and endowed each thing with meaning, Don Quixote set forth from his house into a world he could no longer recognize' (Kundera, 1988a: 6–7). The birth of the novel is equated with the birth of the modern era, of a world that is *Göttverlassenung*, where ambiguity reigns, because it can articulate it. Kundera argues that this is what makes the novel uncomfortable, as 'Man desires a world where good and evil can be clearly distinguished, for he has an innate and irrepressible desire to judge before he understands. Religions and ideologies are founded on this desire. They can cope with the novel only by translating its language of relativity and ambiguity into their own apodictic and dogmatic discourse' (1988a: 6–7).

Kundera argues that literary interpretation – whether by translator, reader, critic or journalist – is liable to constitute a 'translation' into their own values and thus directly oppose what the novel does, i.e. its demystification of epistemological orthodoxy. More than this, the mechanics of this very translation are consistently analysed within Kundera's novels and critical work. His interest in the creation of fiction is in its most human as well as its artistic level: how humans build the castles of their selves through their interpretation of life and ideas and how illusions are bred as defences for these castles. The novel, presenting different viewpoints, presents its complexity in looking through the chinks of these defences, in exposing illusion through the oppositional or complementary illusions of others (as in *The Joke*) or through the ironic distance of the narrator (as in his exile novels). Kundera's characters do not gain self-knowledge in his novels; they have it, but the point is that it is flawed, and while the reader can see it, the character cannot. This is the irony not only of the novel for Kundera, but of life.

Reading books or reading the world is not a transparent process but is presented as such in order to conceal the kind of mechanisms that Kundera returns to in his prose. Literary interpretation has itself to be analysed because it is a human and flawed act – Max Brod's interpretation of Kafka has as much more to do with Max Brod as it has with Kafka. The issue here is that one can argue that Kundera's role as a critic of his own work and others' carries with it the limitations he has set for himself. Kundera's essay on 'Central European' writers has its own agenda of establishing a sense of central, as opposed to eastern, Europe; his establishment of a canon of writers with whom he identifies has the concomitant effect of placing his own work within a pantheon a great writers. Kundera cannot provide a transparent school of Kunderian interpretation, but what he can do – and what he does – is suggest that the reader recognise agendas inherent in the interpretative process. It is easy to hoist Kundera with his own petard, to assume that his critique of others does not extend to himself because he does not provide – and the echo of communist ideology resurfaces – a self-critique. Yet inherent in his novels and in his essays is a constant revelation of interpretation as a translation of values: the field is open to readers to apply this to Kundera, but the question then becomes what are their respective agendas in doing so?

It is not a deflective manoeuvre but one that demands an active responsibility on the part of any interpreter, and it is not a comfortable demand. Some critics have reacted, as we have seen, by condemning Kundera because of his apparent detachment from, and his refusal to critique or even acknowledge, his own rewriting – of both his past and his work. Kundera's claim to be just a novelist has provoked charges that he has retreated into aesthetics, and yet this is exactly the site where issues of literary interpretation and responsibility are located. Kundera's redemption – the redemption of horror by its transformation into existential wisdom (the wisdom of the novel form) – is not the whitewash claimed by his opponents, the convenient forgetting of compromised moments. I suggest it is a responsible, even ethical, consideration of how we interpret the world and ourselves. The transparency that some critics demand – a revelation of Kundera's 'guilty' past – is not only itself portrayed as a transparent interpretation, but also serves to conceal as much as it chooses to reveal, a building of gulags, as Kundera has noted, beside André Breton's glass houses.

However, whatever your view on Kundera and his past, or the function of his paratextual work, what must be taken into account is the style and use of language in Kundera's novels (a style and use that translates into his critical work) as well as the effect of cultural translation and the incumbent loss of cultural shorthand on Kundera's language and on his self-revealing epistemological approach to writing. Kundera takes no prisoners in his paratextual writing, which seems intended not simply as an explanatory coda to his novelistic writing but also as an apology for interpretation. His repetitions of points made in the novels are not answers to them, but a reaction to the critical reception of them, a re-posing of what was missed. Kundera often points to the wilful or inadvertent inadequacies of current 'journalistic' interpretation, which makes little effort to understand. His urge to control his texts and the dissemination of them is based on a disillusioned knowledge and experience of how his own texts – and those of others – have been mediated. The disillusionment pertains not simply to Kundera's work but to his reading of life.

Chapter 6
Conclusion

After 1968, following the creative outpouring of the Prague Spring, the Soviet-backed hard-line regime introduced a period called '*normalizace*' or 'normalisation', which from 1970 onwards banned the works of the protagonists of the reform movement, including those by Milan Kundera. The 'civilised violence' (Šimečka, 1984: 77) of the regime, which introduced 'the re-establishment and consolidation of a Stalinist system' (Zdeněk Mlynář in Šimečka, 1984: 8), led to 'the imposition of strict ideological criteria whereby art in all its forms was to return to the mould of socialist realism and to the role of a didactic and militant instrument in the hands of the party' (Kusin, 1978: 106). The regime's realisation that plays, novels, poetry and songs could instigate significant social unrest and destabilise ideological norms led to overt censorship practices, imprisonment and exile. At the beginning of this politicised fossilisation of the arts, Kundera's work began to be translated in the West, an experience that Kundera described as traumatic and which he equated with the actions of the 'Moscow censors' (Kundera, 1969a: 1259). If one reads Kundera's 1969 open letter to his London publisher and translators in the *Times Literary Supplement*, the tone seems hysterical and pedantic. Yet his accusation of interference in the text in order to sell more books – not simply to the translators, but also, significantly, to the publisher – is embedded in the realisation that in the West too there existed what Translation Studies has identified as a modality of 'normalisation'.

Reading Kundera through the prism of recent movements in Translation Studies affords readers a more holistic sense of the issues surrounding the dissemination of his work and its interpretation, especially in the light of research on normalising practices in the 1980s and 1990s in the translation process. Normalising practices involve 'the exaggerated use in translated texts of features that are typical of the target language' (Kenny, 2001: 65) and 'may be said to occur when translators opt for conventional target-language solutions to problems posed by creative or unusual source text features'. (Kenny, 2001: 66) This may include changes in punctuation where, typically, it is strengthened in the target text in order to simplify the translation and make it 'more clear-cut' for the target-language reader (Baker, 1996: 182). These 'operational norms' (Toury, 1995) manifested in the target text are generally assumed to involve translatorial decisions that may subconsciously or deliberately reflect the current social or ideological norms of the given target culture.

These lexical norms, predicated on given societal norms, are articulated by a society at a given time in order to maintain its power discourse. The 'cultural turn' in Translation Studies, or, as Susan Bassnett argues, what has now become the 'translation turn' in Cultural Studies (Bassnett & Lefevere, 1998: 123), analyses how different cultures at different times use translated texts to consolidate and maintain dominant social and political discourses and practices. Translation, in effect, can become a means of intra- or inter-cultural domination and of appropriative representation of other cultures (Bassnett & Trivedi, 1999; Niranjana, 1992; Robinson, 1997). Social pressures on translators may be overt, as in the kind of ideological norms imposed on the translation process in communist Eastern Europe, or covert, as in the pressure of market demands in the globalised publishing industry today (Gentzler, 2001: 136; Venuti, 1998). The censorship of texts or translated texts, in other words, is not a practice limited to repressive political regimes but also occurs contemporaneously in the 'free' market, which demands that texts subscribe to norms in order to sell them. The dominance of the English-language market, in which only 2% of books sold are translations (Venuti, 1998), demands that those translations conform to paradigms of successful source-language texts. Internationally successful 'translated' writers (i.e. translated in the English-speaking book market), such as the Egyptian Nobel-Prize-winning writer Naguib Mahfouz, are often deemed to be successful because their writing (or the element of their writing chosen to be translated) already conforms to the expectations and norms of the English-language market (Jacquemond, 1992: 153). The effacement of stylistically different or difficult authors in the translation process in the English-language market parallels the effacement of the translation process itself. Michael Cronin divides the notion of translation and censorship into 'anthropoemic censorship' and 'anthropophagic censorship': the first describing an aggressive censorship policy towards translation; and the second describing a more covert censorship that denies translation as a process and the translator as an enabler or agent of translation (Cronin, 2003: 95–96). The 'invisibility' of the translator (Venuti, 1995) and the denial of translation as an issue can lead to a form of 'clonialism' (Cronin, 2003: 127), a desire to reproduce the same as the marketable. However, although the translation process and the skills of the translator are denied in this clonialism, they are also central to its propagation – with Cronin arguing that the notion of simulacra can be a destabilising force and can bring to the fore the beneficial modalities of counterfeiting and of the translator's primacy as an agent-copyist, a reader *par excellence* (Cronin, 2003: 130). In this case, can the translatorial moment destabilise the originary validation of norms in the very application of those norms?

Milan Kundera is an exemplary case and a timely case study for examining the effects of both anthropoemic and anthropophagic censorship and possible liberatory strategies for understanding these modalities and for escaping binary thinking in norms theories in Translation Studies. To date, critics have focused solely on Kundera's relationships with his translators as if this were the whole story, and this reflects a current tendency in Translation Studies to focus on the binary relationship of author / translator *in situ* of published texts in discussing the question of norms and normalisation. The archival material relating to Kundera – the archives of his editor at Knopf, Nancy Nicholas, and the archives of one of his translators, Peter Kussi – illustrate the complexity of the problem and help to situate questions of power, the market, editorial control, translatorial decision-making, the translator–editor relationship, and normalisation in a concrete rather than a speculative way.

A large part of this correspondence in both archives took place while Kundera was still living in Czechoslovakia (before his emigration in 1975) during *normalizace*, when there was an overt censorship of his work, i.e. when it was not published at all except abroad in translation (or, in the case of *Epilog / Farewell Waltz*, in *samizdat* editions). For Kundera, his publication in the West, a necessary lifeline, proved to be a disillusionment in two ways that relate to the question of norms: how his novels were translated and why. Kundera was uniquely famous in the 1960s for resisting the censor's pencil, not simply because of the ideological reasoning behind it, but also because of the lack of knowledge underlying it, the lack of interest in the aesthetics of the text. His reaction to the editorial pencil in the West – the indiscriminate alterations of punctuation, regardless of the aesthetic function of that punctuation – clearly parallels his experiences with more overt forms of censorship. Secondly, the ideological interests of the communist regime, in controlling and eliminating dissent, are also paralleled by the ideological interests in the West in publishing translations of Kundera's work in the first place.

The only golden age of translation into English for Czech writers was the late 1960s and early 1970s, following the Soviet invasion of Czechoslovakia in 1968. Kundera's first translated work, *The Joke*, was published in 1969 (London: Macdonald); Václav Havel's first translated work, *The Garden Party* was published in the same year (London: Cape); Ivan Klíma's *A Ship Named Hope* in 1970 (London: Gollancz); Josef Škvorecký's *The*

Cowards in the same year (London: Gollancz); and Ludvík Vaculík followed three years later with *The Axe* in 1973 (London: Deutsch). Czech writing to this day, 35 years later, is still represented in the English-language mainstream publishing world by four of these five writers: Kundera, Havel, Klíma and Škvorecký (though Havel's plays have been performed only sparsely in the UK). There has been a dearth of interest since the fall of communism in translating and publishing any other Czech writers. Kundera is explicit in his criticism of the uses of Czech writing when he began to be translated, when he believed there was overt political interest in translating 'dissident' voices in order to uphold Western ideological thinking in the Cold War. Translated Czech literature, as with translated Russian literature (May, 1994: 45) had a political function which allowed it to be translated (which the dystopian and disaffected novels of contemporary Russian writers such as Victor Pelevin and Andrey Kurkov may have today in their criticism of post-Soviet Russia and Ukraine).

Kundera is an important voice from the ex-East of Europe because he openly questioned the function of the initial translations of his work. In his 'Author's Note' to the 1983 English-language edition of *The Joke*, Kundera suggests that the problems with the translations were tied to the problems of interpretation, i.e. that the novel was read primarily as a political work that conformed to what the Western European market wanted from the novel. While not openly stated in his editor's archives, it is clear that to his editor, Nancy Nicholas, the import of Kundera's work lay in its content – what it said – rather than in its style – how it said it. For Kundera, the question of style is imperative to the content because the subversive element of writing is in the style of the writing – whether on the macrotextual level of the form of the novel or on the microtextual level of a word or a sentence. In effect, Kundera's two collections of essays, *The Art of the Novel* (1986) and *Testaments Betrayed* (1993), are manifestos to the emancipatory potential of style through the novel form and through the use of features such as repetition and punctuation. Kundera suggests that these new means of articulation can provide a new form of exegesis, just as the rhetorical strategies of philosophers carry the import of their messages (1996b: 112). The import of Kundera's dissent as a writer, in other words, is not rooted in politics but in epistemology.

As style is such a prime issue for Kundera, his work, and the translations of it, provides an instructive case study for Translation Studies. In his paratextual writing as well as in his novels (such as the 'Litost' section of *The Book of Laughter and Forgetting*), Kundera's self-reflexivity on style and the effects of translation foregrounds the difficult symbiotic relationship between form and content that is at the heart of the decision-making process in translation. His demand for fidelity to his writing style (and not, as Venuti argues about Kundera, to the signifieds of his source-language texts) could be seen as an endorsement of Philip E. Lewis's call for 'abusive fidelity', which calls for translators to privilege 'language texture' and the 'clusters of textual energy' in the text over 'a tendency ... to privilege the capture of signifieds, to give primacy to message, content, or concept' (Lewis, 1985: 41–43). Lewis's use of his theory from an analysis of his translation of Jacques Derrida's *La mythologie blanche* (1972) may have isolated his own theory from being used on a wider scale because of the perceived obscurity or trickiness of Derrida's own writing. However, Lewis's notion that style is often the very thing most ignored in translation, being seen as secondary to content, is extremely pertinent to translators for whom style is often, as May points out, a battleground, not only with the author, but, as we see in Kundera's case, with the editors and publishers as well as the censors (May, 1994: 6). In analysing the Nicholas and Kussi archives alongside Kundera's own writing on style, two very important issues arise for Translation Studies: first, the extent of editorial control on importing style; and, second, the implicit ideological stance behind these editorial decisions. In Kundera's case, his style was seen by Knopf and, earlier, Macdonald as being deficient (a) because it was identified as being a peculiarly Czechoslovak style and therefore inadequate for 'Western' norms, and (b) because it was not regarded as a marketable style – in needed to be changed in order to sell it within the constraints of what the publishers envisaged the function of his writing to be, i.e. social criticism.

Kundera situates himself very firmly in a European tradition – this is seen clearly in his references, from that to Cyrano in his very first prose work, and in, for instance, his use of classic French and Greek texts as *points de départs* for his three French-language novels. His decision to write novels is also based on an ongoing admiration for the European novelistic tradition – for Cervantes, Sterne and Diderot. Yet once his novels enter the English-language world, they encounter a resistance from the start, from the publishers through to the reviewers, who regard them as too different from the accepted norms (so therefore they need to be altered) but who also view them as concomitantly deficient (so therefore they need to be improved). These hegemonic assumptions then pervade the translation and, as a result, the reception of the novels, within an intra-European context. This leads to two questions that could usefully be explored in Translation Studies: firstly, if the style of a writer steeped in European traditions and writing is regarded as too different, what other non-European styles are being ignored or left untranslated and unpublished and how detrimental is this to our notion of epistemological understanding? Secondly, how is our notion of European style attenuated by the demands of occidental publishing houses?

Translation Studies has tended to focus on case studies of major world languages: English (in the anglocentric and ex-colonial world), French (in the francophone world), German, Spanish, Italian, Arabic, Chinese and, to some extent, Russian. Case studies such as that of Kundera suggest that there needs to be an analysis of translations from so-called 'minority languages', and certainly one of the areas that has been ignored is ex-Eastern Europe: Central Europe and the Balkans, for instance. While the application of Post-colonial Studies to Translation Studies has provided fertile analyses of the impact of and agendas in cross-cultural transfer, it has tended not to analyse intra-European power relationships, apart from the case of Ireland (Cronin, 1996; Tymoczko, 1999). An analysis of translations from the languages of the 'other Europe' (Rupnik, 1988) may, in effect, open up more diverse avenues for understanding interculturality and plurilingualism within Europe, and in understanding a Europe that is not wholly occidental. 'It often strikes me', Kundera writes, 'that the known European culture harbours within it another unknown culture made up of little nations with peculiar languages [...] The Europe made up of little countries is *another Europe*; it offers another perspective ...' (Kundera, 1985d: 87). Kundera, having written in Czech and French, is as prime an example of a writer from a plurilingual Europe as the far more analysed (in respect of language and translation) Samuel Beckett (Edwards, 1992; Fitch, 1988; Friedman *et al.*, 1987).

Here the questions of style and status of language meet. 'The Czech language, so inaccessible to foreigners', Kundera also wrote, 'has always stood as an opaque glass between Prague and the rest of Europe. Everything known about my country, outside the borders of Bohemia, has been known at second hand' (Kundera, 1985d: 87). Kundera's stylistic tendencies were exacerbated by translation – through the rereading of his novels when checking their translations and in his rewriting (as a result) and writing of novels, in the full knowledge that they would almost entirely be read in translation. In other words, they would always be read 'secondhand'. Kundera, the *scriba duplex*, began writing and rewriting in a secondhand way, self-consciously crafting the linguistic style of the novels in a way in which he could engage with translation at first hand. In essence, taking Lewis's concept of 'abusive fidelity' and Cronin's notion of counterfeiting and simulacra within 'clonialism', I suggest that Kundera engages in a form of abusive writing predicated on a full awareness of a positive second-handedness. The displacement of the language (Czech) of his novels, because his readership was largely non-Czech speaking, becomes central to the epistemological goals of the novels and is intricately tied into their rhetorical style. It is this displacement that has caused most discomfort with Kundera's publishers and reviewers, by whom the style is seen as foreign, and perhaps more so once he begins writing in French. For what Kundera translates (in the sense of transposing) from his Czech writing to his French is this style, borne in a 'minority language' and incubated in translation. In doing this, he postulates that language is itself foreign, destabilised, as often misinterpreted as interpreted.

Kundera's control over his texts (won only after becoming a best-selling author) has itself been read as a form of censorship – Venuti arguing that Kundera 'wishes to control the interpretations put forward by French and English translators [...] on the basis of the author's sheer disagreement with them' (Venuti, 1998: 5). Yet Kundera does not attempt to normalise his texts when he becomes involved in creating definitive versions. Here, the second-handedness of Kundera's writing is spread across the matrices of his 'originals': his manuscripts, Czech versions and definitive French versions, according to Kundera, but also different language editions (i.e. the definitive English editions of his novels or, for instance, the Spanish and German editions of *Laughable Loves*). Kundera certainly abuses his position as a writer with cultural capital, and also his position as a translator, in the sense of which Lewis postulates a notion of abuse. In allowing different definitive versions to exist, in re-engaging in his own texts through retranslation with the 'modalities of expression' and the 'rhetorical strategies' in the texts (Lewis, 1985: 42), Kundera produces a 'threshold' of interpretation (Gaddis Rose, 1997: 7; Mehrez, 1992: 122) rather than an emergency exit.

Umberto Eco, in considering his own experience as a translator and translatee, turns his gaze to James Joyce, who participated in the Italian translation of *Finnegans Wake* and ultimately changed the text quite radically. Eco writes: 'Many have written that, to understand *Finnegans Wake*, it would be a good idea to start with his Italian translation of it. Perhaps, or rather certainly because, on seeing the text wholly rethought in another language, one can understand its deep mechanisms, over and beyond the insistence on this or that play of quotations' (Eco, 2001: 115). Should translation activity, then, involve more interpretation rather than less – a crossing of the threshold rather than an uncertain hovering upon it? Should we not regard the translator's position as advantageous, as a vanguard reader, and is it possible to see the likes of writers such as Joyce and Kundera as prototypes of these translators? Though both inhabited a privileged position as a writer of a supposed (though, in both cases, not actual) 'original text', both were also marginalised in exile, banned in their home countries and forced, almost exclusively, to depend on their translations – both became actively involved in their translations, and translation was a large factor leading to their canonisation. Writers are often privy to the meanings of their texts in a way perhaps that other readers are not, but close readers and collaborators are often very aware of the 'deep mechanisms' of the texts, because these often represent the problematic areas that need to be disentangled, parsed, challenged, reread, translated.

Reading a tri- or pluri-lingual corpus of one author's work, given, in addition, that author's sensitivity to translation and the translation process, is an exegetical threshold that opens onto paths moving towards an understanding of the 'deep mechanisms' of their work. Situating that corpus in the given cultural, intercultural and historical contexts in which the various individual versions appeared allows for additional forms of understanding and interpretation, often through reading the processes of misinterpretation and misunderstandings – indeed, Kundera's case could be seen as one exemplifying a form of 'misinterpreting studies'. It is not the lack of skills of an individual translator that drives this misinterpretation, but rather the general negative or dismissive attitudes towards translation on the part of many institutions and individuals holding cultural power: publishers, editors, newspapers and universities. We should explore further the normalisation of texts as they enter the English-speaking world and the Occident not simply through the lens of the translator's actions but also through examining who or what is pressurising this translator's decisions – through interviewing translators, investigating publishers' archives, analysing university syllabi and in analysing the reception of the translations? Would this allow both Translation Studies and Literary Studies to escape the traditional author–translator dyad as all these areas are related and need to be empirically studied in their interconnections?

Kundera's distrust of outside interventions in any versions of his texts arises in part from a personal and apparently irrational need to control them, but it is also clear that this need was born of experiences of censorship in pre- and post-1968 Czechoslovakia and, then, of his experiences with mainstream publishers in the West. The discomfort with, and more importantly *of*, Kundera's writing is its teleological worth. As with any writing of strong literary worth, it promises new forms of experiential articulation that will always, at first, seem a bad fit because they are foreign to any reader. Yet it is the form, the author's style, that is, Kundera argues, perhaps the most translatable element of a text, even if it is also the most potentially destabilising aspect of it for a receiving culture. Kundera's negotiations, with translators, publishers and readers, through his paratextual work, read together and read with an understanding of the actual translation processes his texts undergo, articulate a modality for reading newness. Herein lies the paradox of negotiation and ultimatum, forced onto Kundera's work (and making it bloom), because, to paraphrase Kundera, it lived in translation: 'One can make compromises with people', Kundera writes, 'but never with words' (Finkielkraut, 1982: 20).

Bibliography

Álvarez, R. and Vidal, M. (eds) (1996) *Translation, Power, Subversion*. Clevedon: Multilingual Matters.
Bailey, P. (1995) Facing the shock of the new. *Daily Telegraph*, 23 September: X pars. *The Telegraph* on CD-ROM. British Library Newspapers, London. (June 2003).
Baker, M. (1996) Corpus-based translation studies: The challenges that lie ahead. In Harold Somers (ed.) *Terminology, LSP and Translation: Studies in Language Engineering in Honour of Juan C. Sager* (pp.175–86). Amsterdam & Philadelphia: John Benjamins.
Bassnett, S. (ed.) (2003) *Studying British Cultures*. London: Routledge.
Bassnett, S. and Lefevere, A. (eds) (1998) *Constructing Cultures*. Clevedon: Multilingual Matters.
Bassnett, S. and Trivedi, H. (1999) *Post-colonial Translation: Theory and Practice*. London: Routledge.
Bauer, M. (1998a) Mystifikátor Milan Kundera. *Tvar* 14, 12–13.
Bauer, M. (1998b) Překladatelská činnost Milana Kundery na přelomu 40. a 50. let. *Tvar*, 5, 6–7.
Bauer, M. (2000) Milan Kundera pod dvěma tyraniemi. *Tvar* 13, 1–5.
Benjamin, W. (1967) *Illuminations*. New York: Schocken.
Bílek, P. (1996) Kunderovské anglofonní reflexe. *Tvar* 14, 17–18.
Billington, G. (1991) The echoing village. *Guardian* 22 July, 30.
Biron, N. (1979) Entretien avec Milan Kundera. *Liberté* (21) 17–33.
Bold, A. (1982) Half-love, half-joke. *Times Literary Supplement (TLS)*, 5 February, 131.
Borges, J.L. (1977) *Prólogos: Con un prólogo de prólogos*. Buenes Aires: Torres Agüero Editor.
Brodsky, J. (1987) *Less Than One: Selected Essays*. Harmondsworth: Penguin.
Chvatík, K. (1989) Milan Kundera and the crisis of language. James Fearns, trans. *Review of Contemporary Fiction* (9) 27–36.
Chvatík, K. (1994) *Svět románů Milana Kundery*. Brno: Atlantis.
Coe, J. (1991) Author in his own intrigue. *Guardian* 16 May, 24.
Connelly, K. (1998) Take that, you damned philistine! *Guardian* 30 September, 10.
Crain, C. (1999) Infidelity. *Lingua Franca* October, 39–50.
Cronin, M. (1996) *Translating Ireland: Translation, Languages, Cultures*. Cork: Cork University Press.
Cronin, M. (2003) *Translation and Globalization*. London: Routledge.
Curtis, A. (1991) Shades of Kafka in a struggle for integrity. *Financial Times* 26 October, 18.
Davidson, M. (1992) Ten years of fiction: Exhuming corpses and ideas – Cult Novels 1982–92. *Daily Telegraph*, 1 September: X pars. *The Telegraph* on CD-ROM. British Library Newspapers, London. (June 2003).
Dyer, G. (1995) Some serious joking. *Daily Telegraph*, 16 September: X pars. *The Telegraph* on CD-ROM. British Library Newspapers, London. (June 2003).

Dyer, G. (2000) No ideas please, we're British. *Guardian* 4 November, 9.
Eagleton, T. (1987) Estrangement and irony. *Salmagundi* (73) 23–32.
Eagleton, T. (1989) Bakhtin, Schopenauer, Kundera. In K. Hirschkop and D. Shepherd *Bakhtin and Cultural Theory* (pp. 178–88). Manchester: Manchester University Press.
Eco, U. (2001) *Experiences in Translation*. Toronto, Buffalo, London: University of Toronto Press.
Edwards, M. (1992) Beckett's French. *Translation and Literature* (1), 68–83.
Elgrably, J. (1987) Conversations with Milan Kundera. *Salmagundi* (73), 3–24.
Fantys, P. (1999) Autor, který provokuje svým dílem i postoji. *Lidové noviny* 31 March, 21.
Finkielkraut, A. (1982) Milan Kundera interview. *Cross Currents* (20), 15–29.
Fitch, B.T. (1988) *Beckett and Babel: An Investigation into the Status of the Bilingual Work*. Toronto: University of Toronto Press.
Friedman, A., Rossman C. and Sherzer, D. (eds) (1987) *Beckett Translating/Translating Beckett*. Pennsylvania: Pennsylvania University Press.
Gaddis Rose, M. (1997) *Translation and Literary Criticism: Translation as Analysis*. Manchester: St. Jerome.
Garfinkle, D. (1999) Betraying K: Milan Kundera on exile and the translator's art. *Modern Czech Studies*. Brown Slavic Contributions (XI), 54–64.
Garton-Ash, T. (1987) Prague – A poem, not disappearing. In Jan Vladislav (ed.) *Václav Havel: Living in Truth* (pp. 213–21). London: Faber and Faber.
Garton-Ash, T. (1998) The moral leader of Europe. *Independent* 21 October, 5.
Genette, G. (1997) *Paratexts: Thresholds of Interpretation*. Cambridge: Cambridge University Press.
Gentzler, E. (1993) *Contemporary Translation Theories*. London and New York: Routledge.
Gentzler, E. (2001) *Contemporary Translation Theories* (2nd edn). Clevedon: Multilingual Matters.
Gilbey, R. (1996) If anyone can, Ken can. *Independent* 5 April, 6–7.
Grayson, J. (1977) *Nabokov Translated: A Comparison of Nabokov's Russian and English Prose*. Oxford: Oxford University Press.
Gross, T. (1994) Cold war divides the authors of Prague's new spring. *Daily Telegraph*, 16 October: X pars. *The Telegraph* on CD-ROM. British Library Newspapers, London. (June 2003).
Gupta, P. (1998) Post- or neo-colonial translation? Linguistic inequality and translator's resistance. *Translation and Literature* (7), 170–93.
Hamšík, D. (1971) *Writers Against Rulers*. D. Orpington, trans. London: Hutchinson.
Hawkins, T. (1999) Good company despite the lists. *Times Higher Educational Supplement* 23 April, 23.
Hawtree, C. (1984) The unbearable lightness of being. *Spectator* 23 June, 29.
Heaney, S. (1999) *Beowulf*. London: Faber and Faber.
Heffer, S. (1993) England expects … *Daily Telegraph*, 18 July: X pars. *The Telegraph* on CD-ROM. British Library Newspapers, London. (June 2003).
Heim, M. (1972) Moravian folk music: A Czechoslovak novelist's view. *Journal of the Folklore Institute* (9), 45–53.
Hoffman, M. (1996) Euro doleurs. *Observer* 10 November, 17.
Hoggart, R. (1991) The abuses of literacy. *Guardian* 27 June, 21.
Hybler, M. (1998) Principálovy starosti. *Revolver Revue: Kritická příloha* (12), 79–83.

Bibliography

Jacquemond, R. (1992) In Lawrence Venuti (ed.) Translation and cultural hegemony: The case of French–Arabic translation. *Rethinking Translation: Discourse, Subjectivity, Ideology* (pp. 139–58). London and New York: Routledge.
Jakobson, R. (1990) On linguistic aspects of literature. *Language and Literature* (pp. 428–35). Cambridge: Belknap Harvard Press.
Jefferson, A. (1991) Counterpoint and forked tongues: Milan Kundera and the art of exile. *Renaissance and Modern Studies* (34), 115–36.
Jungmann, M. (1988) Kunderovské paradoxy. In *Cesty a rozcestí: Kritické stati* (pp.214–54). London: Rozmluvy.
Jungmann, M. (1997) Ironikovy krásné provokace. *Týden* (12), 74–82.
Keane, D. (1994) What I think. *Daily Mail* 22 May, 33.
Keates, J. (1998) The shock waves of recognition. *Independent* 11 April, 15.
Kemp, P. (1984) A personal history. *TLS* 1 June, 614.
Kenny, D. (2001) *Lexis and Creativity in Translation: A Corpus-based Study*. Manchester: St. Jerome.
Knapp, A. (2000) Španělská cesta Milana Kundery. *Respekt* (32), 19.
Kosková, H. (1998) *Milan Kundera*. Prague: H&H.
Kratochvíl, J. (1995) *Príběhy příběhů*. Brno: Atlantis.
Kuhiwczak, P. (1990) Translation as appropriation: The case of Milan Kundera's *The Joke*. In Susan Bassnett and André Lefevere (eds) *Translation, History, Culture* (pp. 118–30). London: Cassell.
Kundera, M. (1960) *Umění románu*. Prague: Československý spisovatel.
Kundera, M. (1962) *Majitelé klíčů*. Prague: Československý spisovatel.
Kundera, M. (1963) *Směšné lásky: Tři melancholický anekdoty*. Prague: Československý spisovatel.
Kundera, M. (1967) *Žert*. Prague: Československý spisovatel.
Kundera, M. (1968) *La plaisanterie*. Paris: Gallimard. (Trans. by Marcel Aymonin.)
Kundera, M. (1969a) The joke. *TLS* 30 October, 1259.
Kundera, M. (1969b) *Žert*. Prague: Československý spisovatel. (3rd edn).
Kundera, M. (1970a) *Směšné lásky*. Prague: Československý spisovatel.
Kundera, M. (1970b) *The Joke*. Harmondsworth: Penguin. (2nd rev. trans. by David Hamblyn and Oliver Stallybrass.)
Kundera, M. (1973) *La vie est ailleurs*. Paris: Gallimard. (Trans. by François Kérel.)
Kundera, M. (1974) *Life is Elsewhere*. New York: Alfred Knopf. (Trans. by Peter Kussi.)
Kundera, M. (1975) *Laughable Loves*. Harmondsworth: Penguin. (Trans. by Suzanne Rapapport,1974.)
Kundera, M. (1976a) *La valse aux adiex*. Paris: Gallimard. (Trans. by François Kérel.)
Kundera, M. (1976b) *The Farewell Party*. London: Faber and Faber. (Trans. by Peter Kussi.)
Kundera, M. (1977) 'Comedy is Everywhere', *Index on Censorship*, 6, pp. 3–7.
Kundera, M. (1979a) *Le livre du rire et de l'oublie*. Paris: Gallimard. (Trans. by François Kérel.)
Kundera, M. (1979b) *Valčík na rozloučenou*. Toronto: Sixty-Eight Publishers.
Kundera, M. (1979c) *Život je jinde*. Toronto: Sixty-Eight Publishers.
Kundera, M. (1980) *La plaisanterie*. Paris: Gallimard. (Trans. by Marcel Aymonin, rev. by Milan Kundera and Claude Courtot.)
Kundera, M. (1981a) *Jacques et son maître*. Paris: Gallimard.
Kundera, M. (1981b) *Kniha smíchu a zapomnění*. Toronto: Sixty-Eight Publishers.
Kundera, M. (1983) Janáček: He saw the coming night. *Cross Currents* (23), 371–80.
Kundera, M. (1984a) A kidnapped west or culture bows out. *Granta* (11), 95–118.

Kundera, M. (1984b) *Risibles amours*. Paris: Gallimard. (Trans. by François Kérel, 2nd rev. by Milan Kundera.)
Kundera, M. (1984c) *The Joke*. Harmondsworth: Penguin. (3rd rev. trans. (1983) by Michael Henry Heim.)
Kundera, M. (1985a) *La plaisanterie*. Paris: Gallimard. (Trans. by Milan Kundera.)
Kundera, M. (1985b) *Nesnesitelná lehkost bytí*. Toronto: Sixty-Eight Publishers.
Kundera, M. (1985c) *The Unbearable Lightness of Being*. London: Faber and Faber. (Trans. by Michael Henry Heim, 1984.)
Kundera, M. (1985d) Prague: A disappearing poem. *Granta* (17), 85–103. (Trans. by Edmund White.)
Kundera, M. (1986a) *Jacques and his Master*. London: Faber and Faber. (Trans. by Simon Callow.)
Kundera, M. (1986b) *L'art du roman*. Paris: Gallimard.
Kundera, M. (1986c) *La valse aux adiex*. Paris: Gallimard. (Trans. by François Kérel, rev. by Milan Kundera.)
Kundera, M. (1986d) *Risibles amours*. Paris: Gallimard. (Trans. by François Kérel, 3rd rev. by Milan Kundera.)
Kundera, M. (1987a) *La vie est ailleurs*. Paris: Gallimard. (Trans. by François Kérel, rev. by Milan Kundera.)
Kundera, M. (1987b) *Le livre du rire et de l'oublie*. Paris: Gallimard. (Trans. by François Kérel, rev. by Milan Kundera.)
Kundera, M. (1987c) *Life is Elsewhere*. London: Faber and Faber. (Rev. trans. by Peter Kussi, 1986.)
Kundera, M. (1988a) *The Art of the Novel*. London: Faber and Faber. (Trans. by Linda Asher, 1988.)
Kundera, M. (1988b) *The Book of Laughter and Forgetting*. Harmondsworth: Penguin. (Trans. by Michael Henry Heim, 1980.)
Kundera, M. (1991a) *Immortality*. London: Faber and Faber. (Trans. by Peter Kussi.)
Kundera, M. (1991b) *Směšné lásky*. Brno: Atlantis (3rd edn).
Kundera, M. (1991c) *Žert*. Brno: Atlantis (4th edn).
Kundera, M. (1992) *Jakub a jeho pán*. Brno: Atlantis.
Kundera, M. (1993a) Krásný jak mnohonásobné setkání. In Patrick Chamoiseau *Solibo Ohromný* (pp.187–204). Brno: Atlantis.
Kundera, M. (1993b) *Nesmrtelnost*. Brno: Atlantis.
Kundera, M. (1993c) *The Joke*. New York: Harper Collins. (4th rev. trans. (1992) by Milan Kundera.)
Kundera, M. (1995) *La lenteur*. Paris: Gallimard.
Kundera, M. (1996a) *Slowness*. London: Faber and Faber. (Trans. by Linda Asher.)
Kundera, M. (1996b) *Testaments Betrayed*. London: Faber and Faber. (Trans. by Linda Asher, 1995.)
Kundera, M. (1996c) The painter's brutal gesture. In France Borel *Bacon: Portraits and Self-Portraits* (pp. 8–18). London: Thames and Hudson.
Kundera, M. (1997a) *L'identité*. Paris: Gallimard.
Kundera, M. (1997b) *Valčík na rozloučenou* (2nd edn). Brno: Atlantis.
Kundera, M. (1998a) *Farewell Waltz*. London: Faber and Faber. (Rev. trans. by Aaron Asher.)
Kundera, M. (1998b) *Identity*. London: Faber and Faber. (Trans. by Linda Asher.)
Kundera, M. (1999a) *Laughable Loves*. London: Faber and Faber. (Rev. trans. by Aaron Asher.)

Kundera, M. (1999b) *The Book of Laughter and Forgetting*. New York: HarperCollins. (Rev. trans. by Aaron Asher, 1996.)
Kundera, M. (2000) *Life is Elsewhere*. London: Faber and Faber. (2nd rev. trans. by Aaron Asher.)
Kundera, M. (2002) *Ignorance*. London: Faber and Faber. (Trans. by Linda Asher.)
Kundera, M. (2003) *L'ignorance*. Paris: Gallimard.
Kusin, V. (1978) *From Dubček to Charter 77*. Edinburgh. Q Press.
Kussi, P. (1991) Několik poznámek o překladání Milana Kundery. *Proměny* (28), 68–70.
Lebrecht, N. (1995) Many strings, several bows. *Daily Telegraph*, 7 August: X pars. *The Telegraph* on CD-ROM. British Library Newspapers, London. (June 2003).
Lefevere, A. (1992) *Translation, Rewriting, and the Manipulation of Literary Fame*. London and New York: Routledge.
Le Grand, E. (1999) *Kundera or the Memory of Desire*. Waterloo: Wilfrid Laurier University Press. (Trans. by Lin Burman.)
Lewis, J. (1977) Fiction review. *The Times* 3 November, 12.
Lewis, P.E. (1985) The measure of translation effects. In J.F. Graham (ed.) *Difference in Translation* (pp. 31–62). Ithaca and London: Cornell University Press.
Liehm, A. (1976) *The Politics of Culture*. New York: Grove Press. (Trans. by Peter Kussi.)
Lodge, D. (1984a) From Don Juan to Tristan. *TLS* 25 May, 567–68.
Lodge, D. (1984b) Milan Kundera, and the idea of the author in modern criticism. *Critical Quarterly* (26) 105–21.
Lukeš, J. (1997) Milan Kundera: Dílo a jeho pán. *Týden* (12), 78–87.
MacGibbon, J. (1969a) The joke. *TLS* 13 November, 1312.
MacGibbon, J. (1969b) The joke. *TLS* 6 November, 1282.
May, R. (1994) *The Translator in the Text: On Reading Russian Literature in English*. Evanston: Northwestern University Press.
Mehrez, S. (1992) Translation and the postcolonial experience: The Francophone North African text. In Lawrence Venuti (ed.) *Rethinking Translation: Discourse, Subjectivity, Ideology* (pp. 120–37). London and New York: Routledge.
Moore, V. (1998) Foreign but familiar. *Daily Mail* 28 March, 39.
Murray, D. (1992) Digging for fire. *Financial Times* 25 March, 17.
Neely, B. (1999) Serbs rewrite history of Racak massacre. *Independent* 23 January, 13.
Němcová-Banerjee, M. (1990) *Terminal Paradoxes: The Novels of Milan Kundera*. London: Faber and Faber.
Niranjana, T. (1992) *Siting Translation: History, Poststructuralism, and the Colonial Context*. Berkeley and Los Angeles: University of California Press.
Oppenheim, L. (1989) Clarifications, elucidations: An interview with Milan Kundera. *Review of Contemporary Fiction* (9), 7–11.
Pilger, J. (1998) Freedom next time. *Guardian* 11 April, 14.
Pizzichini, L. (1998) Paperbacks. *Sunday Independent* 13 September, 13.
Plummer, S. and Holloway, D. (1992) Paperbacks. *Sunday Telegraph*, 12 April: X pars. *The Telegraph* on CD-ROM. British Library Newspapers, London. (June 2003).
Porter, R. (1975) Freedom is my love: The works of Milan Kundera. *Index on Censorship* (4), 41–46
Porter, R. (1981) *Milan Kundera – A Voice From Central Europe*. Aarhus: Arkona.
Rabinovitch, D. (1999) Czech mating game. *The Independent* 28 August, 11.
Rees, J. (1992) Ten years of fiction: The daunting aggregations of consonants. *Daily Telegraph* 1 September: X pars. *The Telegraph* on CD-ROM. British Library Newspapers, London. (June 2003).

Rees, J. (1994) Metamorphosis is the Trial. *Daily Telegraph*, 10 December: X pars. *The Telegraph* on CD-ROM. British Library Newspapers, London. (June 2003).
Rees, J. (1996) Being an icon is almost unbearable. *Independent* 12 April, 6–7.
Remnick, D. (1997) Exile on Main Street. *New Yorker* 15 September, 42.
Ricard, F. (2003) *Agnes's Final Afternoon: An Essay on the Work of Milan Kundera*. New York: HarperCollins. (Trans. by Aaron Asher.)
Richterová, S. (1986) *Slova a ticho*. Munich: Edice Arkýř, Karel Jadrný Verlag.
Rinaldi, A. (1990) Kundera, mort pour la gloire. *L'express*, 19 January, 60–61.
Robinson, D. (1997) *Translation and Empire: Postcolonial Theories Explained*. Manchester: St Jerome.
Rogaly, J. (1991) Metaphors of being. *Financial Times* 18 May, 20.
Rupnik, J. (1988) *The Other Europe*. London: Weidenfeld and Nicolson.
Rushdie, S. (1984) *Shame*. London: Picador.
Rushdie, S. (1999) *The Ground Beneath Her Feet*. London: Picador.
Samson, I. (1998) Life sentence. *Guardian* 12 December, 11.
Saunders, F. (1993) Reluctant lumberjack. *Daily Telegraph*, 22 May: X pars. *The Telegraph* on CD-ROM. British Library Newspapers, London. (June 2003).
Scammel, M. (2001) The servile path: Translating Nabokov by epistle. *Harpers* 308 (May), 52–60.
Sedláček, T. (1995) Všechno bylo pro mne jediné překvapení. *Lidové noviny*. 30 October, 14.
Šimečka, M. (1984) *The Restoration of Order*. London: Verso.
Sinclair, C. (1983) The banana-skin of history. *TLS* 18 February, 149.
Slomek, J. (2000) Ironický a skeptický vypravěč Milan Kundera. *Lidové noviny*, 27 July, 32.
Smith, A. (2001) Last of the action heroes. *Observer* Life Section, 1 April, 6.
Stallybrass, O. (1969a) The joke. *TLS* 20 November, 1339
Stallybrass, O. (1969b) The joke. *TLS* 6 November, 1282–83.
Stanger, A. (1997) In Search of *The Joke*: An Open Letter to Milan Kundera. *New England Review* (18), 93–100.
Steiner, G. (1998) She's scared to blink in case her man turns into somebody else. *Observer* 19 April, 15.
Theim, J. (1995) The translator as hero in postmodern fiction. *Translation and Literature* (4), 207–18.
Tonkin, B. and Miller, L. (1997) Paperbacks. *Independent* 4 January, 7.
Toury, G. (1995) *Descriptive Translation Studies and Beyond*. Amsterdam and Philadelphia: John Benjamins.
Tymoczko, M. (1999) *Translation in a Postcolonial Context*. Manchester: St Jerome.
Uhdeová, J. (1993) Mini-interviews Jitkou Uhdeovou. *Labyrint* (9–10), 4.
(Unattrib.) (2000) Classicwatch: New editions of old favourites. *Observer* 24 September, 14.
(Unattrib.) (1996) The best of summer reading. *Independent* 14 July, 28–29.
(Unattrib.) (1973) Women award Prix Femina to male writer. *The Times* 27 November, 9.
Venuti, L. (1992) (ed.) *Rethinking Translation: Discourse, Subjectivity, Ideology*. London and New York: Routledge.
Venuti, L. (1995) *The Translator's Invisibility: A History of Translation* (London and New York: Routledge.
Venuti, L. (1998) *The Scandals of Translation: Towards an Ethics of Difference*. London and New York: Routledge.

Bibliography

Verecký, L. (2001) Milan Kundera: Spisovatel, který se skrývá. *Lidové noviny*, 29 November, 6.
Walker, P. (1997) Free to take your clothes off. *Sunday Independent* 27 July, 26.
Weiss, J. (1986) An interview with Milan Kundera. *New England Review and Bread Loaf Quarterly* (8), 407–10.
Weissbort, D. (1998) His own translator: Joseph Brodsky. *Translation and Literature* (7), 101–12.
Whittell, I. (2001) Liverpool are back. *Observer* Sport, 18 February, 9.
Williams, R. (1996) First man who needs a sting in his tale. *Guardian* 31 December, 22.
Woods, M. (2001) Original and translation in Milan Kundera's Czech fiction. *Translation and Literature* (10), 200–21.
Woods, M. (2002) Lost letters: Translating Milan Kundera's Czech fiction. PhD thesis, Trinity College Dublin.
Woods, M. (2003) A very British Bohemian? The reception of Milan Kundera and his work in Great Britain. *Kosmas* 16 (Spring), 27–43.
Wullschlager, J. (1992) The lightness of being. *Financial Times* 3 October, 17.
Zimra, C. (1991) From lightness to immortality: Kundera's incestextual abyss. In Aaron Aji (ed.) *Milan Kundera and the Art of Fiction* (pp. 320–47). New York: Garland.

Index

Aaron Asher Books, 40
Alfred A. Knopf, 31-7, 40, 57, 68, 83, 182, 184
Allende, Salvador, 174
American Poetry Review, 33
Arena, 164
Aristophanes,
 – *Lysistrata*, 12
Asher, Aaron, vii, 3, 26, 37-41, 45, 50, 51-2, 54, 56-7, 67, 80, 81, 83, 102, 108, 110, 111
Asher, Linda, 40
Atherton, Mike, 170
Aymonin, Marcel, 28, 70

Bailey, Paul, 167
Balzac, Honoré de, 120
Basnický almanac, 60
Bassnett, Susan, 12, 15, 161, 181
Bauer, Michal, 6, 65, 87, 96, 103, 154-5, 157, 160
Beckett, Samuel, xi, 2, 15, 127, 185
 – *Quatres poèmes*, 15
Benjamin, Walter, 9
Bílek, Petr, 155
Boccaccio, Giovanni, vii, 51, 94
Bold, Alan, 171
Borges, Juan Luis, 84, 169
Brandys, Kazimierz, 119, 149
Breton, André, 178
Broch, Hermann, 76
Brod, Max, 177
Brodsky, Joseph, xi, 15, 16, 27, 119

Calvino, Italo, 169
Černý, Václav, 149
Cervantes, Miguel de, 184
 – *Don Quixote*, 177
Chamoiseau, Patrick, 21

Chopin, Frédéric, 68
Chvatík, Květoslav, 21, 60, 72, 105, 146, 153, 155-9
 – *Svět románů Milana Kundery*, 60
Clementis, Vladimír, 19, 90
Coe, Jonathan, 171
Connelly, Kate, 167
Crain, Caleb, 4, 6, 65, 145, 159-160
Cricketer's Who's Who, 170
Cronin, Michael, 13, 181-2, 185

Davidson, Max, 169, 170
Denon, Vivant, 21, 122, 123, 125-127
 – *Point de Lendemain*, 21, 125-6
Derrida, Jacques, 10, 15, 19, 184
 – *La mythologie blanche*, 10, 184
Diderot, Jacques, 15, 20, 67, 134, 175, 184
 – *Jacques Le Fataliste*, 134
Drabble, Margaret, 173
Dubček, Aleksandr, 165, 174
Dyer, Geoff, 168, 171

Eco, Umberto, 160, 169, 186
Esquire, 32

Faber & Faber Publishers, 61, 166
Fantys, Petr, 151-2
Faulkner, William, 7, 35
Fikar, Ladislav, 60
Flaubert, Gustave, 63, 99
 – *Dictionnaire des idées reçues*, 63
 – *Madame Bovary*, 99, 101
Frank, Anne, 12
Fučík, Julius, 19, 70-1, 87, 95-7,
Fuentes, Carlos, 25

Gaddis Rose, Marilyn, 17
Gallimard, 31-4, 36-7, 68, 73

Garton-Ash, Timothy, 166
Genette, Gérard, 60
Goethe, Johann Wolfgang von, vii, 93, 94, 95
Gott, Karel, 69
Gottwald, Klement, 19, 87, 90
Grass, Günther, 169
Grayson, Jane, 15
Gřebeníčková, Růžena, 153
Green, Graham, 168
Gross, Tom, 167
Grove Press, 38
Guevara, Che, 174
Gupta, Prasenjit
– *Stories of Bengalee Life*, 13

Halas, František, 94
Hamblyn, David, 29, 39, 45, 46, 162
Hamšík, Dušan, 27-8, 66
Harper and Row Publishers, 37-8
HarperCollins Publishers, 40
Hašek, Jaroslav
– *The Good Soldier Švejk*, 166
Havel, Václav, 88, 149, 166, 167, 168, 182, 183
– *The Garden Party*, 182
Hawtree, Christopher, 169, 171
Heaney, Seamus, 21
Heim, Michael Henry, vii, 34-40, 45, 46, 51-3, 82-3, 107, 110-11, 135, 165
Hemingway, Ernest, 7, 35, 125, 170
Homer, 21, 136
– *The Odyssey*, 21, 136, 137
Host, 64, 86
Houllier, Gérard, 170
Hrabal, Bohumil, 7, 87, 120, 149, 156, 160, 166, 167, 171
Hrbata, Zdeněk, 153
Husák, Gustav, 69
Hybler, Martin, 153-4

Jakobson, Roman, 9, 17
Janáček, Leoš, 7, 22, 70, 89, 91, 100, 147
John Murray Publishers, 34-5, 55
Joyce, James, 7, 22, 43, 99, 173, 186
Jungmann, Milan, 4-5, 6, 86, 91, 103, 153, 160, 175, 176
– *Kunderovské paradoxy*, 4, 86

Kachlík, Antonín, 73
Kafka, Franz, 11, 43-4, 60, 71, 76, 99, 144, 147, 157, 166, 167, 177
– *The Trial*, 76
Kapuścinski, Ryzsard, 89
Keane, Dillie, 170
Keates, Jonathan, 168
Kemp, Peter, 164
Kérel, François, vii, 54, 107, 110-12
Kiš, Danilo, 149
Klíma, Ivan, 87, 166, 167, 182-3
– *A Ship Named Hope*, 182
Knapp, Aleš, 152-3
Kohout, Pavel, 87, 91
– *Phenomenon Kohout*, 87
Kołakowski, Leszek, 119
Konwicki, Tadeusz, 149
Kosková, Helena, 60, 72, 105, 153, 155-9
– *Milan Kundera*, 153, 155
Kožmín, Zdeněk, 149
Kratochvil, Jiří, 20, 44, 60, 113, 155, 158-9
– *Příběhy příběhů*, 60, 155
Kuhiwczak, Piotr, 14, 29, 162-3
Kundera, Milan
– *Člověk zahrada šírá*, 19, 65, 97
– 'Doctor Havel After Ten Years', 73
– 'Don't Be Yourself', 33, 73, 75, 76
– *Druhý sešit směšných lásek*, 73
– *Dvě uši, dvě svatby*, 65
– 'Edward and God', 32, 33, 73
– *Epilog*, 3, 68, 182
– *Farewell Waltz*, 1, 3, 18, 21, 40, 52, 64, 66, 68, 80, 86, 101, 121, 132, 135, 143, 146, 153, 176, 182
– 'First Variation on Death', 71
– 'I am Someone Else', 73, 75, 76-7
– *Identity*, 2, 21, 40, 74, 86, 117, 130-4, 152, 168, 170, 174
– *Ignorance*, 2, 19, 21, 40, 45, 86, 117, 132, 136-43, 153
– *Immortality*, 1, 38, 39, 40, 58, 59, 62, 64, 67, 75, 76, 85, 86, 93, 94, 117, 120, 127, 132, 168, 169, 171
– 'I, the Mournful God', x, 18, 33, 72-7, 120, 127, 132, 135, 158
– *Jacques and His Master*, 1, 64, 86, 91, 134-5, 143

- *Jakub a jeho pán*, 1, 86, 134-5
- *La lenteur*, 2, 86, 121-9
- *L'art du roman*, 2, 64, 151, 175
- *Laughable Loves*, x, 1, 3, 18-19, 31, 33, 38, 40, 54, 55, 57, 58, 64, 65, 66, 67, 72-3, 77, 82, 86, 87, 91, 106, 112, 132, 134, 154, 171, 186
- *Laughable Loves: Three Melancholy Anecdotes*, 73
- *La valse aux adieux*, 1, 3, 68
- *La vie est ailleurs*, 1
- *Le livre du rire et de l'oublie*, 1
- *Les testaments trahis*, 2
- 'Let the Old Dead Make Room for the Young Dead', 73
- *L'identité*, 2, 86, 130, 132
- *Life is Elsewhere*, 1, 3, 17, 18, 23, 31, 32-5, 38, 40, 48, 53, 55-6, 58, 59, 66, 67, 80, 82, 83, 84, 86, 92, 94, 100, 102, 111, 113, 120, 134, 135, 153, 158
- *L'ignorance*, 2, 86, 132, 136-7, 140-3
- *L'immortalité*, 1
- *L'insoutenable légèreté de l'être*, 1
- *Majitelé klíčů*, 23, 65
- *Man, the Broad Garden*, 19
- *Monologues*, 19, 66, 71, 87, 92, 146
- *Monology*, 19, 66, 71
- 'Mother', 33, 77
- *Nesmrtelnost*, 1, 85, 86
- 'Nobody Will Laugh', 31-2, 73
- 'Nurse of my Nurses', 72, 73, 91, 100
- *Poslední máj*, 19, 65, 66, 70, 95
- *Ptákovina*, 65, 91, 134, 135, 146
- 'Second Variation on Death', 71
- 'Sixty-Three Words', 63, 89, 99, 105, 115, 125
- *Slowness*, 2, 21, 40, 86, 117, 121-9, 153, 168
- *Směšné lásky*, 1, 86
- *Směšné lásky: Tři melancholický anekdoty*, 73
- 'Song of a Great Runner', 71
- 'Symposium', 73
- *Testaments Betrayed*, 2, 22, 40, 43, 60, 84, 86, 89, 93, 118, 143, 153, 157, 172, 176, 183
- *The Art of the Novel*, 2, 40, 44, 63-5, 67, 84, 86, 91, 120, 121, 153, 158, 168, 175, 176, 183
- *The Book of Laughter and Forgetting*, vii, x, 1, 3, 18, 19, 20, 21, 32, 33, 36, 37, 40, 51, 58, 62, 65, 66, 67, 68-9, 71, 72, 75, 76, 77, 83, 86, 90, 93, 95, 105, 106-110, 113, 115, 116, 120, 123, 126, 133, 141, 143, 171, 172, 183
- 'The Cap of Clementis', 33, 34, 77
- *The Farewell Party*, 3, 33, 34, 40, 52, 58, 68, 134, 165, 171
- 'The Golden Apple of Eternal Desire', 54, 73, 75, 132, 134
- 'The Grand March', 91, 97
- 'The Hitchhiking Game', 55, 73
- *The Joke*, 1, 3, 4, 5, 14, 18, 19, 21, 23, 28, 29-30, 37, 38, 39, 40, 45-8, 59, 63, 64, 66, 69, 70, 76, 77-9, 82, 83, 84-5, 86, 87, 95-7, 132, 145, 148, 149, 154, 156, 157, 160, 161, 162, 165, 168, 173, 177, 182, 183
- *The Keepers of the Keys*, 23, 65, 72, 84, 146, 149-50, 158, 176
- *The Last May*, 19, 65, 66, 70-1, 87, 95
- 'The Messenger', 73
- *The New Yorker*, 33, 106
- *The Second Notebook of Laughable Loves*, 73
- 'The Sentence', 11
- *The Third Notebook of Laughable Loves*, 73
- *The Unbearable Lightness of Being*, x, 1, 3, 4, 18, 19, 20, 38, 40, 45, 52-3, 65, 66, 67, 68, 75, 76, 86, 91, 97-99, 105, 106, 111, 112-13, 114-15, 126, 132-3, 135, 137, 155, 161, 165, 166, 169, 171, 173
- 'The Unloved Child of the Family', 22
- 'Third Variation on Death', 71
- *Třeti sešit směšných lásek*, 73
- *Umění románu*, 44, 64, 65, 120
- *Valčík na rozloučenou*, 1, 3, 86
- 'Words Misunderstood', 20, 114-16
- *Žert*, 1, 84, 86

Kurkov, Andrey, 183
Kussi, Peter, vii, ix, 3, 6, 7, 16, 31-40, 43, 44, 48, 50, 52, 53, 55, 56, 57-9, 62, 65, 66, 67, 68, 72, 81, 83, 100, 120, 182, 184

- *Několik poznámek o překládání Milana Kundery /A Few Notes on Translating Milan Kundera*, 58-9

Laclos, Choderlos de
- *Les Liaisons Dangereuses*, 21, 126
Le Débat, 63
Lefevere, André, 8-9, 12-13
Le Grand, Eva, 156-7, 176
- *Kundera or The Memory of Desire*, 153, 155
Lermontov, Mikhail, vii, 93, 94
Lewis, Philip E., 10, 11-12, 184, 185, 186
L'Express, 120, 152
Liehm, Antonín, 31
Literární noviny, 28, 160
Lodge, David, 165, 171
Lukács, Gyorgy, 177
Lukeš, Jan, 6, 91, 151
Lumumba, Patrice, 174

Macdonald Publishers, 14, 28-30, 77, 162, 182, 184
MacGibbon, James, 29
Mácha, Karel Hynek
- *Máj*, 70-1
Mahfouz, Naguib, 181
Malmstad, John, 13
Mann, Thomas, 78
May, Rachel, 13, 14, 184
Mehrez, Samia, 14
Menzel, Jiří
- *Lark on a String*, 160-1
Miłoscz, Czesław, 89, 119, 149, 167
Moore, Victoria, 174

Nabokov, Vladimir, xi, 2, 15, 16, 25, 125
Němcová-Banerjee, Maria
- *Terminal Paradoxes*, 41
Nicholas, Nancy, vii, 31-8, 43, 54, 56, 57, 59, 60, 182, 183, 184
Niranjana, Tejaswini, 14

Opelík, Jiří, 149
Oxford Guide to English Literature, 173

Pelevin, Viktor, 183
Penguin, 61
Perec, Georges, 169
Petrarch, Francesco, vii, 51-2, 94
Petro, Peter, 154
Prague Spring, 14, 119, 180

Proust, Marcel, 169, 170

Rabelais, François, 43, 67
Random House, 37
Rappaport, Suzanne, 31-2, 54-6
Rees, Jasper, 166, 168, 172
Ricard, François
- *Agnes's Final Afternoon*, 41
Richterová, Sylvie, 60, 155
- *Slova a ticho*, 60
Rimbaud, Arthur, 53, 54, 93, 94, 120
- *Une saison en enfer*, 53
Rinaldi, Angelo, 120, 152
Rogaly, Joe, 168
Rostand, Edmound, 21
- *Cyrano de Bergerac*, 18, 21, 73, 74, 120, 130, 132, 143, 184
Roth, Philip, 31, 32-3, 37, 62, 68
Rushdie, Salman, 172-3
- *Shame*, 172
- *The Ground Beneath Her Feet*, 172
- *The Satanic Verses*, 172

Salinger, J. D., 5
Salivarová, Zdena, 88
Scammel, Michael, 16
Schoenberg, Arnold, 7
Sebald, W.G., 169
Shelley, Percy Bysshe, 94, 120
Sinaivsky, Andrei, 119
Sinclair, Clive, 165
Sixty-Eight Publishers, vii, 1, 3, 68, 80, 85, 88
Škvorecký, Josef, 1, 2, 31, 68, 88, 120, 156, 166, 171, 182, 183
- *Two Murders in My Double Life*, 88
- *The Cowards*, 182
Slomek, Jaromír, 152
Stalin, Josef, 96, 145
Stallybrass, Oliver, 29, 39, 45, 46, 60, 77, 162
Stanger, Allison, 4, 5, 6, 16, 65, 67, 79, 160
Steiner, George, 173
Sterne, Laurence, 67, 172, 173, 184
Strindberg, August, 22

The Daily Telegraph, 166, 168, 169, 170
The Financial Times, 168

The Guardian, 166, 168, 171
Theim, Jon, 16
The Observer, 168, 170
The Spectator, 171
The Times, 165
Times Literary Supplement, 28, 30, 164, 165, 180
Trotsky, Leon, 76, 77, 174
Turlington, Christy, 170

Uhdeová, Jitka, 60

Vaculík, Ludvík, *The Axe*, 149, 183
Vančura, Vladislav, 44, 64, 158-9,
Venuti, Lawrence, 3-4, 8-9, 11, 13, 15, 16, 17, 184, 186
Verecký, Ladislav, 152
Voltaire, vii, 94
von Arnim, Bettina, 94

Walker, Peter, 170
White, Edmund, 39
Williams, Nigel, 164
Wolker, Jiří, 94

Yesenin, Sergei, 94
Ying, Hong, *Summer of Betrayal*, 170

Zimra, Clarissa, 76
Zinoviev, Alexander, 119

For Product Safety Concerns and Information please contact our EU Authorised Representative:

Easy Access System Europe

Mustamäe tee 50

10621 Tallinn

Estonia

gpsr.requests@easproject.com

www.ingramcontent.com/pod-product-compliance
Lightning Source LLC
Chambersburg PA
CBHW070607300426
44113CB00010B/1443